T0384630

CONSENT AND TRADE

In a time of changing trade norms, when free trade seems to be giving way to new kinds of nationalism, some fundamental questions about trade are still not being asked. Is trade consensual or coercive? Is "free trade" as currently practiced really free? If not, what difference can trade law make in addressing economically oppressive practices that nationalistic trade policies cannot? In this book Frank J. Garcia offers an examination of trade law's roots in consensual exchange, highlighting the central role of consent in differentiating trade from legally facilitated coercion, exploitation or predation. The book revisits the premise of consensual exchange that underlies the rhetoric of "free trade," and then examines the social and political conditions that are a necessary part of a more genuine trade law system, in service of the idea that recovering consent in trade law can promote human flourishing on a global scale.

FRANK J. GARCIA is Professor of Law and Dean's Global Fund Scholar at the Boston College Law School, Massachusetts. A Fulbright Scholar, he has lectured widely on globalization and international economic law in Europe, South America and the Asia/Pacific region. Professor Garcia has held various leadership positions within the American Society of International Law, and currently sits on the editorial board of the *Journal of International Economic Law*, where he is the chief book review editor. He is the author, most recently, of *Global Justice and International Economic Law: Three Takes*, published by Cambridge University Press (2013).

Consent and Trade

TRADING FREELY IN A GLOBAL MARKET

Frank J. Garcia
Boston College Law School

CAMBRIDGE
UNIVERSITY PRESS

CAMBRIDGE
UNIVERSITY PRESS

University Printing House, Cambridge CB2 8BS, United Kingdom

One Liberty Plaza, 20th Floor, New York, NY 10006, USA

477 Williamstown Road, Port Melbourne, VIC 3207, Australia

314–321, 3rd Floor, Plot 3, Splendor Forum, Jasola District Centre, New Delhi – 110025, India

79 Anson Road, #06–04/06, Singapore 079906

Cambridge University Press is part of the University of Cambridge.

It furthers the University's mission by disseminating knowledge in the pursuit of education, learning, and research at the highest international levels of excellence.

www.cambridge.org
Information on this title: www.cambridge.org/9781108473255
DOI: 10.1017/9781108569255

First published 2019

Printed and bound in Great Britain by Clays Ltd, Elcograf S.p.A.

A catalogue record for this publication is available from the British Library.

Library of Congress Cataloging-in-Publication Data
Names: Garcia, Frank J., author.
Title: Consent and trade : trading freely in a global market / Frank J. Garcia,
    Boston College, Massachusetts.
Description: United Kingdom ; New York, NY : Cambridge University Press Cambridge, 2019.
Identifiers: LCCN 2018029218 | ISBN 9781108473255 (hardback) |
    ISBN 9781108461092 (pbk.)
Subjects: LCSH: Free trade. | Commercial policy. | Commercial treaties. | International trade.
Classification: LCC HF1713 .G37 2019 | DDC 382/.71–dc23
    LC record available at https://lccn.loc.gov/2018029218

ISBN 978-1-108-47325-5 Hardback

For Joseph Vining, James J. White and
James Boyd White,
for teaching us what a warm, intelligent, vigorous love
of the Law looks like,
and for all my teachers.

Where there is voluntary agreement, there is justice.

Plato, *Symposium*

...justice will take us millions of intricate moves

William Stafford, "Thinking for Berky"

CONTENTS

CONTENTS

ACKNOWLEDGMENTS

This book has been twelve years in the making, and over those twelve years I have been privileged to present these ideas in workshops at a number of law, philosophy and political science faculties and conferences around the world. Among them I would like to thank Sorbonne University, Nanterre University, Warwick University, Monash University, Boston University, the Graduate Institute of Geneva, Durham University, the University of Cambridge, the University of Richmond, the University of the Andes (Bogotá, Colombia), Harvard University and my own Boston College.

This kind of research does not happen without patient and consistent support from one's home institution. I would like to thank the two most recent deans of the Boston College Law School, John Garvey and Vincent Rougeau, for their ongoing support from the Law School Fund. Nor would it see the light of day but for the support of editors like the Press's John Berger for interesting and unusual work – this is certainly the latter, and I hope the former as well.

I feel very fortunate to have many generous friends and colleagues who have read all or part of the manuscript at various stages in its formation and helped refine these ideas. Among them are Paulo Barrozo, Betty and David Buchsbaum, Jeffrey Dunoff Jim Henle, Joseph Killough, David Lefkowitz, Pietro Maffetone, Vlad Perju, Diane Ring, Asif Qureshi, Mattias Risse, Gary Whited and Katie Young. I owe a special debt of gratitude to Sonia Rolland and Fiona Smith for reading through the entire manuscript at the end, with their customary insight and acumen.

Over these twelve years I have also been supported by a small army of research assistants, who have invested of themselves and made my project theirs. I would like to thank Ritika Bhakhri, Alex Galliani,

Frances Ha, Kirrin Hough, Jennifer Kay, Thomas Lampert, Khoa
Nguyen, Aaron Staudinger, Erika Steinbauer and Michael Tomasini –
and apologies if I have missed any of you; of all people, you know how
my memory and record keeping are! Many among this group have been
trained by Xin "Sherry" Chen, our wonderful international research
librarian, who has also helped me countless times find the sources I have
needed to land this plane.

As with my last book, a substantial portion of the thinking and
writing for this book took place while seated in the warm and friendly
environs of the Petit Passage Cafe, East Ferry, Nova Scotia, my
summer "office." My heartfelt thanks to Brenda, Debbie, Vicki and
the gang for the bottomless cup of coffee, the equally bottomless
reservoir of good cheer even on foggy days and the great pie.

Finally, I want to acknowledge the ongoing intelligent, perceptive
and creative support I have received from my partner Kim Garcia, in
all aspects of this project as in literally everything else. She has been
and continues to be my most important teacher, and in that sense this
book is also dedicated to her.

INTRODUCTION

This book is an investigation into the nature of trade and trade agreements. I am interested in the words we use to capture the meaning of trade as a human experience, and a cluster of associated words, ideas, norms and practices centered on exchanges of various kinds. In particular, this book is a reflection on what we mean by the idea of "trade" itself, and by trade's relationship to freedom, by which I mean consent – trade as a consensual economic exchange. Finally, I am interested as a legal scholar in how trade and its relationship to consent are reflected – or not – in our understanding of "free trade," our trade laws and in the transnational commercial relationships, both public and private, of our globalizing world today.

I A REFLECTIVE INVESTIGATION OF TRADE

My goal for this book is to say something meaningful about the nature of trade as a human experience, which I hope will help inform our understanding of the economic relationships we have built so far, and our collective decisions as to what kinds of economic relationships we want to build going forward. In this sense, my purpose is more in line with that of phenomenological writing (although this is not a work of phenomenology) than with trade law scholarship per se: to capture something essential about an experience that has implications for our practice.[1] My hope is that if we can identify what is essential to trade *as trade*, we can better understand how to facilitate, protect and enhance

---

[1] *See* Max van Manen, *Practicing Phenomenological Writing*, 2 PHENOMENOLOGY + PEDAGOGY 36, 38 (1984).

it, and thereby better understand how to promote a flourishing system of global economic relationships. In other words, I am proposing that we begin by looking at what trade *is*, and then see what trade, properly understood, *asks of us* if we are to protect and promote it – what it means, in fact, to engage in trade at all, and not something else.

Today we most often come upon the word "trade" already embedded in a phrase that is quite common and often assumed – mistakenly, as it turns out – to be well understood: "free trade." The idea of free trade has come to mean a policy of freeing trade from government restrictions, often of a protectionist nature, that interfere with the natural patterns of exchange that private parties might otherwise establish and follow toward their own – and our collective – good.[2]

There is, however, much more to trade and its relationship to the word "free" than is readily captured by this conventional understanding. On closer inspection, the phrase "free trade" invokes the idea of freedom in two ways. The conventional meaning of the phrase, as mentioned, is that trade is free if it is not subject to governmental regulation that distorts it from economically efficient patterns of exchange, and that is certainly a meaningful view.

The second, less obvious resonance (think "freely traded" or "trading freely") is that there is an element of freedom in the economic exchange itself – trade must be "free," i.e., consensual, in order to be trade at all. In this sense, it seems that what we call trade must involve consensual exchange; it must have the consent of those involved in the trade (whether as people or as states), or else the absence of protectionist regulation is beside the point – it is not even trade anymore, but something else. Offering an account of that "something else," and of this second kind of freedom and its relationship to what we call "trade,"[3] is at the heart of this book.

---

[2] So, at least, says the theory of trade. *See* DOUGLAS A. IRWIN, AGAINST THE TIDE: AN INTELLECTUAL HISTORY OF FREE TRADE 5 (1996). Irwin offers a fascinating intellectual history of the doctrine of free trade.

[3] I've put the word "trade" in quotes here and elsewhere at times to suggest that once we begin to investigate the nature of this complex phenomenon, it becomes apparent that we can't always or easily be sure how the word is being used, and whether in fact it is meant to signal genuine trade, as that notion will be developed here, or a pathology of trade, as is too often the case. I am not fully consistent in this usage, but at least we are all now on notice.

II WHY CONSENT?

I first became interested in the relationship between trade and consent through Simone Weil's penetrating studies of consent and oppression in economic life.[4] In her two foundational essays "Analysis of Oppression" and "*The Iliad*, Poem of Might," I discovered a fundamental insight with great resonance for the trading system today.[5] Writing in the shadow of Fascism early in the twentieth century, Weil understood that oppressive tendencies are inherent in all forms of socioeconomic organization, that they are best resisted by protecting consent in these relationships and that one cannot seek consent where there is no power of refusal.[6]

In the *Symposium*, Plato offers one definition of justice as mutual consent.[7] In a similar vein, Weil also writes that justice has as its object the exercise of the faculty of consent in human relations.[8] If socioeconomic relationships are not just – understood here as consensual – then by institutionalizing them we risk gratifying what Weil terms that "shameful, unacknowledged taste for conquest which enslaves under the pretense of liberating."[9]

While the root of this violence is for Weil nature itself – "all force originates in nature"[10] – oppression is more subtle: it depends first on privilege, or the position of a relative few in control over the work and the needs of many. There are many sources of privilege among people, but economic privilege comes when the need to organize into more complex forms of social organization, such as markets for the exchange

---

[4] To be accurate, I was directed to Weil by my partner, the poet Kim Garcia, who in the midst of her omnivorous reading said to me one day out of the blue, "You really should read Simone Weil in connection with this trade stuff."

[5] Indeed, with great resonance for law itself. The legal scholar James Boyd White has written an entire book of essays on law with Weil's *Iliad* essay as his departure point, to which I am much indebted. *See* JAMES BOYD WHITE, LIVING SPEECH: RESISTING THE EMPIRE OF FORCE (2006).

[6] SIMONE WEIL, *Justice and Human Society*, *in* SIMONE WEIL 123–25 (Eric O. Springsted ed. 1998). This will hereinafter be referred to as *Justice and Human Society*.

[7] "... where there is voluntary agreement, there ... is justice" (Benjamin Jowett trans.)

[8] *Justice and Human Society*, *supra* note 6, at 125.

[9] *Id.* at 126.

[10] SIMONE WEIL, *Analysis of Oppression*, *in* THE SIMONE WEIL READER 126, 133 (George A. Panichas ed. 1977).

of goods or firms for the deployment of capital, places a few persons in an exclusive position of control over the system on which all depend for their livelihood.

Weil is emphatic that this understanding of oppression is not limited to capitalism, but applies to all forms of social organization:

> Whenever, in the struggle against men [sic] or against nature, efforts need to be multiplied and coordinated to be effective, coordination becomes the monopoly of a few leaders as soon as it reaches a certain degree of complexity, and execution's primary law is then obedience; this is true both for the management of public affairs and for that of private undertakings ... [A]ll these factors enter into play under all systems of oppression; what changes is the way they are distributed and combined, the degree of concentration of power, and also that more or less closed and consequently more or less mysterious character of each monopoly.[11]

The response to this fundamental dilemma of changing one form of servitude (natural) for another (social) – and there is no solution to it, in the sense of eliminating it, but only a response – is to seek to protect and promote consent in all aspects of the social order. Consent is the expression of an essential human freedom that resists and balances what Weil elsewhere calls "the empire of force" (I will be returning to this in the final chapter).[12]

Consent is thus the keystone for all efforts to resist the oppressive tendencies inherent in all forms of socioeconomic organization, including perhaps (as we shall see) the global trading system, the most extensive form of socioeconomic organization we share today. Consent is the antidote, if you will – that element within social organization that insists on maintaining human beings as ends, that keeps us human within an oppressive system, rather than objects.[13] Otherwise, Weil

---

[11] *Analysis of Oppression, supra* note 10, at 134.

[12] SIMONE WEIL, *The Iliad, Poem of Might, in* THE SIMONE WEIL READER 181 (George A. Panichas ed. 1977). Panichas translates the phrase as "empire of might," but I prefer James Boyd White's translation, quoted here.

[13] She locates this analysis in her penetrating reading of the *Iliad*: "... in this ancient and wonderful poem there already appears the essential evil besetting humanity, the substitution of means for ends." *Analysis of Oppression, supra* note 10, at 138.

writes that "the law of all activities governing social life" – I would say the tragedy of it – "is that here each one sacrifices human life – in himself and in others – to things which are only means to a better way of living."[14]

This insight echoes through many dimensions of politics and economics, as well as the law, both private and public, as Weil herself understood.[15] Her life ultimately proved too short for the fullest exploration of these implications, and in any event, Weil was no systematizer. Rather, her genius lay in the personal intensity of her political reflections, an instinctive sympathy for and understanding of the oppressed and the breadth of her intuitive reach. For me, the intriguing possibility opened up by Weil's insight is that by analyzing trade's relationship to consent, we might find both the mechanisms through which oppressive tendencies are being realized in today's global economy and, one hopes, the pathways toward global economic freedom.

The farther I read into and reflected on trade and its relationship to consent, the more convinced I became that here was buried a forgotten key. Integrating this discovery with my twenty-five years of teaching and writing about international trade law has led me to the conclusion that the absence, or impingement, of consent is at the root of the numerous pathologies of trade that today complicate both transnational "trade" relations and the domestic politics of "trade." Simply put, it is the presence of consent, even when cabined by economic pressures and necessities, that renders an exchange "trade." When consent leaves the room, so to speak, trade goes with it, no matter how papered over any subsequent "agreement" might be by

---

[14] *Analysis of Oppression, supra* note 10, at 138.

[15] For this reason Weil has been called the "philosopher of oppression." *See* ADRIENNE RICH, *For a Friend in Travail, in* AN ATLAS OF THE DIFFICULT WORLD: POEMS 1988–1991, at 51 (1991). ("*What are you going through?* she said, is the great question. / Philosopher of oppression, theorist/ of the victories of force.") "She" being Weil, who wrote, "The love of our neighbor in all its fullness simply means being able to say to him: 'What are you going through?'" *See* SIMONE WEIL, WAITING FOR GOD 115 (1959). It has fallen to others to explore the many structural implications of her work through law, humanities and the arts, and Weil studies are undergoing something of a renaissance today. *See, e.g.,* Oche Onazi, *Justice Dictated by the Surfeit of Love: Simone Weil in Nigeria,* 28 LAW & CRITIQUE 1 (2017); KAIJA SAARIAHO & AMIN MAALOUF, LA PASSION DE SIMONE (Barbican Centre, Los Angeles Philharmonic and Lincoln Center for the Performing Arts 2006).

legal formalities, which only serve to make appear as trade what is really something else: coercion, exploitation or worse.

This means that in order to understand how a globalizing economy can at the same time be both an oppressive weight on human freedom, and a progressive force for human flourishing, we need to take a closer look at how consent fares in international trade law, and international economic law more generally. Weil's account highlights the futility of creating alternative futures or economic systems – capitalist or Marxist – that do not directly confront through consent the oppressive tendencies of any form of social organization.[16] Instead, a consensual engagement in social organization is itself the way forward, turning the necessity of social organization itself into an expression of the flourishing of human nature. Weil expresses this paradox most trenchantly as follows: "This world is the closed door. It is a barrier. And at the same time, it is the way through."[17]

The key to "the way through" is to closely analyze the mechanisms of oppression involved in any specific form or aspect of social organization.

> The problem is, in short, to know what it is that links oppression in general and each form of oppression in particular to the system of production: in other words, to succeed in grasping the mechanism of oppression, in understanding by what means it arises, subsists, transforms itself, by what means, perhaps, it might theoretically disappear.[18]

In this passage, Weil articulates, in her characteristically urgent style, the rationale for the consent analysis of trade I offer here. Insofar as the global economy is the system of production that all human beings on the planet find themselves to one degree or another subject to, it is this

---

[16] Although Weil rejected Marx's prescription, his mode of analysis remained central to her project: "If Marx's system, in its broad outlines, is of little assistance, it is a different matter when it comes to the analyses he was led to make by the concrete study of capitalism, and in which, while believing that he was limiting himself to describing a system, he probably more than once seized upon the hidden nature of oppression itself." *Analysis of Oppression,* *supra* note 10, at 131. *See generally* LAWRENCE A. BLUM & VICTOR SEIDLER, A TRUER LIBERTY: SIMONE WEIL AND MARXISM (2009).

[17] SIMONE WEIL, GRAVITY AND GRACE 145 (1952).

[18] *Analysis of Oppression, supra* note 10, at 126.

structure that we must analyze if we are to know the links between oppression in general and the oppressiveness of the global economy in particular, and it is this same structure, suitably reformed, which we must also rely on to safeguard consent: it is both the closed door, and the way through.

Weil reminds us that the analysis of oppression must be tailored to the specific "instruments" of power deployed in a given area of social life, for after all "you do not command in the same way, by means of soldiers with bows and arrows, spears and swords, as you do by ... exchanges in economic life."[19] Trade agreements and trade negotiations are their own unique instrument of power, and therefore at the heart of any analysis of the nature of the global economic relationships we are building through trade.

In her own work, Weil outlines an approach to this task – to the analysis of specific instruments of oppression and injustice – that she believes will result in the kind of clarity about and resistance to oppression that she advocates:

> It would be necessary first of all to define by way of an ideal limit the objective conditions that would permit of a social organization absolutely free from oppression; then seek out by what means and to what extent the conditions actually given can be transformed so as to bring them nearer to this ideal; find out what is the least oppressive form of social organization for a body of specific object-ive conditions; and lastly, define in this field the power of action and responsibilities of individuals as such.[20]

In other words, this must be a deeply contextual inquiry – a simple analysis of oppression in general will not unlock the oppressive nature of particular social systems. For that one needs a detailed analysis of the specific conditions within which a social system operates. Similarly, the phenomenon of consent may not look the same in all circumstances: "[t]he forms and expressions of consent vary greatly in different traditions and milieu."[21]

---

[19] *Analysis of Oppression, supra* note 10, at 141.
[20] *Id.* at 130.
[21] *Justice and Human Society, supra* note 6, at 126.

Therefore, in order to understand the oppressive tendencies inherent in the global economy today, we need to understand the consensual and nonconsensual elements within contemporary trade agreements and how they are negotiated. Through these agreements we are building the world, and as such these agreements are both the closed door, and the way through. However, before embarking on this study, I think it would be helpful to first look briefly at how consent is understood in other fields, sometimes in line with Weil's insight, and sometimes not.

III CONSENT IN OTHER FIELDS

The role of consent in human social behavior, law and politics is of course a vast and fundamental inquiry that touches many areas of concern and opens many possibilities, only some of which I can hope to address here. As James Boyd White reminds us, when the human mind meets and tries to use the language that surrounds it in responding to the world, a rich array of intellectual, ethical and political commitments are at work.[22]

Expressions of consent can play a constitutive role in everything from who we share our lunch with, and who we take as romantic partners or life partners, to who we choose to govern us, the economic bargains that we make or reject, and the laws that frame what bargains we *can* make and how; in short, the entire system of social, economic, political and legal relationships we are born into and at least implicitly presented with as a choice.

Political consent is of course a cornerstone of liberalism and democratic theory generally, with an illustrious history dating back at least to Socrates in Plato's *Crito*.[23] Within liberalism we continue to maintain that consent plays a normative role as the basis of the domestic legal order, at least in the social contract model of liberal societies, despite

---

[22] WHITE, *supra* note 5.

[23] Consent has ancient roots. *See generally* TOM O'SHEA, CONSENT IN HISTORY, THEORY AND PRACTICE 1–11 (2011), https://autonomy.essex.ac.uk/wp-content/uploads/2016/11/Consent-GPR-June-2012.pdf. Last accessed June 5, 2018.

challenging theoretical critiques of consent theory.[24] Consent also features prominently in global political theory, for example in the work of David Held, in which consent is the third of four core cosmopolitan principles.[25]

Political consent can have a theoretical as well as pragmatic role. For example, Brian Barry suggests that we ask of any rule or principle if it would emerge from a negotiation involving equality and freedom.[26] Implicit in this formulation is the expectation that it be a rule or principle freely consented to, since we assume that to be the outcome of negotiations involving equality and freedom. Similarly, John Rawls's famous "original position" can also be seen as an exercise to invoke our notions of consent: under the conditions he prescribes, what principles of justice would we consent to?[27] Scanlon, by contrast, could be said to invoke the other side of consent, namely, what principles would we have reasonable grounds to reject?[28]

As with political theory, there is an extensive literature on the many roles that consent plays in the law.[29] Consent plays a key doctrinal role within many specific substantive bodies of law, in which a series of consequences to one's life and liberty depend upon a determination of consent as defined by the law.[30] For example, Beyleveld and Brownsword open their comprehensive analysis of consent across many fields of law with an illustration of the changing law of consent in marital sexual relations. Under the early English common law, consent on the part of the wife was presumed in law by the state of marriage itself, a legal construction we now reject. Growing in part from these troubled roots, the modern criminal law of

---

[24] *See generally* RICHARD DAGGER & DAVID LEFKOWITZ, *Political Obligation,* THE STANFORD ENCYCLOPEDIA OF PHILOSOPHY (Aug. 7, 2014), https://plato.stanford.edu/archives/fall2014/entries/political-obligation/ (last accessed June 5, 2018).

[25] David Held, *Cosmopolitanism: Globalisation Tamed,* 29 REV. INT'L STUD. 465, 470–71 (2003).

[26] BRIAN BARRY, THEORIES OF JUSTICE 343 (1989).

[27] JOHN RAWLS, A THEORY OF JUSTICE 17 (1971).

[28] *See* T. M. SCANLON, WHAT WE OWE EACH OTHER (1998).

[29] *See generally* DERYCK BEYLEVELD & ROGER BROWNSWORD, CONSENT IN THE LAW (2007) (reviewing this literature and analyzing the role of consent in public and private law).

[30] *Id.* at 1–2.

sexual relations now depends fundamentally on a careful examination of consent in all its complex forms and degrees.[31]

This analogy to marriage in early common law also illustrates the relationship in law between consent, power and inequality that is a subject of this book as well. It can be said to be axiomatic of human behavior, at least as understood through law, that inequalities in power often lead to infringements of consent.[32] Law plays a key role in creating, reinforcing or masking this relationship, but can play an equally key role in unmasking and transforming it as well – both the closed door and the way through.[33]

The notion of consent also plays an important role in international law, quite relevant for us here since trade agreements are legal instruments under international law. In international law, consent is a formal principle of legitimacy and a necessary element in the creation of legally binding obligations.[34] Without consent, international law would be an imperial order and not a legal order in the Westphalian sense.[35] In fact, as the International Court of Justice has pointed out, consent is at the heart of international law, at least with respect to its formal indicia (treaty ratification, for example, or state decisions as reflective of state practice).[36] There are, however, significant limits to the power of such a doctrine of formal consent when it comes to safeguarding

---

[31] So does the law of contract, which has also had a complex relationship to the question of consent under conditions of inequality, in particular with respect to gender. *See* Fiona Smith, *Book Review*, 2 INT'L J.L. CONTEXT 419 (2006) (reviewing FEMINIST PERSPECTIVES ON CONTRACT LAW [Linda Mulcahy & Sally Wheeler eds. 2005]). I shall have more to say about contracts in Chapter 1.

[32] Certainly, Weil would have said so. *See supra* note 10 and accompanying text.

[33] *See* BEYLEVELD & BROWNSWORD, *supra* note 29. The common law's evolution with respect to consent in marital sexual relations also illustrates law's capacity for reform as our understanding changes.

[34] For an overview of consent in international relations and the role of consent as a legitimizing factor in international law, *see* DAVID LEFKOWITZ, *The Legitimacy of International Law, in* GLOBAL POLITICAL THEORY 78 (David Held & Pietro Maffetone eds. 2016).

[35] Of course, there are many who claim that modern international law is an imperial order, despite the formal role of consent, for reasons that are quite relevant to the subject of this book. *See, e.g.,* B. S. Chimni, *International Institutions Today: An Imperial State in the Making*, 15 EUR. J. INT'L L. 1 (2004). I shall have more to say about this throughout the book.

[36] *See* Chios Carmody, *Theory and Theoretical Approaches to WTO Law*, 13 MANCHESTER J. INT'L ECON. L. 152, 154–55 (2016) (discussing the *Maritime Delimitation* case).

actual consent in international relations and elsewhere, which I shall have more to say about as this book progresses.

Turning to private law, the classical notion of consent in contract as the "meeting of minds" illustrates the key role of consent in identifying enforceable private exchanges: "If it is made clear that there has in fact been no such meeting of the minds, the court will not hold a party bound by a contract varying from the party's own understanding."[37] Consent also serves as a conceptual "trigger" invoking the applicability of specific areas of law such as the law of contracts, where the presence of a possibly consensual exchange is what designates contract law as the relevant body of law, rather than for example, the criminal law of extortion.

What these consent doctrines have in common with the consent approach to trade is the shared idea that in any society that takes ordinary people and their choices seriously, consent will play a key role in the law.[38] The risk, as Weil warns us (echoing Hume), is mistaking the form of consent for actual consent, in both political and economic matters.[39] I would add legal relationships to this at-risk list, as Onora O'Neill so eloquently states: "Even the clearest formulas of consent, such as signatures and formal oaths, may not indicate consent when there is ignorance, duress, misrepresentation, pressure, or the like."[40] In international law, for example, issues of oppression and coercion in treaty making and the doctrinal recognition of "treaties of adhesion,"[41] as I will discuss in Chapters 2 and 3, all illustrate the limits of a formal consent doctrine when aiming to capture the richness and complexity of our experience of consent.[42]

---

[37] *See* ARTHUR LINTON CORBIN, CORBIN ON CONTRACTS §1.4 (rev. ed. 1993) (describing the necessity of mutual assent – the so-called meeting of the minds.).

[38] BEYLEVELD & BROWNSWORD, *supra* note 29, at 3–4.

[39] *Justice and Human Society, supra* note 6, at 126.

[40] Onora O'Neill, *Between Consenting Adults*, 14 PHIL. & PUB. AFF. 252, 254 (1985).

[41] On the notion of an adhesion treaty, *see, e.g.*, Donald P. Harris, *Carrying a Good Joke Too Far: TRIPS and Treaties of Adhesion*, 27 U. PENN. J. ECON. L. 681 (2014).

[42] For an interesting argument that international law preserves meaningful space for actual consent, *see* Matthew Lister, *The Legitimating Role of Consent in International Law*, 11 CHI. J. INT'L. L. 663, 663–91 (2011) (arguing that international law preserves a role for actual consent among states, in relation to the jurisdiction of international tribunals, and is therefore more fully consensual in this aspect than even domestic law); *see also*

In short, it is no surprise that consent – how we express and incarnate our intellect, conscience, will and agency – should be at the center of so many disciplines and reflective traditions since its exercise is so fundamentally human. Ultimately we are all of a piece as human beings, despite the analytical convenience (and occasional analytical violence) of temporarily isolating our activities into their component elements. However, despite consent's centrality and ubiquity it has been considered impossible on a theoretical level to draw out a unified account of consent as it works in all disciplines and fields – even political and legal consent, so closely linked, have divergent strands.[43]

Nevertheless, independently of this vast enterprise of theoretical reflection on consent, I believe we can all recognize at an elemental level *when* we have expressed our consent – and how freely – and when we have not, and it is this touchstone to which I hope to continually return us.[44] As I speak at various points to the personal, the social, the political, the legal and the economic in trying to follow and map the role of consent in trade, I hope this builds to a fuller and richer chord, and not a discordant noise.

IV THE PLAN OF THIS BOOK

In Chapter 1, I am going to begin by reflecting on the role of consent in economic arrangements, specifically on how consent plays a key role in making trade "trade." I will set out the reasons why I have come to consider that trade must at heart involve consensual bargains to be trade *at all*: in other words, the key to the nature of trade *as* trade, and not predation, coercion or exploitation, *is* consent.[45] In Weil's terms, where there is no power to refuse, there is no trade, because there can be no consent.

LEFKOWITZ, *supra* note 34 (noting coercion and representation problems affecting consent's validity).
[43] Dagger & Lefkowitz, *Political Obligation, supra* note 24.
[44] There is an earthy expression in English – I don't know if other languages have parallel sayings – that "even a dog knows the difference between being tripped over and being kicked." It could be helpful to keep this folk insight in mind as the discussion proceeds.
[45] I develop this view further in Chapter 2.

This insight is both simple and potentially transformative. It is simple, in that it bears a direct relationship to our deepest intuitions about our economic selves, that "propensity in human nature ... to truck, barter, and exchange one thing for another."[46] If the parties to a specific exchange are not satisfied with their bargain, they may well accept it anyway, with the understanding that they will not be doing business with that person, or that way, ever again. That is one of the freedoms a well-functioning market offers. However, if we consider trade as a *pattern* or series of exchanges, and the parties are not over the long run basically satisfied, then exchange itself breaks down, and with it the social relationships built around exchange, as every businessperson knows.

This insight can be transformative, in that the neoliberal trading system today only imperfectly fulfills the conditions of consent inherent in the nature of trade itself – it is not "liberal" enough, in the classical sense of liberalism as freedom.[47] Many aspects of current trade law and policy shift what is ostensibly trade into something else: exploitation, coercion or predation.[48] By tracing consent and its absence or impairment through an illustrative set of these arrangements, which I will do in Chapter 2, I hope to shed light on subtle but important dynamics in contemporary trade relations, particularly as they involve substantial inequalities in power among participating states.

These inequalities and their effect on trade rules and trade negotiations undercut the fairness and sustainability of the global economy through their effects on the rules of the game and on the possibility of truly consensual exchanges. When considered in the light of Weil's insight, one must conclude that the many unequal trade relations currently structured and managed through unequal agreements are

---

[46] ADAM SMITH, THE WEALTH OF NATIONS, BOOKS I–III 121 (Andrew S. Skinner ed. 1999) (1776). I am indebted to Judith Wise for introducing me to this aspect of Smith's work.

[47] The core commitment of classical liberalism is liberty itself. *See* GERALD GAUS & SHANE D. COURTLAND, *Liberalism*, THE STANFORD ENCYCLOPEDIA OF PHILOSOPHY (Dec. 22, 2014), http://plato.stanford.edu/archives/spr2015/entries/liberalism/ (last accessed Dec. 22, 2015).

[48] *See* JOSEPH E. STIGLITZ, MAKING GLOBALIZATION WORK 62 (2007). In part, free trade has not worked because we have not tried it – trade agreements of the past have been neither free nor fair. I am arguing that for these reasons they have not been trade agreements at all.

not consensual in a fundamental sense, because one of the parties –
state or private – often has no real power of refusal.

Having described where we are now in terms of trade and consent
in Chapter 2, I will in Chapter 3 take up the questions of how we got
here, why we should be concerned and what we can do about it if we
are. The most important thing we can do if we care about trade is to let
our understanding of the role of consent in trade reorganize our ideas
of trade, trade law, trade policy and trade negotiations, such that what
we expect from trade (and of our political leaders and trade negotiators), and what we are willing to allow in its stead, can evolve. In
practical terms, this could involve changes to how trade agreements are
negotiated and some new approaches to what to do with the troubling
aspects of agreements currently in force.

Understanding this might also open up new possibilities for us as a
society built around markets, which I will explore in Chapter 4. The
question of consent goes to the heart of trade law's social justification
and political sustainability: in order for free trade as a policy to deliver
fully on its social promise of mutually beneficial, welfare enhancing
exchanges toward increased human flourishing, it must be both "free"
and "trade."

For example, when one considers how contemporary trade policy is
currently under fire and hotly contested by democratic polities around
the world, one can see that the perceived absence of consent is not
merely a developing world complaint, but is also being voiced by many
at the heart (and heartland) of the United States and other advanced
democracies currently undergoing a populist crisis. As I came to
understand during the 2016 US presidential election, we in the United
States have a "country within the country," and many of the pathologies of trade I am tracing here can be applied within this new frame as
well, to help us better understand the roots and tenor of the current
crisis in trade policy.

Similarly, a consensual understanding of trade might allow us to
come at the problem of fairness from an entirely different perspective –
not the theoretical debates on global justice in terms of political philosophy (cosmopolitanism versus communitarianism, egalitarianism
versus libertarianism, liberalism versus Marxism, etc.), important as

they are, but instead something closer to the ground. At a minimum, it might help us understand what it means to us as human beings that we trade, that we have built a trading society, and what we might hope from of such a society. This is particularly important as we become a global market society built around trade, as I will also explore in the Conclusion.

For such an inquiry the place to start, however, we must begin with trade itself as a human social practice.

1 CONSENT AND TRADE

When did we begin to trade with each other, and why? Paleoanthropologists suggest the answers may be rooted in the far distant past, when the first genetically modern human beings began to produce abstract images and more complex tools and pierce shells, some sixty to eighty thousand years ago.[1] This, coupled with the development of language at about that same period, created the conditions for the kinds of exchanges that would grow into what we would recognize as trade today.[2]

Efforts to regulate and ultimately govern such exchanges grew in tandem, as human beings organized themselves into more and more complex social units, often intimately associated with trading patterns.[3] It is fair to say, then, that trade, speech, social life and trade regulation are inextricably bound together and are as old as we are. Language is integral to both trade itself (although we need not share a language to trade, as I will discuss presently), and to our ideas, words and norms around trade, and our exploration of the nuances of what is trade and what is not.

---

[1] WILLIAM J. BERNSTEIN, A SPLENDID EXCHANGE: HOW TRADE SHAPED THE WORLD 21 (2008).

[2] *Id.*

[3] *See* THOMAS HALE ET AL., GRIDLOCK: WHY GLOBAL COOPERATION IS FAILING WHEN WE NEED IT MOST (2013) (economic governance dates back to earliest history of trade between communities of human beings).

I WHAT DO WE DO WHEN WE TRADE?

Both our language and our collective experience of trade suggest many possible aspects or dimensions of that experience that are worth exploring as we try to understand just what trade is.[4]

A Exploring the Many Dimensions of Trade

I begin here with the notion of trade as a species of exchange, one rooted in a rich experience of encounter, opportunity, risk and inequalities in power.

1 Trade as Exchange

To begin, trade involves an exchange. When we trade, we engage in a transaction – something changes hands, so to speak. I exchange a good with you for the good you have that I want. In this sense, trade is a basic everyday experience among people. It was none other than the economist/philosopher Adam Smith who noted "a certain propensity in human nature ... to truck, barter, and exchange one thing for another."[5] A more contemporary economist/philosopher, Amartya Sen, puts it this way: "The freedom to exchange words, or goods, or gifts does not need defensive justification; they are part of the way human beings in society live and interact with each other ..."[6]

We also speak of trade, in a specifically international sense, as exchanges involving the crossing of geographic and political boundaries. This kind of trade, in which we go beyond the known limits of our village or locale, is closely tied to the etymological roots of the English word "trade," as "track" or "tread" – in other words, to trudge from one place to another bringing goods to exchange.[7] It also

---

[4] By speaking in the plural, I mean to invite the reader to consider whether they find what I say to be consistent with their own experience, rather than to presume that I can speak for any of us or "all" of us in some definitive sense.

[5] ADAM SMITH, THE WEALTH OF NATIONS, BOOKS I–III 121 (Andrew S. Skinner ed. 1999) (1776).

[6] AMARTYA SEN, DEVELOPMENT AS FREEDOM 6 (1999).

[7] Trade, OXFORD ENGLISH DICTIONARY, https://en.oxforddictionaries.com/definition/trade (last accessed June 25, 2018).

poses for us an interesting question, given the dangers, rigors and uncertainties of travel – in the words of William Bernstein,

> Why would anyone risk life, limb, and property on journeys that might carry him from hearth and home for years on end, yielding only meager profits? Simple: the grim trading life was preferable to the even grimmer existence of the more than 90 percent of the population who engaged in subsistence-level farming. An annual profit of one hundred dinars – enough to support an upper-middle-class existence – made a trader a rich man.[8]

This kind of venture evokes other dimensions of trade as well, such as trade as exploration, where economic need rouses us out of the known into the unknown; and trade as risk or adventure: Will this gamble pay off? Will the merchant ships arrive? Will my fortune grow or be lost?

One powerful evocation of this in Western literature is Shakespeare's *The Merchant of Venice*, in which the loss of Antonio's ships is one of the dramatic forces propelling the primary story of *The Merchant of Venice*.[9] This story, interestingly enough, raises several other dimensions of trade that are also quite relevant to our inquiry, such as the risks inherent in trade, and also the interaction of trade and inequalities of various kinds, culminating in the key question of the play, namely, which kinds of exchanges we will and will not allow and why.[10] I will have more to say about this in a moment.

2 Trade as Encounter

The desire to exchange brings us into contact with one another; when we cross boundaries to engage in trade, it has meant encounters with the "Other."[11] Thus, trade is one of the prime forces bringing peoples in contact with other peoples. What is distinctive about trade, as

---

[8] BERNSTEIN, *supra* note 1, at 7.

[9] *See generally* WILLIAM SHAKESPEARE, THE MERCHANT OF VENICE (1605).

[10] It has been suggested that this play shadows all our inquiries into trade, markets and capitalism itself. *See* SEBASTIANO MAFFETTONE, *Is Market Capitalism Morally Acceptable?*, *in* ETHICAL CHOICES IN ECONOMICS, SOCIETY AND THE ENVIRONMENT 95, 95–97 (Simona Capece ed. 2008).

[11] On the many ramifications of the "Other," the canonical source is EDWARD W. SAID, ORIENTALISM (1978).

opposed to conquest or the desire for land, is that trade by its nature brings people together on terms that might result in a mutually beneficial exchange. In this way, trade can also be a primal form of communication across difference, expressing who we are, what we make, what we value, what we want and how we exchange.

One of the marvelous aspects of trade is that it can involve communication and exchange where there is no shared language, culture or history – only the mutual desire to exchange. In this way, trade involves a form of what Stanley Cavell calls "acknowledgement" – the recognition that the Other exists as a separate, recognizable human person with the treatment due a person, even if we cannot directly or fully know the person's mind.[12]

A remarkable example from classical sources of this kind of trade is Herodotus' account of trade between the Carthaginians and a race of African peoples with whom they did not share a language. The example, even if mythologized, is worth quoting in full, as it is quite suggestive of the phenomenon we are exploring here:

> On reaching this country, [the Carthaginians] unload their goods, arrange them tidily along the beach, and then, returning to their boats, raise a smoke. Seeing the smoke, the natives come down the beach, place on the ground a certain quantity of gold in exchange for the goods, and go off again to a distance. The Carthaginians then come ashore and take a look at the gold; and if they think it represents a fair price for their wares, they collect it and go away; if, on the other hand, it seems too little, they go back aboard and wait, and the natives come and add to the gold until they are satisfied. There is perfect honesty on both sides; the Carthaginians never touch the gold until it equals in value what they have offered for sale, and the natives never touch the goods until the gold has been taken away.[13]

Without sharing a language or a system of value, the participants to such trade arrive at a mutually beneficial exchange, through a process that allows for a kind of bargaining within understood safeguards or conventions.

[12] STANLEY CAVELL, THE CLAIM OF REASON 329–426 (1979).
[13] HERODOTUS, THE HISTORIES 307 (1968).

Of course, encounters with the Other are not always beneficent. We can try to profit from the lack of shared language, or other information asymmetries, to engage in sharp dealing – trade as trickery or deceit. We have many colloquial examples of this, including offers to sell one another the Brooklyn Bridge, or the fable about Manhattan being "purchased" from indigenous Americans for a "handful of beads."[14]

More ominously, we can see in *The Merchant of Venice* how the proposed flesh trade in the play dramatizes several of the negative dynamics of trade to be examined in this chapter: in the face of inequalities in social power and the breakdown of acknowledgement along ethnic, religious and gender lines, we see elements of coercive, exploitative and oppressive conduct, and a kind of commercial overreaching. The most memorable speeches of the play are in fact calls for acknowledgement across and in spite of such differences.[15]

3 Trade as Domination

The darker side of trade on an interpersonal level raises another serious aspect of trade on a social/cultural level: trade as conquest. I do not mean this in the literal sense: conquest is conquest. However, the history of trade sadly offers many examples from all parts of the world that illustrate the fluid interrelationship between the concepts of commerce, conquest and confiscation, allowing us to see a darker side of trade as domination under the guise of trading.[16]

For example, Antony Anghie chronicles the way in which trading companies were used during the colonial period to assert sovereignty and extend the colonizing states' dominion over vast territories that the European states were not yet ready to administer directly.[17] In Asia we see examples of this in the "trade" relations of the East India

---

[14] See Peter Francis, Jr., *Beads and Manhattan*, WORLD HISTORY ARCHIVES, www.hartford-hwp.com/archives/41/415.html (last accessed July 12, 2017).

[15] See SHAKESPEARE, *supra* note 9. I am indebted to Kim Garcia for pointing this out.

[16] See, e.g., ANTONY ANGHIE, IMPERIALISM, SOVEREIGNTY AND THE MAKING OF INTERNATIONAL LAW (2005); James Thuo Gathii, *Commerce, Conquest and Wartime Confiscation*, 31 BROOKLYN J. INT'L L. 709 (2006); Omar Saleem, *The Spratly Islands Dispute: China Defines the New Millennium*, 15 AM. U. INT'L L. REV. 527, 554–56 (2000) (documenting commercial exploitation, lack of reciprocity and legacy of bitterness arising from unequal treaties).

[17] ANGHIE, *supra* note 16, at 68.

Company, or the notorious "Unequal Treaties" between China and the West following the Opium Wars.[18]

Turning south, Eduardo Galeano writes passionately how "Latin America's big ports, through which the wealth of its soil and subsoil passed en route to distant centers of power, were ... built up as instruments of the conquest and domination of the countries to which they belonged, and as conduits through which to drain the nations' income."[19]

In Africa, James Gathii documents the role of free trade rhetoric in legitimating Belgium's monopoly on exploitation of the Congo under the "freedom of commerce" principles agreed upon at the Berlin Conference.[20] By arguing that trade should be free, the colonial powers effectively left the stage open for unregulated exploitation of the Congo.[21]

These examples sadly and vividly illustrate how trade can seem to function as a form of dominance over the Other.[22] I say "seem," not because this is not domination (it is), but because as shall be seen, these examples are in fact an inversion of trade and not, I will argue, trade at all. Such exchanges exploit the mutual need and encounter across difference that characterize trade as a pretext for acts of violence and domination, and yield the opposite of trade as bargains: thefts.

Once again, *The Merchant of Venice* offers us an eloquent window into these dynamics. The secondary storyline of the play is also about domination, about choosing a woman, Portia, not as a commodity but as a person.[23] Shakespeare makes the point that there is no marriage if she is a commodity, just as there is no trade if it involves domination. At the heart of both marriage and trade, then, are consent, in particular the consent of those involved when the exchange crosses lines of

---

[18] *See Opium Wars*, NEW WORLD ENCYCLOPEDIA, www.newworldencyclopedia.org/entry/Opium_Wars (last accessed Aug. 27, 2017).

[19] EDUARDO GALEANO, OPEN VEINS OF LATIN AMERICA 197 (1973).

[20] JAMES THUO GATHII, *How American Support for Freedom of Commerce Legitimized King Leopold's Territorial Ambitions in the Congo*, in TRADE AS GUARANTOR OF PEACE, LIBERTY AND SECURITY? CRITICAL, EMPIRICAL AND HISTORICAL PERSPECTIVES 97 (Padideh Ala'i et al. eds., 2006).

[21] *Id.*

[22] *Id.* at 98 (citing SAID, *supra* note 11, at 3).

[23] *See* SHAKESPEARE, *supra* note 9.

power, gender and difference. Viewed in this light, the play is also about the limits of the marketplace in view of these darker possibilities, as for example when Bassanio is given a ring he is not to give away.

Historically, we can read the play as responding to a contemporaneous wave of globalization and the European encounter with the "New" World, raising difficult and timely questions for Elizabethan England and for us. Can we deny our own and others' humanity for economic gain, whether in the form of religious discrimination, or as slavery, the mines and Spanish *encomienda*-style serfdom?[24] Can we use "bargains" to enact racial and religious prejudice and shame the Other, or extract wealth and resources? Most importantly, does a "new" world mean it is all up for grabs, that maybe the old rules won't apply in this new economic space?

Such questions are never far from the surface in international trade, particularly in an era of globalization and its transformed social spaces.[25] From one perspective, the fact that globalization connects us to each other and to locales around the world in unprecedented ways could lead to the conclusion that there is no longer an "over there" or a "somewhere else," that it is all simultaneously "here" and "now." And yet, the newness and transnationality of this experience, and the seeming vastness of the digital world, can tempt us into believing it is a "new" world, hence under-regulated, beyond the pale and ripe for exploration, encounter and exchange, or domination, extraction and conquest.

II INVESTIGATING TRADE AS A TRANSACTION

I would now like to take a few of these aspects of trade and explore them more systematically in order to construct a preliminary picture of

---

[24] We hear echoes of Bartolomeo de las Casas here. BARTOLOMÉ DE LAS CASAS, A SHORT ACCOUNT OF THE DESTRUCTION OF THE INDIES (Nigel Griffin trans. 1992) (1552).

[25] As I write this, the United States and Western Europe are currently living through the early days (one hopes, the flood tide) of an anti-globalization backlash involving racism, nationalism and xenophobia, triggered in part by a fear of economic dislocation and loss of identity arising from "trade" as currently managed – in short, the questions are sadly not far from us even now, perhaps ever.

trade as a human experience. Key to that experience is the notion of *transaction*. I will first explore trade as an experience of transactions between individuals, and then take a look at trade as what happens or not between states when they facilitate, manage or impose such transactions.

A Trade as Private Transactions: Consensual Exchanges

1 Trade as an Exchange of Value

We engage in many types of transactions or exchanges throughout our lives, whether involving money, goods, ideas, services, affinity or information. However, if we think of what distinguishes trade from the many other exchanges we participate in, one element is that trade involves a transfer of economic value. By "economic value" I mean, in a general sense, goods, services, information or currency – as opposed to other qualities such as affection that have great value but are not economic in this sense. I am also not assuming any objective theory of value – for our purposes here, we can take value as determined by preferences and functioning markets.[26]

There are many different types of transactions involving a transfer of economic value, but not all of them are trade.[27] For example, gifts are transactions involving a transfer of economic value, but one of their distinguishing characteristics is their unilateral nature: the gift giver transfers something of economic value for nothing in return. I mean to

---

[26] In fact, as shall be seen presently, it is precisely because we don't have a satisfactorily objective theory of value that consent becomes so important. Under these circumstances, the freedom of the exchange is the only way we have to determine that the exchange is welfare enhancing for both participants – both freely participate because they expect to be better off as a result of the exchange. See *infra* notes 44–58 and accompanying text. A nonconsensual exchange is in this sense not even part of the rationality of the market system itself, i.e., the enhancement of individual and collective welfare. I am indebted to Pietro Maffetone for this insight. *See also* Florian Ostmann, *Two Ways of Conceiving of Moral Constraints on Prices in International Market Transactions* (2017) (unpublished manuscript) (on file with author). There has been renewed interest in the question of moral constraints on prices.

[27] Hillel Steiner notes three paradigms or types of transfers: gifts, exchanges and thefts. Hillel Steiner, *A Liberal Theory of Exploitation*, 94 ETHICS 225 (1984). Rather than map this onto trade, he takes this categorization in a different direction, toward the basis on which to develop an account of a fourth type of exchange, an exploitation. I shall return to that account later in the chapter. *See infra* notes 80–84 and accompanying text.

distinguish this sense of gift, which I would call the true sense, from a gift given in expectation of a return of noneconomic value: affinity, loyalty, etc. The latter may still be a gift in the sense of a unilateral transfer of economic value, but it starts to verge closer to trade in the *expectation* of a mutual exchange.

In contrast, trade transactions are all about the expectation of a mutual exchange – they are bilateral, or mutual, in nature, involving a *bilateral* exchange of economic value. We can experience this in both a positive and a negative dimension. The simultaneous face-to-face barter transaction is perhaps the paradigmatic experience and image of trade, and embodies this bilaterality in its positive form: I hand you something of value to you, and in return you hand me something of value to me. If it is not set up as a simultaneous face-to-face exchange, and we hand over our value, and nothing ever returns, we discover that what we have been engaged in is not a trade at all, but something else, perhaps a fraud or a theft – I shall have more to say about that shortly.[28]

We can edge into the definition of trade as bilateral exchange through another negative experience as well. For example, we have probably all had the experience of receiving what is ostensibly a gift, but discovering there was an expectation of an economic return, and we know how that changes the sense of the exchange from a gift into a form of trade, to the detriment of the gift-giving sensibility: "Oh, so this is just business," or, "that turned out not to be a gift at all." That sense of disappointment, even disillusionment, can be a signal, insofar as it accompanies the discovery that what we thought was a unilateral gift, turned out to be the expectation of a bilateral form of exchange.

Theft is another type of unilateral transaction, helpful in clarifying the nature of trade. A theft involves an *involuntary* transfer of value. It could be said that a theft is not a trade because it is unilateral, but a simple thought experiment clarifies that this is not the essence of the distinction. A thief in the paradigmatic "your money or your life"

---

[28] The documentary sale of goods, a brilliant mercantile invention, is designed to preserve and enforce the bilateral nature of trade in the face of the risks of *not* being able to execute a simultaneous face-to-face exchange, whether for reasons of distance, or timing, etc. Merchants have been wrestling with the nature and exigencies of trade for as long as there have been merchants, long before we had commercial law as we know it.

scenario could give you a cheap watch in return for your wallet, but it would still be a theft despite its bilateral quality. We would not call this a trade, nor would we call it even a coerced exchange, as will be discussed presently. The "exchange" element in this hypothetical is cursory or symbolic only – the essence of the experience is the complete involuntariness of the transfer of the victim's wealth, except in the "voluntary" sense of exchanging one's money to keep one's life.

Thus, trade must also be voluntary, which introduces the key notion of consent – both parties must consent to the transaction or there is some element of theft or violence. Return for a moment to the example of the paradigmatic face-to-face exchange I began this section with, and now imagine a third person, standing behind one of the two exchange parties, holding a gun at her back to drive the exchange forward. Our understanding of the nature of the moment changes entirely – whatever it is, it is not trade. I shall have more to say about what that in fact might be later in the chapter and throughout the book.

This key role for voluntariness is reflected in our language.[29] We can speak of good trades versus bad trades in terms of meeting our expectations of net value, and yet we distinguish even bad trades from "rip-offs" or thefts. We would not refer to the experience of being robbed as a "bad trade," except in a deliberately ironic sense.

Another aspect of the voluntariness of bilateral exchange can be expressed through the notion of bargain. Bargaining, or the process of reaching mutually agreeable terms, is often a necessary element in reaching consent, reaching a "bargain." Even where parties to an exchange do not actually bargain, the exchange presumes the freedom of both parties to consider and propose a variety of possibilities on the road to saying yes or no. Otherwise, if either of the parties were not able to bargain freely, the resulting transaction might still be voluntary in a

---

[29] I am of course working in English, as that is the language whose nuances I understand best. By saying "our language," I do not mean to assert that English is a universal language or that its terms are universally generalizable; I mean to invite the reader to assess these observations against their own language. Perhaps for commercial matters English is indeed a fairly generalizable language, but more than that I wouldn't want to suggest here (and I am not even sure about that). A definitive phenomenology of trade intended for an argument on global economic justice would need to undertake a linguistic interrogation of trade in many languages.

basic sense, but something has been lost (remember the gun?). This would be more akin to coercion than trade, as I will discuss further.

The centrality of the idea of bargaining can be understood through an investigation of its role in contract law, an institution "central to our social and legal systems, both as reality and as metaphor,"[30] and "long ... recognized as one of the most powerful statements of the nature of freedom in our society."[31] The notion of consensual bargain is foundational to the field of contract law.[32] The significance of bargained-for consent is reflected in the law of contract at the mythopoeic level through the concept of a "meeting of minds." The meeting of minds in contract law, even as a constructive notion, is key to the whole system for enforcing promises.

Beyond the mythopoeic, if we look at the core justifications under which a contract is declared void or voidable – mistake, duress or fraud – we see that they reflect the absence of or an impingement upon bargained-for consent.[33] Thus contract law is a key resource for understanding the consensual nature of trade, insofar as it embodies centuries of reflection on the nature of bargains of various kinds and their absence, and the implications for social life. In the following section, I will return to these legal ideas to help us further explore this intuition about the social significance of consent, and its absence, in economic relationships such as trade.

To summarize, by examining our experiences and language of economic exchanges of many kinds, I have sketched out a notion of trade as consisting of voluntary, bargained-for exchanges of value among persons for mutual economic benefit. I believe this account of trade is both plausible and coherent with our everyday uses of the term.[34] I hope at this point in the account that at least some of the examples and distinctions I have drawn might ring true in the reader's

---

[30] Melvin Aron Eisenberg, *The Bargain Principle and Its Limits*, 95 HARV. L. REV. 741 (1982).

[31] Todd Rakoff, *Contracts of Adhesion: An Essay in Reconstruction*, 96 HARV. L. REV. 1173, 1235 (1983).

[32] Eisenberg, *supra* note 30, at 741.

[33] *See infra* notes 35–43 and accompanying text.

[34] *See* Mathias Risse & Gabriel Wollner, *Trade Justice* (unpublished manuscript) (on file with the author) ("trade is cooperative in nature, mutually beneficial and by and large voluntary").

own experience of exchanges, even if the reader is still withholding judgment on the larger argument.

2 What Is Not Trade, and Why

Based on this preliminary inquiry, I would now like to turn to an examination of several alternatives to trade (i.e., other economic interactions that we do not consider trade), in order to paint a fuller picture of what trade is and what it is not. Exchanges and their pathologies have been around for a very long time, so we have much to draw upon.

a Predation

In the previous discussion, I introduced the concept of theft as a contrast to trade. Essential to this distinction is the absence of consent on the part of the one surrendering economic value. As Weil writes, one cannot seek consent where there is no power of refusal.[35] This rings true. Perhaps we are fortunate enough not to have been subjected to an actual theft, as the law would define it, and yet we may well have found ourselves in situations in which we felt we had no power to refuse an economic transfer of some kind, much as it felt against our will. However we understood the equities and imperatives of the situation as we handed over the subject of the transfer, it is unlikely we experienced that moment in the same way we experience consensual exchanges, even exchanges in which we give our consent reluctantly. To obey reluctantly is not the same as to consent reluctantly. Rather, the former experience comes closer to what we describe as predation, which in its classical roots is akin to plunder, or the seizing of property as booty, following the subjugation of one's will through an act of violence.

At the private-party level, contract law recognizes this difference through the concept of duress, a defense to the finding of a contractual obligation. In other words, where one party's formal consent to a contract was not freely given, but was given under some form of pressure, the law will not recognize this as a meeting of minds and will

[35] SIMONE WEIL, *Justice and Human Society, in* SIMONE WEIL 123 (Eric O. Springsted ed. 1998).

not find a contract. Thus through contract law's exploration of this subtle terrain of consent and economic relationships, we have as a society identified a space short of the criminal law of theft, within which the absence of consent nevertheless has important consequences. Within that space, we withhold the apparatus of contractual obligation and enforcement because we have determined that such apparent agreements are not in fact contracts – deals, bargains, promises – despite the formal appearance of consent.

b Coercion

Short of predation, we can recognize a subtler weakening of consent, involving what I will call coercion. Coercion occurs when a transaction is mutual, and in some basic way consensual, but something weakens the fullness or freedom of the consent, short of outright theft or duress.[36] Returning to our earlier thought experiment, in which we obeyed reluctantly, we can imagine other situations – we have very likely experienced them ourselves – in which we reluctantly agree to an economic transfer of some kind, against deep misgivings or resentments as to whether this is really in our self-interest. If we spend a moment here, in the difference between obeying against our will, and agreeing under pressure and in the face of great reluctance, we can gain some insight into the nature of coercion as opposed to theft or predation.

The experience of coercion often involves a restriction on the range of possible bargains that the parties are free, or not free, to propose and consider. To take the paradigmatic case, if I want the flat-screen plasma television, I have to surrender my right to judicial resolution of any disputes, accepting the nonnegotiable arbitration clause embedded in the form contract.[37] Thus, coercion can presuppose an inequality in bargaining power, where one party works to limit the range of possibilities "on the table," so to speak. The resulting agreement will in

---

[36] *See* Robert Hale's groundbreaking essay *Coercion and Distribution in a Supposedly Non-Coercive State*, 38 POL. SCI. Q. 470 (1923) (even voluntary market exchanges can be coercive in the presence of disparities in bargaining power, resources or knowledge). I am indebted to my friend Jeffrey Dunoff for introducing me to Hale's work.

[37] *See* Rakoff, *supra* note 31, at 1265–66 (discussing the problem of the enforceability of arbitration clauses in contracts of adhesion).

an important sense be voluntary, yet in an equally important sense will be motivated less by a desire to do the act in question, than by "a desire to escape a more disagreeable alternative."[38] In the end I may well opt for the television, but not because I tried and failed to negotiate a better bargain in terms of arbitration, but *in spite of* the fact that I was not allowed to negotiate that provision at all.

As with duress, contract law also wrestles with this issue and reflects this distinction between coerced and voluntary agreements.[39] As with predation, here again contract law, as our collective reflection over time on the nature of promises we should stand behind and promises we should not, opens a space within which we can see both the ubiquity and risks of economic transfers in which one party in some way pressures the other to agree. The coerced party may well agree in the end, but something important has happened, which our own experience of reluctance, resentment or misgiving indicates as well. However, as Robert Hale points out, since coercion is a market reality independent of the law, the law cannot eliminate coercion – at most, it can change the terms of coercion for better or worse.[40]

For this reason, contract law provides particular protections for consumers and those with weaker bargaining power when they deal in what the law calls "adhesion contracts": contracts with commercial parties or manufacturers who possess greater bargaining power, and which are presented in a "take it or leave it" manner.[41] In such cases, where a dealer says "if you want this good, these are the terms and the only terms," leaving the consumer unable to negotiate, courts will look carefully before assuming the consumer consented to the adverse terms of the contract, despite the fact that, in all other material respects, it looks as if a contract was voluntarily entered into. The bargain may stand, and coercion may inevitably be a part of it, but under scrutiny and with moderation through law. Courts

---

[38] Hale, *supra* note 36, at 472.

[39] On the difficult, but possible, task of drawing a line between coerced consent and no consent at all, *see* DERYCK BEYLEVELD & ROGER BROWNSWORD, CONSENT IN THE LAW 345–46 (2007).

[40] Hale, *supra* note 36, at 493–94.

[41] *See* Rakoff, *supra* note 31 (reconceptualizing the law of adhesion contracts).

will not automatically void such a contract, as would be the case
with duress, but they will look closely at the contract and may not
enforce all of its provisions, particularly provisions such as a mandatory arbitration clause that gives away valuable legal rights and
remedies.[42]

Circling back to Hale, insofar as coercion is an element in many
kinds of market and nonmarket transactions that we decide nevertheless should go forward, we have accepted at some level that economic
(and even noneconomic) relationships are complex phenomenon with
many mixed motives and crosscutting dynamics involved.[43] Simply to
accept coercion as part of trade with no further attention or recourse,
or alternatively to reject any exchange as valid trade if there is a
coercive element, may well go too far in either direction and distort
the subtle nature of our experience. I shall have more to say about this
in Chapter 3.

c Exploitation
When investigating the nature of theft and coercion, one dimension
common to both turns out to be that the party violating our consent,
or pressuring us for it, is present within the transaction, so to speak,
as is the offending behavior. What about a situation in which the
violation or pressure have occurred outside the four corners of the
transaction, yet throw a profound shadow over the resulting bargain,
the range of choices, and the decision to consent or not? We are left
with an uneasy sense that there is something unfair or abusive in the
transaction, yet it does not fit our experience of theft or coercion per
se. In considering this possibility, we are uncovering the nature of
exploitation.

To get at the nature of the experience of exploitation, theorists have
used a range of approaches, focusing either on the fairness of the

---

[42] In Rakoff's view, enforcing boilerplate terms "trenches on the freedom of the adhering
party," whereas failing to enforce them does not violate any abstract notion of "freedom of
contract" deployed in defense of the commercial firm, which as a hierarchical and
bureaucratic entity lacks any meaningful sense of "freedom" requiring judicial protection.
Rakoff, *supra* note 31, at 1236–37.

[43] *See* Hale, *supra* note 36; Onora O'Neill, *Between Consenting Adults*, 14 PHIL. & PUB. AFF.
252 (1985) (complexities of understanding coercion in commercial and intimate relationships).

transaction or its degrading or abusive quality.[44] Because I am focusing in this project on market transactions, and not the full range of personal and other interactions that might be exploitative, I will lean toward the fairness approach as most relevant for the market, although I aim to be neutral between the two.[45]

"Fairness" theorists seeking to characterize a situation as exploitative, must first offer an account of what constitutes fairness, or at least how it would be determined.[46] Alan Wertheimer, for example, a leading theorist of exploitation, suggests we evaluate the fairness of a transaction in terms of the agreement that might have been reached between the parties in a hypothetical competitive market.[47] Similarly, David Miller characterizes exploitation as the use of special advantages to deflect markets away from equilibrium, defined as exchanges involving equivalent value.[48] Hillel Steiner also uses notions of equal value and hypothetical markets to explore the nature of exploitation, but in a different way, as shall be seen in this chapter. In any event, this notion of an exchange on roughly equal terms or of roughly equal value – a "private" commercial notion of fairness – is key to both exploitation in commercial settings and the legal analysis of contract enforceability as well.[49]

Steiner's approach to equal value is particularly congenial to the exchange analysis of trade I am working with here, since he also analyzes the phenomenon of exchange as requiring that the transaction both bilateral and voluntary, and adds a third element: that the two transfers be of roughly equal value.[50] By rough equality, I take Steiner to mean that both parties consider the exchange fair – there is an appropriate relation, in their eyes, between what they are giving and

---

[44] See Matt Zwolinski, *Structural Exploitation*, 21 SOC. PHIL. & POL'Y 154, 157 (2012).

[45] As Zwolinski does in his own account of structural exploitation. *Id.* I also don't mean to foreclose the usefulness of the "degrading" approach in exploring a range of market situations, such as the labor market or the market for sexual services.

[46] Similarly, "degrading" theorists need to offer an account of what makes a transaction degrading or abusive. *Id.*

[47] ALAN WERTHEIMER, EXPLOITATION 230 (1996).

[48] DAVID MILLER, MARKET, STATE AND COMMUNITY: THEORETICAL FOUNDATIONS OF MARKET SOCIALISM 175 (1989).

[49] Rakoff, *supra* note 31, at 1230.

[50] Steiner, *supra* note 27, at 226.

what they are receiving. Where two transfers are not of equal value, yet the exchange is voluntary, Steiner characterizes this as evidence of possible exploitation.[51]

Steiner offers as illustration a market in which the top bid, the one the offeree ultimately accepts, does not reflect the maximum possible value of the items auctioned, but is simply the top bid in that market at that time. However, Steiner does not rely on an objective theory of value to characterize the bid as inadequate, but suggests we look at other parties who might have bid, and perhaps bid more, but were prevented from bidding by their rights being violated, such that the potential offerors either lacked the resources to bid, despite an interest in doing so, or were prevented from participating in the auction.[52] In either case, the result for the offeree is that they accept a voluntary mutual exchange with the resulting offeror, but for less than they might otherwise have received. In other words, the transaction is consensual and mutual, yet exploitative, because a potentially higher-paying third party was not able to participate in the auction and the resulting successful bidder took advantage of that opportunity.[53]

While I find Steiner's account particularly useful here, I don't intend to stump for a particular approach to exploitation, as I think that together they most fully develop our intuitions regarding what is disturbing about the hypothetical situation I outlined at the beginning. As Zwolinski writes, "the unfairness that constitutes exploitation ... is not the sort of thing that can be assessed by means of any precise formula."[54] What the various accounts share in common is the notion of unfair advantage taking.[55] This occurs when there is a flaw in the circumstances of the transaction – Risse and Wollner call it a moral

---

[51] *Id.* at 226–28.

[52] *Id.* at 232–34.

[53] *Accord* MILLER, *supra* note 48, at 177, 186 (it is in the nature of exploitation that the exploited party is unable to consider alternative, more attractive hypothetical transactions, due to the exploiter's use of unfair advantage).

[54] Zwolinski, *supra* note 44, at 178; *accord* Mathias Risse & Gabriel Wollner, *Three Images of Trade*, 1 MORAL PHIL. & POL. 201, 216 (2014) (favoring an ecumenical approach to diverse competing accounts of exploitation).

[55] WERTHEIMER, *supra* note 47; Risse & Wollner, *supra* note 54, at 214; Zwolinski, *supra* note 44.

defect in a distribution and its history[56] – that, whether due to an injustice in the background conditions, a vulnerability,[57] a rights violation or some other form of disrespect, results in one apparently free party seemingly inexplicably accepting a bargain that is not *fair*, but without evidence of direct coercion.[58] We take the party benefitting from the flaw to be exploiting the situation, and the vulnerable party as the exploited party.

When applied to trade, this suggests that where a party benefits from a defect in the background conditions, say, or a unique economic vulnerability, to the detriment of the other party, the resulting exchanges are not trade, but rather exploitation. They are not trade, because exploitation affects the consensual nature of the resulting transaction. The offeree's consent was granted within a restricted range of choices, a restriction that worked in favor of the offeror to permit a bargain that would otherwise be considered unfair. In a sense, it is a kind of trick or mistake: one consents to a set of circumstances that has been manipulated to the advantage of the other party, whether by one's counterparty or by others. If we participate in a transaction of this kind, we are participating in an exploitation, rather than a mutually beneficial and freely bargained exchange of roughly equal value. We are exploiting others, not trading with them.

Exploitation thus differs from coercion in that the force, pressure or rights violation occurs generally or with respect to others, including potential third parties, and not between the two primary parties to the transaction. In fact, one distinctive feature of exploitation is that the transaction may be voluntary, in the sense that it is free from direct coercion, and yet the exploited party was never given the opportunity to consent to the better deal that, but for the other party's intervention, might have been on offer.[59] Thus any consent

---

[56] Risse & Wollner, *supra* note 54, at 215.

[57] "Vulnerability" is a useful term to describe the situation that makes one ripe for exploitation, whether an individual or a state. *See* Robert E. Goodin, *Exploiting a Situation and Exploiting a Person, in* MODERN THEORIES OF EXPLOITATION 166 (Andrew Reeve ed. 1987).

[58] Zwolinski, *supra* note 44, at 158–61.

[59] *See* Zwolinski, *supra* note 44, at 156 (noting that "[t]o the extent that exploitative interactions are mutually beneficial, even if unfair, exploited parties will often have good reasons to go into them.").

happens in response to an unfair advantage taking that is essential to
the "deal" having been struck at all.

d Summary
The foregoing investigation of several of trade's pathologies, such as
predation, coercion or exploitation, have I hoped further developed the
core intuition of trade as consensual exchange, by highlighting other
types of transactions where some or all of trade's core elements are
absent or diminished. I have aimed in this discussion to present an
account of trade as consensual exchange that a reader might find as
intuitively plausible, in terms of their own experience of both consensual exchange, and (regrettably) any experiences of theft, coercion or
perhaps even exploitation. I would not like to turn to the more complex
patterns of consent, predation, coercion and exploitation that arise
when states get involved in trade.

B Trade as Public Transactions: Consensual Flows or
Patterns of Exchange

Let us assume, then, that the initial intuition holds, regarding the sense
of trade as essentially about consensual exchange between private
parties. What about what we call trade between states?

We can begin with the notion of trade between states as a transnational pattern of private exchanges, often (but not necessarily) facilitated by state action (here is one place where notions of trade and "free
trade" touch). At a purely economic level, we can measure commercial
flows of various kinds between states, and certainly this is at least an
element of what might be trade between states (commercial flows seen
as patterns of exchange).[60] At one level, our everyday speech registers
that this must be so. But we can draw on the same thought experiments

---

[60] It is certainly a key element of economic globalization. *See* DAVID HELD ET AL., THE
GLOBAL TRANSFORMATIONS READER 67 (2d ed. 2003) ("flows facilitated by infrastructure" being a key dimension of globalization). This raises an important question: if we
conclude that mere economic flows are not enough to count as trade, then much of what is
currently constituting economic globalization and justified publicly as "global trade" may
not in fact be trade but something else. This ominous possibility chimes with elements of
the current globalization backlash. I will return to this point in the concluding chapter.

regarding theft and private exchange, to dig a bit deeper into patterns of exchange between states, as we did for exchanges between individuals.

1 Theft and Economic Flows Between States

Imagine if we came newly onto the scene and witnessed commodity flows between states – we could be justified in thinking this to be trade, understood as patterns of exchange of economic value. Imagine, however, that we then discovered that one state had recently conquered the other, and the flows we could see and measure were in actuality the spoils of war. Would we then be as confident that this was trade? I'm not so sure.

What I am exploring here is whether our sense of trade versus theft at the private level, is in some way equally characteristic of similar patterns of exchange at the public level between states, when goods are exchanged by force or as the result of the past exercise of force, or perhaps even the ongoing threat of force. History furnishes us many examples of such commercial flows on which to reflect (some mentioned earlier), such as the steady stream of ships bringing gold, silver and precious gems from the New World to the Old, Galeano's "open veins." We would not be inclined, I think, to consider such wealth extraction to be "trade," though the commodity flows are undeniable, even essential, to the relationship, whatever we may decide to call it.

My sense is that the analogy holds. In socioeconomic terms, the aggregate equivalent to theft – transactions that are not mutual and where consent is not present – can be called wealth extraction, plundering or predation; add a political element and we call it imperialism or colonialism.[61] In these cases, there is a pattern of economic benefit flowing from one party to the other, but it is not mutual in a meaningful sense, and most importantly, it is not consensual. Rather, the flow of economic benefit in these cases is achieved

---

[61] For an interesting account of the wrongs of colonialism with respect to equality, reciprocity, agency and relationship, *see* Lea Ypi, *What's Wrong with Colonialism*, 41 PHIL. & PUB. AFF. 158 (2013).

through power inequalities as expressed by economic or military force – there is no power of refusal.[62]

If we are confident that at the private level we can readily distinguish between the experience of an exchange, and the experience of a theft, this public experience of wealth extraction by force would seem to hit the same markers. The reader may remain unconvinced, but for the moment, perhaps we can agree at least to register a sense of disquiet about what we initially took to be trade under these circumstances, and keep digging.

2 Coercion and Economic Flows Between States
What if we came upon the same scene, and discovered that, in addition to the commercial flows we can see and measure, there was a treaty between the two states, calling itself a trade agreement, covering these commercial flows? Would this then assure us that what we are indeed in the presence of trade, given that the treaty was duly ratified, indicating at least formal consent? I'm not so sure. Consider if we dug further as before, and discovered again that there had been an armed conflict between these states, that one state had won, and the victorious state had insisted as a condition of cessation of hostilities that the losing state sign an agreement formalizing a process of wealth extraction or "market opening."

What would we make of this? Once again history furnishes us actual examples of such events, such as the unequal treaties mentioned earlier that opened China to British trade following the Opium Wars. I suspect that on further reflection we would register the same disquiet as in the earlier example about theft, out of concern that what we are in the presence of is something other than trade, whatever the name of the agreement and perhaps in spite of any agreement at all.

The analogy to my earlier account of coercion between private parties seems valid here regarding forced agreement at the public level. States can coerce other states just as readily as individuals coerce other individuals, perhaps even more so if we consider the monopoly on violence that many states hold vis-à-vis private citizens. Coerced

---

[62] *Id.* There remains the difficult issue of determining the limits of acceptable "influence" or persuasion between states (for example, through forms of soft power), which the later discussion of coercion only partly answers.

patterns of exchange between states seem just as much to be something other than trade, as coerced exchanges between individuals.

How can we best read private law's reflection on coercion within contracts back into the state trade situation? Here we are saying that a pattern of exchange is consensual in some important way, and yet nonconsensual in another important way. It seems too much to conclude that this is a theft, as we did with the examples of predation earlier in the chapter.[63] And yet, to say it is simply "trade" and go no further, also seems to miss the mark. Such a move would be akin to concluding under contract law that a coerced exchange is a contract, full stop, and ending our scrutiny of the bargain there because there was in fact some degree of voluntary consent. In the private law context, we have decided we need to go further.

One answer may lie in the way courts will modify a coerced bargain to improve its terms, thereby aiming to approximate what the bargain might have looked like absent the coercion. In the trade context, this may mean concluding that coerced trade or a coerced trade agreement is really a composite transaction, with elements of trade (the consensual parts) and elements of coercion (the nonconsensual parts).[64] Much as the idea of a mixed case of trade and non-trade seems an uncomfortable amalgam, this is not merely a scholastic exercise of abstract distinctions. I suspect, but the reader will have to judge, that the discomfort lies in the nature of the experience itself, and not simply in our attempts to capture it in words.[65] More than one kind of dynamic is taking place, and we – and the law – are uncomfortable with ambiguity. I will have more to say about this in Chapter 3.

---

[63] Accord DAVID LEFKOWITZ, The Legitimacy of International Law, in GLOBAL POLITICAL THEORY 98, 108 (David Held & Pietro Maffetone eds. 2016) (costs of nonagreement on the part of a weaker state may not be so severe as to render the agreement nonvoluntary, yet still raise serious consent issues affecting the agreement's legitimacy).

[64] This hearkens back to Llewelyn's foundational if limited analysis of adhesion contracts as containing a mixture of what he called "specific assent" to negotiated terms, and "blanket assent" to the inclusion of terms that were not negotiated at all. See Rakoff, supra note 31, at 1199–1200. While Rakoff is critical of Llewelyn's analysis as incomplete and incoherent, Llewelyn does clearly label the fiction of considering the latter terms as "assented to," a useful distinction in the context of trade agreements as well.

[65] See O'Neill, supra note 43, at 255 (determining presence and scope of actual consent beyond formal indicia is a fraught exercise).

3 *Exploitation and Economic Flows Between States*

What about exploitation? Does the characterization of exploitation between private parties explored in the previous section also hold true at the public level?

Consider again the same example of coming across a pattern of commercial flows between states that looks like trade, and may even be carried out under an agreement calling itself a trade agreement. What if we dug further again, and discovered that a few decades earlier one of the states, the more powerful of the two, had taken active diplomatic and even military steps to warn other powerful commercial states away from that hemisphere, declaring it to be uniquely the province of that powerful state? Suppose further, that upon the success of this policy, this newly hegemonic state then used its local preeminence to deepen financial and commercial ties with the hemisphere's other, weaker, states such that when it came time to negotiate commercial agreements, the existing ties with the hegemon were so deep, the market relationships so important and the market presence of other rival states so comparatively weak, that the smaller hemispheric states had little choice but to accept poor terms or even unilateral terms in negotiating such agreements?

This thought experiment is clearly designed to illustrate one form of exploitation or unfair advantage taking – Steiner's account of actions taken to limit a market's potential rival bidders – but it is far from purely hypothetical. Commercial and political relationships in the Americas of the nineteenth and twentieth centuries reveal just such a pattern of behavior, and one can readily summon examples from other regions as well, which map in important ways onto the private experience of exploitation I characterized earlier as being something other than trade.

In such cases, taking Steiner's earlier bidding example but transposing it to states, one state takes steps away from the table to ensure that other potential bidding states are not in a position to offer a competing bid, and therefore its lower bid becomes the high bid in the ensuing negotiations.[66] Just as between private individuals, we

---

[66] Hillel Steiner, *Liberalism, Neutrality and Exploitation*, 12 POL. PHIL. & ECON. 335 (2013); Hillel Steiner, *Exploitation Among Nations* (2005)(unpublished manuscript) (on file with author).

would consider this pattern between states as a form of unfair advantage taking, despite the fact that it involves bilateral exchanges, perhaps even some negotiation and even a degree of consent, and may even be formalized by a treaty.[67]

Exploitation in transnational settings has increasingly become a subject of normative and legal reflection, no doubt due to the salience of unequal economic relationships in many global contexts, such as capital and labor in foreign investment.[68] In the interstate context, exploitation or unfair advantage taking may take the form of a range of policies, structures and institutional behaviors, which for one reason or another result in a situation where a state accepts from another state a poorer bargain than it otherwise could have pursued but for the vulnerability of its circumstances.

Critically for our purposes, the negotiation of trade agreements themselves can be form of structural exploitation – following Zwolinski's intuition, the trade agreement is not just an element in the background conditions for other private and public relationships that might be exploitative, it *is* the exploitation.[69] This can operate on at least two levels. First, the trade agreement can set unfair terms of trade between a more powerful state and a weaker state – it can *be* the unfair advantage taking.[70] States can take advantage of one another in trade negotiations in a variety of ways, which I shall have much to say about in Chapter 2.[71] Here again we are also presented with the question of

---

[67] *See* Risse & Wollner, *supra* note 54, at 211–12 (Exploitation is a powerful concept for the analysis of trade because "[a] core aspect of exploitation is that it may occur even if everybody's fate is improved through the activity in question, and even if everybody participates voluntarily. Trade exhibits these features ...").

[68] *See, e.g.*, Zwolinski, *supra* note 44.

[69] Zwolinski, for example, explores the possibility that unfair or abusive state behavior does not merely set the background conditions for exploitation, it *is* the exploitation, with implications for its own citizens that could be readily extended toward other states and the citizens of other states as well. *Id.* at 175–77.

[70] *See* Risse & Wollner, *supra* note 54, at 211 ("States can take unfair advantage of each other. Bigger states can exploit their bargaining power in negotiations, bilaterally or within the WTO.").

[71] *See id.* at 218–19 ("Moral problems suitably captured in the language of exploitation also arise in the context of trade if one party is 'no match in games of advantage' in relative terms, for example if abilities and skills of one party are significantly inferior. Common worries about lack of expertise of developing country representatives in WTO negotiations raise problems of exploitation in this sense.").

what level of advantage taking would be acceptable in an agreement we might still consider "voluntary" and therefore a trade agreement, and what rises to the level of exploitation, making it an "exploitation" agreement. It is easier to mark the clear cases at one end of the spectrum (illegal use of force, human rights violations) than it is to map out the middle zone. I will return to this question in Chapter 3.

Second, the trade agreement can create the conditions for subsequent private exploitations of the citizens of the weaker state. I am thinking for example of a treaty whose market access provisions open an industry to unsustainable levels of competition, or at an unsustainably fast pace, for reasons that benefit the more powerful state.[72] This puts the export industries of the dominant state – perhaps unwittingly (perhaps not) – into the position of exploiters, since the treaty's lopsided market access provisions are now background conditions to their new market dominance. Moreover, this may result in a large number of displaced workers who are then ripe for employment under exploitative circumstances, for example in the move from agriculture to sweatshops.[73]

Thus a "trade" agreement may be both exploitative *in itself*, and create the background conditions for further exploitation by other actors. It may even be the case, as Zwolinski suggests, that the high-unemployment state, or more accurately its elites, were complicit in this process in order to attract MNEs and reap private benefits from this exploitative process.[74] Such a pattern is not only an exploitation but a breach of the state's fiduciary duty to its citizens in the negotiation of the treaty, a related problem that I will explore in Chapter 4.

---

[72] *See, e.g., id.* at 219–20 (discussing Vrousalis's account of exploitation as domination for self-enrichment) ("Some economists argue that trade liberalization may, under certain circumstances, be detrimental to a country's prospects for growth and poverty alleviation (e.g., Rodrik 2007). Some such cases can be understood as exploitative. Powerful actors, states like the United States or organizations like the WTO, that require particular institutional set-ups or the pursuit of specific trade and industrial policies detrimental to the prospects of weaker actors, engage in exploitation as domination.")

[73] On exploitation and the sweatshop problem *see, e.g.,* Robert Mayer, *Sweatshops, Exploitation, and Moral Responsibility,* 38 J. Soc. Phil. 605 (2007); Zwolinski, *supra* note 44.

[74] Zwolinski, *supra* note 44, at 176–77.

4 Summary

What I have tried to offer in this brief exploration is not a definitive normative account of the ethics of commercial relationships between states, far from it – that is not the aim of this project. Instead, I have sought to ground our sense of trade between states in our earlier sense of trade between individuals, and to mark how in both cases consent seems equally relevant to our discrimination between trade on the one hand, and predation, coercion or exploitation on the other.

Fundamentally, this is the thread running through the account of trade that I offer in this book: there is a deep coherence between our individual experience of trade, and its pathologies, between private parties; and our shared public experiences of trade, and its pathologies, between states. In both cases, what makes trade recognizable as *trade*, and not something else, is consent.

III WHY CONSENT IN TRADE MATTERS

If this account of consent and trade continues to seem to the reader at least intuitively plausible, then the stage is set for an investigation of contemporary trade agreements in Chapter 2. The goal in that chapter will be to evaluate to what extent these agreements are or are not about trade at all, or something else, regardless of their name or formal characteristics. Insofar as they are about something else, we may then have options for making "trade" agreements about trade again, and perhaps moving closer to the social benefits we count on trade to deliver, which I will examine in Chapter 3.

Before moving on to this, however, I want to take up a criticism that might be in the reader's mind at this point, namely that I have not offered an account of *why* we ought to prefer trade, as defined here, to coercion, predation or exploitation. That is intentional on my part. What I am attempting here, as I said earlier in the chapter, is a reasonably accurate picture of trade as a human experience, which I hope makes it intuitively clear why consent matters. I do not consider it my task to offer a full-blown normative account of consensual trade, nor do I consider myself, as an academic trade lawyer, necessarily the best person to do so. However, having spent almost three decades

working in and around the field of international trade law, I have begun
to recognize certain patterns and opportunities when it comes to what
makes trade *work*, and what it takes to bring out the fullness of trade's
potential for individual and social good, and it is those patterns and
intuitions I have sought to present.

We must also recognize that trade, consent and trade agreements
do not operate in a vacuum – on the contrary, they work within, and
help shape, the institutions and relationships that constitute economic
life in our complex market societies. Our experience of trade and its
pathologies helps determine how we experience that economic life in
terms of freedom and opportunity, or oppression. It is not a question of
conforming or confining twenty-first-century trade to the evocative
writings of a twentieth-century social reformer and essayist. Rather,
insofar as Weil is right about how oppression works, then we have an
opportunity in how we build our socioeconomic relationships through
trade to avoid some of the more obvious costs that come from building
oppressive social structures, whether intentionally or out of ignorance.

While remaining deliberately agnostic, then, as to any explicitly
normative reasons we should care about consensual trade, I want to
end this chapter by suggesting some of the more pragmatic reasons
why minimizing oppressive tendencies in social relationships could be
important regardless of one's normative commitments. In order to do
so, I want to borrow the language of game theory and first look at what
kind of "game" trade is, and the rules of the game we are in fact
creating; and then at some of the social costs of this kind of game.

A The Trade "Game"

There are powerful reasons why we should be concerned about the
health of consent in trade agreements today, reasons that don't depend
on one's adherence to any particular normative view. Weil's analysis of
oppression reminds us that consent and oppression matter in very
concrete and important ways to any society and its well-being. Consent
is not merely an abstract social value or political ideal; rather, consent –
and its opposite, oppression – are everyday concrete realities for everyone involved in production of any kind around the world, with specific
economic and noneconomic costs.

However, restoring consent and reforming trade won't work if this depends on some mistaken idea that powerful actors will just decide to be "nice" – lawyers at least can't proceed that way. Even if one is not particularly troubled by oppression in itself, or deems oneself to be happily favored by the outcomes of oppression, there are nevertheless concrete, pragmatic reasons why consent and oppression might be worth considering.

1 What Kind of Rule-Based Game Are We Creating?

The fundamental reason to reframe trade toward consent is that consensual trade makes pure pragmatic common sense, if one correctly understands the kind of game that trade is. Respecting consent will therefore simply mean limiting the use of one's power in one's own long-term self-interest. Doing so brings us certain benefits, and helps us avoid certain costs.

One way to begin is to envision the role of trade institutions as that of playground monitor, charged with maintaining a beneficial process of interaction, but allowing a great deal of latitude to the participants in establishing their own relationships, and conducting their own transactions. As with playground games, there will be transitory winners and losers, but the monitor's role is to watch out for bullying. Bullying may appeal to the bully, and to others who might imagine themselves at some point attaining the bully's role and prerogatives, but in actuality the whole game breaks down.

In highly unequal trade agreements such as CAFTA, the law is no playground monitor; the powerful party, the United States, is relatively free to achieve its goals "unilaterally" despite a ratified and implemented multilateral agreement, since as will be seen in the next chapter the agreement itself bears its unilateral stamp. In this way, trade law of this sort is not capable of playing one of its key functions, that of structuring a reciprocal relationship toward mutual benefit. So, what kind of game *are* we creating?

In order to more fully understand the incentives for even powerful actors to moderate their rapacity, game theory can help us. The economic literature on games offers us ways to model and conceptualize the effects on others and on our future selves of certain kinds of opportunistic behavior. As a set of tools to articulate rational behavior in the face of a variety of types of decision matrices, game theory offers a useful way to analyze bargaining strategies and their consequences.

The key insight from applying game theory to trade is that *trade is a repeat game,* in which partners contemplate a series of ongoing exchanges with no clearly determined end point.[75] The self-interested calculation of what strategies and tactics to employ changes when one contemplates a repeat game, as opposed to a single iteration. Approaches that may seem attractive for their short-term gains might seem less attractive if they depend on exploitation, coercion or manipulation, which can all poison the well for future iterations of the game. Over time, the oppressive nature of such agreements becomes clearer, and as does their consequently diminishing returns.

The result is that if we correctly understand trade as a repeat game, then we are led to favor pro-consensual strategies as rationally self-interested strategies. For this reason we could alternatively call the consent approach to trade law as a "smart businessperson's theory of justice," since this is something every successful businessperson learns. Just because you have the power to drive home an unfair deal, a deal that is insufficiently mutually beneficial, doesn't mean it is always smart to do so. Businesses that survive and thrive learn that how you behave in the market can have long-term consequences against your own self-interest.

That is no more, and no less, than what a consent theory of trade seeks to bring home at the level of treaty, policy and politics. If you ignore consent, you undermine the basis for future bargains, since trade is a repeat game embedded in a complex set of structural relations. We have concrete self-interested reasons to care how we are structuring such games and relationships through our "trade" agreements.

This matters of course to the states involved, but it also matters a great deal to parties conducting business under these rules. The rules set the limits of what private bargains are possible, and set some of

---

[75] This can alter the incentives of the players toward cooperation. *See* George Norman & Joel P. Trachtman, *The Customary International Law Game,* 99 Am. J. Int'l L. 541, 559–60 (2005). *See generally* GEORGE J. MALAITH & LARRY SAMUELSON, REPEATED GAMES AND REPUTATIONS (2007); Jeffrey L. Dunoff & Joel P. Trachtman, *Economic Analysis of International Law,* 24 YALE J. Int'l L. 1 (1999).

the terms (for example, the terms of market access) of the game within which market actors will play. For example, as we shall see in the next chapter, the rules often determine the shape of private law as a condition of the agreement, therefore directly altering private bargains and the terms of bargains. They can also directly affect the dispute settlement options available to private parties, as well as the recourse available to their states when complaining of treaty violations and oppressive behavior. We will see both aspects illustrated vividly with respect to CAFTA and law reform, through which agents and distributors in Costa Rica have had the enforceability and stability of their private transactions forever altered by the CAFTA treaty. Such rule changes also affect the terms of competition among private parties within the states and between the states, and through investment chapters the relative position of domestic and foreign capitalists.

This is just one set of illustrations as to why consent matters in trade. Again, my goal here is not a moral argument in favor of consensual trade, but instead that we correctly evaluate our own economic self-interest. The rules of a framework agreement like a CAFTA or NAFTA need to protect the space and conditions for consensual exchanges, creating possibility of flourishing commerce, or there will be reduced space for such exchanges, to the detriment of us all.

2 The Social Costs of Nontrade
Insofar as we make consensual bargains and not other kinds of exchanges, we preserve and enhance the opportunity to engage in future beneficial consensual bargains, and we reduce the social costs of overreaching. On the other hand, to the degree we engage in predation, coercion or exploitation, we may lose potential partners for future beneficial transactions, and we certainly increase the social costs of making and enforcing such bargains.

a The Social Costs of Oppression
One way to begin to understand these costs is to look at the social psychology literature on justice. Social psychologists interested in justice have studied our subjective human experience of fairness and unfairness, or justice and injustice, and the social consequences of

perceptions of injustice.[76] Their research suggests that our emotional response to perceptions of injustice is among the most powerful reactions measured, and hence a powerful motivator in the human psyche toward emotions, judgments and behaviors – indignation, resentment, hostility and conflict, to name a few – that create personal and social costs.[77]

This is quite relevant to our examination of trade and consent, because of the risk that being subject to predation, coercion or exploitation – in a variety of ways, being forced to accept bad bargains or no bargain at all – will be perceived as the injustices that they are (in a subjective sense), and provoke precisely these same costly actions and reactions. Harder to quantify is the failure to thrive – for want of a better term – that an economic relationship subject to these forces will manifest, reminiscent of the suboptimal performance of Soviet-style command economies.[78]

For such reasons, our sense of whether we are engaged in trade or something else matters, not only to us as market participants, but also to those concerned with the optimal performance of the market, and with the minimization of social conflict over transboundary economic relationships.

b Trade and Security
Nonconsensual trade agreements do not simply create social and economic costs – they can create political and security costs as well. Trade agreements that are not consensual create conditions for blowback. Perceptions of injustice are strong motivators, leading to civil conflict, instability and violent counterreaction.[79] Over recent history we have seen manifestations of blowback from all points in the

---

[76] See generally KJELL TORNBLOOM, The Social Psychology of Justice, in JUSTICE: INTER-DISCIPLINARY PERSPECTIVES 177 (Klaus R. Scherer ed. 1992).

[77] See FRANK J. GARCIA, Trade, Justice and Security, in TRADE AS GUARANTOR OF PEACE, LIBERTY & SECURITY? CRITICAL, HISTORICAL AND EMPIRICAL PERSPECTIVES 78, 78–80 (Padideh Ala'I et al. eds. 2006).

[78] See, e.g., ALAN A. BROWN & EGON NEUBERGER, Basic Features of a Centrally Planned Economy, in INTERNATIONAL TRADE AND CENTRAL PLANNING 404 (Alan A. Brown & Egon Neuberger eds., 1968); Richard Rose & Ian McAllister, Is Money the Measure of Welfare in Russia, 42 REV. INCOME & WEALTH 75, 75–90 (1996).

[79] See Garcia, supra note 77, at 80.

spectrum, from an earlier upsurge of leftist authoritarian populism in Latin America,[80] to the current upsurge of rightist authoritarian populism around the world in response to globalization, its current "trade" patterns and their costs.[81]

If trade agreements are negotiated under circumstances in which our trade partners have no real possibility of consent, and significant sectors of their domestic societies have no way of expressing their consent or lack of consent, such a treaty is not going to promote an effective trading environment. Instead, such a treaty promotes over-reaching and instability to the degree to which it is coercive or exploitative, provoking resentment and unrest that often lead to violence by both citizens and governments.[82]

Eschewing opportunities for coercive or exploitative trade agreements might allow a region's people to finally enjoy the gains of trade while simultaneously weakening the tide of authoritarianism. Thus there is a mutually reinforcing relationship between consensual economic relations and our collective security.

c The Social Costs of Monopolies

Short of outright conflict, we also cannot risk that trade relations take on the properties of a monopoly, because of the well-recognized social

---

[80] To many in the region, the unequal terms and social unrest caused by agreements such as CAFTA represent failures of democracy. Hence, for example, the rhetoric and appeal of former Venezuelan President Hugo Chavez, his Bolivarian Revolution and his increasing influence in the region. *The Return of Populism*, THE ECONOMIST (Apr. 15, 2006), www.economist.com/node/6802448. I am indebted to Dan Blanchard for drawing this point to my attention.

[81] This has direct consequences for the viability of trade law today, and direct roots in the breakdown of political consensus – read as consent – in trade politics. See Frank J. Garcia & Timothy Meyer, Restoring Trade's Social Contract, 116 MICH. L. REV. ONLINE 78 (2017). *See generally* Steven Erlanger, *Britain Votes to Leave E.U.; Cameron Plans to Step Down*, N.Y. TIMES (June 23, 2016), www.nytimes.com/2016/06/25/world/europe/brit ain-brexit-european-union-referendum.html; James McAuley & Karla Adam, *Europe's Harsh New Message for Migrants: "Do Not Come,"* WASH. POST (Mar. 3, 2016), www .washingtonpost.com/world/french-british-leaders-meet-amid-migrant-crisis-concern-over-eu-exit/2016/03/03/9b0ee319-6128-4d06-b897-ef13a4044d31_story.html; Jane Perlez, *China-Led Development Bank Starts with $509 Million in Loans for 4 Projects*, N.Y. TIMES (June 25, 2016), www.nytimes.com/2016/06/26/world/asia/china-led-devel opment-bank-starts-with-509-million-in-loans-for-4-projects.html.

[82] *See* Garcia & Meyer, *supra* note 81.

costs of monopoly practices.[83] Trade relations become a monopoly when one partner has the market power sufficient to allow it to unilaterally dictate the terms of engagement, and behave in this sense like the classic monopolist with a dominant position. Returning to the playground metaphor, one expects to see some turnover as to who plays which role, who is winning and losing – it is rare for the same child to always win, and if this happens, the rules or the teams are usually changed to return the game to the realm of healthy competition, or else the other children lose interest and the game stops.

Unequal trade agreements such as the CAFTA treaty set up a system that resembles the sort of playground in which the same child wins most of the time, and is perceived as continuously trying to formulate self-serving rules, with little effective restraint, and with the leverage to force everyone else to play along. In that sense, such trade agreements would fail most tests for monopolistic concentrations of power: the dominant partner can set the terms of engagement regardless of the behavior of other competitors or the "consumers" themselves.

At the private level, monopolies impose well-recognized economic costs to society in terms of higher prices and the longer-term costs to competition and the innovation and cost benefits competition can bring. At the public level, such a system is usually maintained at great cost to private citizens through bureaucracies and enforcement mechanisms, a higher cost than if the system could count on willing participants. This means that a "monopoly agreement" is actually increasing certain kinds of social costs of trade to private actors and consumers, even as it seeks to reduce others. From an economic perspective, this doesn't necessarily allow for the emergence of the best products and services.

3 Trade Agreements and the Coherence of Liberalism

The importance of competition and individual economic opportunity to society, and the costs of their diminishment, are key tenets

---

[83] See Keith Cowling & Dennis C. Mueller, *The Social Costs of Monopoly Power*, 88 Econ. J. 727 (1978).

of classic economic liberalism.[84] This brings us back around to normative political theory, but I hope still in a "pragmatic" sense. By this I mean out of a concern for basic policy coherence: a state that considers itself to be part of the liberal political tradition, has reasons to be concerned that its foreign policy not violate its own founding principles.[85] Liberal states risk compromising their basic values and undermining their political legitimacy and public effectiveness when they fashion or accept trade agreements that vitiate the consent of the states or peoples they involve, because consent is a core value for liberal societies.

This can create a kind of externality problem for liberal states. One of the functions of law in economic matters is to restrain the human tendency to seek profit for one's self and to shift cost and risk onto other parties. Economists describe this as the process of creating externalities. It is no surprise that human beings in economic relationships should seek to advance their own interests, trying to shift risk and costs to others. That is one reason we have law: to plan ahead for this tendency and build in certain safeguards. In corporate law matters, for example, we expect that corporate actors will seek to maximize profit, transfer risk and externalize cost, and we legislate with that in mind. We consider economic law successful when it is effective in ensuring that parties who exercise control and derive profit bear an appropriate degree of risk and internalize their costs.[86]

"Externalizing" the costs of oppressive trade creates costs for the societies involved and ultimately for all of us. For one thing, citizens of liberal states pursuing illiberal trade are often faced with the subsequent prospect of supporting authoritarian regimes abroad solely to maintain the economic opportunities we have created through

---

[84] *See* WILLIAM D. GRAMPP, ECONOMIC LIBERALISM: THE CLASSICAL VIEW (1965).

[85] On the link between a state's foreign conduct and its own political legitimacy, *see* LEA BRILMAYER, JUSTIFYING INTERNATIONAL ACTS (1989); *see also* FRANK J. GARCIA, GLOBAL JUSTICE AND INTERNATIONAL ECONOMIC LAW: THREE TAKES 67–136 (2013) (one mode of justice is as integrity to one's normative commitments, regardless of the commitments of others).

[86] *See* JOSEPH VINING, FROM NEWTON'S SLEEP 287–90 (1995); *see also* Larry D. Thompson, *The Responsible Corporation: Its Historical Roots and Continuing Promise,* 29 NOTRE DAME J. L. ETHICS & PUB. POL'Y 199 (2015).

predation or coercion.[87] If the use of such force is not internalized as a cost of that production, then the goods coming from a factory in such countries might seem cheaper, since labor costs are lower. However, this would not be a true price, and consumers would not have an accurate reflection in the price of the costs they may also have to bear as taxpayers and citizens, resulting from the violence necessary to enforce that bargain. If, on the other hand, the costs of enforcement are internalized (through the possibility of imposing a social tariff, for example), then the full nature of the bargain will be clearer to consumers and to society as a whole, and it will be seen as the bad bargain it is.[88] Such an approach in the trade area would be similar to the "political risk" calculations made in the foreign investment area, and would be equivalent to adding a "social tax" to the cost of such goods.

This is just one example of a kind of externality that liberal states may inadvertently create in pursuing trade policies inconsistent with their core values. In designing instruments to create global markets through treaties, liberal states must take care that they do not talk the rhetoric of trade while instead creating the reality of coercion or exploitation, thus aiming to reap what might seem to be the short-term economic gains of oppression, while externalizing abroad the social consequences of coercion or exploitation. Such an agreement would be morally compromising for liberal states, whatever else its costs, because for liberal states trade agreements lose their moral justification when not free.

IV CONCLUSION

Consent is at the heart of what makes trade "trade": voluntary, mutual, bargained-for exchange of roughly equal value. I have suggested three other types of transactions that, while they may look somewhat like trade, do not in fact meet the definition: predation, coercion, and exploitation. Participants in any of these three transactions will see

---

[87] One striking example is the Unocal case alleging human rights violations by the oil giant in Burma. *See* Daphne Eviatar, *A Big Win for Human Rights*, THE NATION (May 9, 2005), at 20.

[88] For an evaluation of such a tariff from the environmental protection debate, *see* CHRISTIANE KRAUS, IMPORT TARIFFS AS ENVIRONMENTAL POLICY INSTRUMENTS (2000).

economic value exchange hands, and society may reap some economic benefit, but this occurs under conditions involving the absence or impairment of consent, which introduces its own costs and risks. I have also suggested reasons why we should care about such risks, costs and consequences that have to do with our own self-interest and the benefits we expect to see from trade.

If we begin with an understanding of trade itself as consensual exchange, we can then look aspects of the current trading system that undercut these social and economic opportunities, because they build oppressive relationships rather than consensual ones. We can look at the pathologies or mechanisms whereby oppression in general is linked with the trading system in particular as a system of production: mechanisms or dynamics that allow or constitute predation, coercion and exploitation in transnational economic relationships. We can then look at ways to build an ideal trading system around "the forms and expressions of consent," and then see how current trading systems and trade negotiations can be brought nearer to this goal. That will be the task of the chapters that follow.

**CONSENT, OPPRESSION AND
CONTEMPORARY TRADE
AGREEMENTS**

If it turns out that consent plays a role in safeguarding what is life-giving in trade, then we will want to understand the degree to which consent is reflected, or not, in the trade agreements we have negotiated thus far. In the words of Weil, if consensual trade can be an "ideal limit" allowing for economic transactions free from oppression, it is important to understand "the conditions actually given" before determining what changes are necessary to bring these conditions nearer to this ideal.[1]

In this chapter, I will take the view of trade as consensual exchange developed in the last chapter, and through that lens examine several bilateral and regional agreements currently in force, then contrasting them to the WTO as a multilateral agreement, to get a sense of the state of consent in our contemporary trade practice. I have chosen the WTO, and several regional and non-regional FTAs between the United States and moderately unequal or highly unequal partners (Korea and Colombia as the former, Central America as the latter, although the Colombian economy is weaker than Korea's), to illustrate the broadest possible range of issues, and also that such issues are not confined to a certain region or kind of partner or, indeed, to non-multilateral agreements.

This analysis can also help us see into the link between what Weil highlights as the nature of oppression in general, and the oppressive aspects of a particular system of production such as global trade, where

---

[1] WEIL, *Analysis of Oppression*, in THE SIMONE WEIL READER 126, 133 (George A. Panichas ed. 1977). I am using the term "ideal" here, as I believe Weil intends it, not as the antonym to "real" but as an archetype of what is *most* real about trade, most true.

commercial relations take place across a broad spectrum of inequalities in economic and other forms of power, all of which affect consent. Understanding this link could help us understand the capacity of the global economic system, as currently constituted through trade agreements, to preserve or undercut consent, and therefore to resist or enact on a global scale the oppressive tendencies in social organization. If we are fortunate, this might help lay a foundation for us to see opportunities to move the system toward the ideal of consensual trade agreements.

I want to start by briefly introducing the reader to the nature of trade agreements today, before moving on to the analysis in chief. The specialist reader should feel free to skip Section I and proceed directly to Section II, where I undertake the main investigation of the chapter. With the fruits of that analysis in hand, we can then begin considering in Chapter 3 how we got where we are today, and what kinds of agreements, substantive provisions and negotiation strategies would be necessary to promote, rather than undercut, consensual economic relationships.

I CONTEMPORARY TRADE AGREEMENTS

A Overview of the Trade Agreement Process

There are four main stages in the trade agreement process, each of which can also play a key role in understanding the full arc of consent and its absence in trade agreements today: the negotiations, the resulting substantive trade rules themselves, the ratification process and implementation of the agreement. In this book I am focusing in particular on the transnational elements, i.e., the process of negotiation between states, and the negotiated text of the treaty itself. Ratification processes and politics differ with each state and are essentially domestic, although I will touch on them in a few places as they concern, or should concern, other states involved in the negotiations. The same goes for the implementation process, though I will explore one aspect – the role of trade adjustment assistance – in Chapter 4 as an illustration of important "internal" analogues to consent between states, that are newly foregrounded in today's fraught trade policy environment. Nevertheless, I will briefly review all four elements here.

Negotiation matters, of course, because it is in the process of negotiation that we reach consent as negotiating parties, and through which the terms of any bargain are hammered out. Negotiation is also where inequalities in power will surface in their most acute forms, and thus where we see domination, coercion or exploitation at work in framing (or denying) possible bargains. The more asymmetric a trade agreement, the more reason we have to be concerned that the negotiations were skewed by marked inequalities in power. Finally, in negotiation (as with ratification), the political contest over whose voice is represented, by whom, at what point in the process and with what fidelity (bringing in notions of fiduciary responsibility, principal–agent theory and the underlying social contract of representative government itself), comes to a head.

The substantive provisions that result from any process of negotiations are significant, first, because they express the bargain struck by the negotiating states, and therefore the terms of their structural economic relationship. Consent, its impairment or its absence, will all be manifest in the nature of the rules as negotiated. But these rules have a second kind of importance, for private parties. These treaties – as economic framework agreements – set the rules that, if adopted, will in domestic law set the terms for many economic exchanges by private parties in the adopting states. In other words, the treaties by their nature set or remove limits on the kinds of bargains private parties can strike, and can in some cases reach right into the private agreements themselves and change them, thus directly impacting their scope and nature.

The ratification process is key to the role of consent in the domestic politics of trade, because that is where each constituency of trade, through its relevant national political institutions, expresses (or withholds) its consent to the trade agreement as negotiated. Alongside negotiation, this is another site where political consent and the social contract meet economic consent and the nature of trade, with important consequences. The mechanisms that each society has in place for its deliberations on the prudence of adopting trade agreements will matter in political terms when it comes to the formal legitimacy of the adoption of the treaty,[2] but they also matter in concrete economic terms, since an agreement adopted without voice, if it creates economic harm, can be understood as working a form of domination or theft on the voiceless citizenry (or subgroup of voiceless citizens) of the adopting state, thereby undermining its substantive legitimacy as well.

This brings me to the fourth and final element, how trade agreements are implemented, which can involve a host of formal and informal regulatory adjustments, compromises and agreements, any of which may respect or undermine any consensual agreements reached in the ratification process, or indeed the consensual basis of trade itself. In particular, I am interested in how trade liberalization fits into the larger social fabric of the adopting state. This forms part what I am calling the social contract of trade: insofar as free trade represents a commitment to a social policy that is likely to displace some workers even as it employs or enhances the condition of other workers in pursuit of a collective good (the benefits of trade), then to seek ratification of a free trade agreement is to ask (or compel) certain members of a society to undertake a risk for the collective good.

In concrete political terms, the support of workers and organized labor for trade agreements is in fact often secured through the promise of mechanisms to compensate them for any trade losses. Whether and to what extent a society delivers on this explicit or implicit promise in the implementation phase matters for whether an agreement equitably and consensually distributes wealth or works as a form of theft, extracting wealth from one segment of society and transferring it uncompensated to another.

With this brief overview of the trade policy process behind us, I will now offer a brief introduction to some of the key substantive areas that make up the modern free trade agreement, before turning to the consent analysis in chief.

---

[2] See DAVID LEFKOWITZ, *The Legitimacy of International Law, in* GLOBAL POLITICAL THEORY 98 (David Held & Pietro Maffetone eds. 2016) (noting coercion and representation problems affecting consent's validity); Matthew Lister, *The Legitimating Role of Consent in International Law*, 11 CHI. J. INT'L. L. 663, 663–91 (2011) (arguing that international law preserves a role for actual consent among states, in relation to the jurisdiction of international tribunals, and is therefore more fully consensual in this aspect than even domestic law).

B The Modern Free Trade Agreement

The scope and complexity of trade agreements – even bilateral agreements – have increased dramatically in the postwar period. The United States has been an active proponent of such a broad FTA agenda in its own regional/bilateral treaty practice, and includes both traditional subjects like market access for goods and services, and new subjects such as domestic law reform, investment protection, intellectual property obligations and macroeconomic policy coordination.[3] This brings with it both the potential to achieve substantial social good, and the possibility for imposing seriously unbalanced commitments and poorly understood obligations that work deep within domestic legal systems, to the detriment over the long term of all parties to the agreement and of the global market itself.[4]

What follows is a quick tour of the major categories of substantive provisions found in most contemporary trade agreements.

1 Market Access and Core Principles

At the core of any trade agreement are the rules that govern the terms of access to goods and services markets, or market access provisions as they are called in trade jargon. In multilateral trade, market access is regulated by a set of negotiated tariff commitments, or bindings, listed on each country's schedule.[5] Regional or bilateral FTAs are somewhat different, in that the presumption is "free" trade or the elimination of

---

[3] Young-Shik Lee et al., *The United States–Korea Free Trade Agreement: Path to Common Economic Prosperity or False Promise*, 6 U. Pa. E. Asia L. Rev. 111, 123 (2011).

[4] On the potential regulatory benefits of "deep integration" through regionalism, *see* James H. Mathis, *Regulatory Regionalism in the WTO: Are Deep Integration Processes Compatible with the Multilateral Trading System?*, *in* Bilateral and Regional Trade Agreements: Commentary and Analysis 142 (Simon Lester et al. eds., 2d ed. 2015). The risks can come through some of the same mechanisms Mathis highlights (MFN for example) if we assume highly unbalanced norms imposed by coercion, rather than organic and balanced law reform.

[5] *See* Asif H. Qureshi & Andreas R. Ziegler, International Economic Law 354–55 (3d ed. 2011). Since 1994 the multilateral agenda has grown to include services. *See generally* Federico Ortino, *Regional Trade Agreements and Trade in Services*, *in* Bilateral and Regional Trade Agreements: Commentary and Analysis, *supra* note 4, at 213, 215–24 (discussing market access and other core principles of the services trade in the multilateral trade context under GATS).

tariffs on substantially all trade in goods between the participating states.[6] This may take the form of a graduated process of tariff reductions, and may still maintain a few negotiated exceptions, but "free" trade is the normative model.[7]

Closely associated with market access concessions are the two core antidiscrimination principles, Most Favored Nation (MFN) and National Treatment (NT), together with their associated exceptions. These obligations prohibit states from discriminating between like products from different states, or between imports and like domestic products, respectively.[8] At the multilateral level, MFN and NT are subject to important exceptions, such as for development-related preferential trade arrangements such as GSP (in the GATT Enabling Clause). Important for our subject here, it is the GATT Article XXIV exception that allows states to pursue "free" trade in the form of FTAs and Customs Unions despite their inherent discrimination in favor of participating states and against nonparticipating states.[9]

At the bilateral or regional level, MFN and NT obligations can also be conditioned in a number of ways, despite the trade liberalization commitment being generally more extensive than in multilateral trade. NAFTA, for example, allows numerous exceptions to MFN and NT in the reservations the NAFTA states entered into the NAFTA Annexes.[10] In the services sector where liberalization also tends to be less comprehensive than in goods, states can choose between the "negative list" approach, whereby MFN and NT

---

[6] Services trade liberalization tends to move more slowly than goods liberalization even in an FTA. *See generally* ORTINO, *supra* note 5, at 230–35 (discussing market access and general obligations of FTAs in the services context).

[7] QURESHI & ZIEGLER, *supra* note 5, at 357. *See generally* ANDREW D. MITCHELL & NICOLAS J. S. LOCKHART, *Legal Requirements for PTAs Under the WTO*, *in* BILATERAL AND REGIONAL TRADE AGREEMENTS: COMMENTARY AND ANALYSIS, *supra* note 4, at 81.

[8] *See* QURESHI & ZIEGLER, *supra* note 5, at 359–61. For variations in the possible approaches to MFN and NT in the services sector, *see* ORTINO, *supra* note 5, at 230–31.

[9] *See* QURESHI & ZIEGLER, *supra* note 5, at 360; *see also* MITCHELL & LOCKHART, *supra* note 7, at 83–92 (discussing the scope of the General Agreement on Tariffs and Trade [GATT] Article XXIV).

[10] *See, e.g.*, North American Free Trade Agreement, art. 1108, Can.–Mex.–US, Dec. 17, 1992, 32 I.L.M. 289 (1993) (hereinafter NAFTA) (allowing states to maintain exceptions to MFN and NT in the investment sector by listing them in Annexes I and III).

obligations apply to all sectors by default except those that are excluded by the schedule, and a "positive list approach" whereby the MFN and NT obligations do not extend to any service not positively listed on the schedule.[11]

The gatekeepers for these more favorable trade benefits are known as "rules of origin." In a regional or bilateral FTA context, rules of origin set out the criteria by which goods qualify for the trade benefits that are specific to regionally produced goods, especially zero-tariff treatment.[12] Participating states can adjust the regional value content requirements to determine precisely how much economic value must be the result of activity within the free trade zone, as a condition of regional origin designations. These requirements can significantly influence production and investment decisions, and therefore have important industrial policy implications.[13]

2 Trade Disciplines and Remedies

Trade agreements also institute rules governing various kinds of trade-related measures states employ in a variety of situations, that have both a substantive justification or role, and a possible protectionist dimension. States have many ways to circumvent their tariff reduction commitments, through what are collectively known as nontariff barriers or NTBs, and trade agreements therefore can contain a range of anti-circumvention provisions.

Perhaps the most important is the prohibition against quantitative restrictions, either total (embargoes) or partial (quotas), and against measures having equivalent effect.[14] As with other trade rules, this prohibition is subject to many exceptions, such as in the case of balance of payments crises (e.g., GATT Article XII). Other anti-circumvention provisions include measures disciplining the application

---

[11] See ORTINO, supra note 5, at 221–22.

[12] QURESHI & ZIEGLER, supra note 5, at 366; MATHIS, supra note 4, at 95–96. The origin of services is determined less "quantitatively," by the "modes of supply," the patterns of source and destination jurisdictions of the service provider and the customer, respectively. See WTO General Agreement on Trade in Services, Apr. 15, 1994, Marrakesh Agreement Establishing the World Trade Organization, Annex 1B, 1869 U.N.T.S. 183; ORTINO, supra note 5, at 216, 225–26.

[13] QURESHI & ZIEGLER, supra note 5, at 367.

[14] Id. at 355.

of sanitary or phytosanitary measures (SPS) or technical barriers to trade (TBTs)[15] so as to minimize the potential for protectionist abuse; measures governing customs administration and valuation procedures; and other technical matters.

Trade agreements also recognize the need to allow for temporary exceptions to trade rules in a range of cases involving economic stress and crisis. When the crisis involves temporary and lawful import surges, such measures are called safeguards.[16] Negotiating the rules allowing for safeguard actions in designated cases, and governing their use and duration is therefore an important element in concluding trade agreements, since they essentially allow protection from what is considered "fair," negotiated trade.[17]

"Unfair" trade is the subject of state antidumping and countervailing duty laws, and trade agreements also often regulate how states employ their antidumping and countervailing duty measures to address sales at less than fair value and state subsidies, respectively.[18] Sadly, such rules are often employed by states beyond their substantive justification, as protectionist tools to offset the economic benefits their trading partners expect from liberalization commitments found in bilateral or regional FTAs.[19]

Subsidies, or government grants offsetting a cost of production, have been a vexed and vexatious issue in multilateral trade for decades, with some progress against explicit export subsidies, but little process on otherwise distorting subsidies, through the WTO Agreement on Subsidies and Countervailing Measures, or SCM. One reason subsidy policy has been perhaps the most controversial of all trade subjects is that for the subsidizing state it reaches deep into the heart of the state's

---

[15] *Id.* at 370–78.
[16] *Id.* at 398–99.
[17] *Id.* at 399.
[18] *Id.* at 379.
[19] *See, e.g.*, Chapter 2, pp. 83–85 (discussing such US tactics in the case of Korea and the KORUS negotiations. *See generally* Lee et al., *supra* note 3, at 132–33 (arguing that the Korea–US free trade agreement did not result in a large amount of trade liberalization for Korea because many of their major exports already benefited from low tariffs and the "actual impediments to Korean exports to the US were antidumping measures, countervailing duties, and extraterritorial applications of antitrust laws ….").

industrial policy and economy-priming tool bag. For such reasons, states generally do little to address subsidy concerns in bilateral or regional agreements, preferring to advance (or delay) this effort in a multilateral forum instead, where any commitments they may be willing to make can have the broadest possible reciprocal benefit to their economies from the sheer number of other members imposing the same discipline. However, subsidy policy remains stalemated at the multilateral level, causing ongoing difficulties for states on the receiving end of subsidized exports, either in their domestic markets or in third markets where they must also compete against the subsidized goods. The current multilateral stalemate on subsidies is a costly one for all concerned.

3 Macroeconomic Policy Coordination

A distinctive element in contemporary trade agreements is the inclusion of provisions aimed at coordinating macroeconomic policies. Typical subjects include key sectors such as competition policy, IP, transportation, agriculture and technical standards, among others. Such a provision will generally aim to establish agreed standards and policy frameworks, often adopting as a goal the harmonization of national policies and standards in the relevant area.[20]

Such policy coordination has historically been associated with deeper levels of integration such as typically found in Customs Unions and Common Markets, with the European Union as the paradigm case. However, provisions aiming at macroeconomic coordination can now be found in most FTAs, at least in United States treaty practice. This has proven controversial, since under conditions of asymmetry, as will be discussed in Section 6, harmonization can consist of the forced adoption of the more powerful state's standards and policies.[21] Given the nature of the subject matter, this kind of harmonization reaches deep into the domestic policy framework of the imposed-upon state.[22]

---

[20] See generally MATHIS, supra note 4.
[21] See infra notes 152–54 and accompanying text (Korean complaints about forced harmonization).
[22] Lee et al., supra note 3; MATHIS, supra note 4.

4 Investment

Similarly, FTAs today also typically fold into their provisions a chapter on investment, generally consisting of one party's – generally the dominant one's – current model bilateral investment treaty (BIT), perhaps modified through the trade negotiation.[23] This recent development (dating to the 1994 NAFTA treaty) thus links trade agreements to the history of foreign investment protection, and represents an important yet fraught convergence in contemporary international economic law.[24]

While foreign investment and the law protecting foreign investment have a long history,[25] modern international investment treaties arose during the twentieth-century decolonization period, when economic nationalism led to increased anxiety among foreign investors, often nationals of former colonial parent states, as to the vulnerability of their investment.[26] BITs addressed that anxiety through clauses granting foreign investors specific rights involving fair and equitable treatment and national and most-favored-nation treatment, as well as rules governing expropriation, enforceable through binding arbitration against host states.[27]

The fairness of the investment treaty regime is currently being hotly debated, in part due to the asymmetry of its normative framework, and in part due to its origins in the colonial pattern of foreign investment.[28]

---

[23] See generally JOSHUA P. MELTZER, Investment, in BILATERAL AND REGIONAL TRADE AGREEMENTS: COMMENTARY AND ANALYSIS, supra note 4, at 245.

[24] Sergio Puig, Conflict or Convergence? On the Relationship of International Trade & Investment Law, 33 BERKELEY J. INT'L L. 1 (2015). I will say more about this convergence in the concluding chapter.

[25] See MELTZER, supra note 23, at 246–50 (recounting the history of investment provisions in international trade agreements from seventeenth- and eighteenth-century treaties of "Friendship, Commerce and Navigation" to the World Trade Organization).

[26] M. Sornarajah describes investment law as a power struggle between capital-exporting developed countries and capital-importing countries developing states. M. SORNARAJAH, THE INTERNATIONAL LAW ON FOREIGN INVESTMENT (3d ed. 2010); see Nicholas A. DiMascio & Joost Pauwelyn, Non-Discrimination in Trade and investment Treaties: Worlds Apart or Two Sides of the Same Coin?, 102 AM. J. INT'L L. 48, 52 (2008).

[27] See MELTZER, supra note 23, at 245 (providing a discussion and analysis of investment provisions in regional and bilateral free trade agreements). See generally JONATHAN BONNITCHA ET AL., THE POLITICAL ECONOMY OF THE INVESTMENT TREATY REGIME (2017).

[28] Frank J. Garcia et al., Reforming the International Investment Regime, 18 J. INT'L ECON. L. 861 (2015).

It is possible that states may achieve some progress toward more balanced investment provisions through bilateral and regional FTA negotiations.[29] However it is equally possible that the trade leverage which FTA negotiations apply to the incorporation and negotiation of investment provisions may also perpetuate unbalanced investment rules. Given the highly asymmetric nature of much FTA negotiation, and the fact that the asymmetry often mirrors and indeed reproduces the original colonial patterns, and it becomes a matter of real concern.[30] Thus the incorporation of model BITs into FTAs, while perhaps substantively justifiable given the interaction of trade and investment in the global economy, is far from simple.

5 Dispute Resolution

Trade agreements today contain some form of institutional mechanism for the settlement of disputes (DSM), and bilateral or regional FTAs are no exception.[31] The most typical involves an arbitration-style process between the state parties, usually with reference to some institutional setting or home for the arbitration, and associated rules.[32] While some FTAs do provide for the creation of administrative bodies to oversee the dispute resolution process, none of these reach the institutional level of the World Trade Agreement. Rarely are these administrative bodies involved in the actual disputes but they may help create procedural rules for dispute resolution processes, serve a

---

[29] For example, commentators cite the investment chapter of the EU-Vietnam FTA, http://trade.ec.europa.eu/doclib/press/index.cfm?id=1437, as achieving some progress in dispute resolution provisions. See Igor Sarkissian, Are We Moving Forward? A New Generation of Trade Agreements for the EU, POLITHEOR, http://politheor.net/are-we-moving-forward-a-new-generation-of-trade-agreements-for-the-eu/; see generally MELTZER, supra note 23, at 296–98 (discussing the prospects for investment provisions in free trade agreements moving forward and addressing the issues posed by ISDS provisions, expropriation provisions for noncapital heavy countries and the scope of the fair and equitable standard, among other issues).

[30] See Chapter 4 173–77 (discussing incorporation of investment rules into FTAs).

[31] For a more complete discussion on the practical function of dispute resolution mechanisms in regional and bilateral free trade agreements, see VICTORIA DONALDSON & SIMON LESTER, Dispute Settlement, in BILATERAL AND REGIONAL TRADE AGREEMENTS: COMMENTARY AND ANALYSIS, supra note 4, at 385.

[32] An example would be NAFTA Article 20. See NAFTA, supra note 10, at art. 20.

role in selecting panelists for dispute resolution bodies and serve other administrative functions.[33] NAFTA, for example, establishes that any dispute between the Parties that cannot be resolved through consultation, can be referred to a five-member arbitral panel hosted by the NAFTA Secretariat and conducted under sui generis procedural rules.[34]

Such an approach would seem by its nature respectful of consent, since at a formal level it appears to submit disputes to an impartial rule-of-law-based procedure.[35] However, the devil is in the details, as not all arbitration procedures are equally binding or equally reflect the rule of law, as shall be seen in subsection B.3.[36]

6 Law Reform

Trade agreements by their nature effect changes in domestic law, whether that means changes in tariff or customs procedures or in the law of public procurement, for example. It is entirely reasonable for states to create obligations in this area, requiring Parties for example to "(a) administer domestic laws in a reasonable, objective and impartial manner; (b) establish review and appeal mechanisms for

[33] Most often, trade agreements focus on four key issues in the selection of members to dispute resolutions panels: "(1) whether a roster or list of possible panelists is to be maintained; (2) qualifications and requirements for panel service; (3) the appointment process [of the panelists]; (4) procedures to prevent parties from blocking the appointment process." DONALDSON & LESTER, supra note 31, at 389–90.

[34] NAFTA, supra note 10, at ch. 20, §B, arts. 2008, 2012. This assumes of course that the complaining Party or a third Party does not successfully request the dispute be moved to the World Trade Organization (WTO), assuming subject matter jurisdiction. Id. art. 2005. By contrast, CAFTA Article 19.3 does not create a new administrative body but requires the parties "to identify an existing body or individual within its territory that will serve as part of a 'secretariat' in order to provide support and co-ordinate, as necessary, with its counterpart in the territory of the other party to the PTA." Dominican Republic–Central America Free Trade Agreement, Costa Rica–Dom. Rep.–El Sal.–Guat.–Hond.–Nicar.–US, art. 19.3, Aug. 5, 2004 (hereinafter CAFTA).

[35] Indeed, Canada mentions this on their NAFTA website as one reason it considers Chapter Twenty as essential to NAFTA. Dispute Settlement Under the NAFTA, GLOBAL AFFAIRS CANADA (July 13, 2015), www.international.gc.ca/trade-agreements-accords-commerciaux/agr-acc/nafta-alena/settle.aspx.

[36] See, e.g., Frank J. Garcia, "Americas Agreements" – An Interim Stage in Building the Free Trade Area of the Americas, 35 COLUM. J. TRANSNAT'L L. 63, 117–22 (1997) (noting how, technically, NAFTA parties are not bound to resolve the dispute according to the panel report, thus reopening the door to power politics).

administrative decisions; (c) ensure that measures relating to qualification requirements and procedures, technical standards and licensing requirements do not constitute unnecessary barriers to trade in services (so-called necessity requirement) and (d) use relevant international standards."[37]

However, in asymmetric trade agreements such as the regional or bilateral FTAs between developed and developing countries, it is also not unusual to find provisions requiring changes to the weaker party's non-trade domestic laws as an element of the overall negotiated agreement. This raises some concerns. While some may arguably involve legitimate trade-related or global social policy concerns, such as labor and the environment, even requirements in these areas have been contested as disguised protectionist efforts to blunt legitimate comparative advantage.[38] Moreover, for other areas, the trade relationship (and interventionist purpose) is even more suspect. We can see examples of this in the CAFTA (agency & distribution contracts) and the KORUS (health care policy), both of which will be discussed further in subsection B.4.[39]

Such measures differ in nature from the trade-related legal changes one would expect to see mandated in a trade agreement, and constitute in my view a form of conditionality.[40] The reference to the IMF's controversial conditionality policies is deliberate – in my view, trade conditionality typically serves the interests of the more powerful party, introducing measures of questionable relevance that advance the interests of key constituencies within the imposing state. I shall have a lot more to say about this in later sections.

---

[37] See ORTINO, *supra* note 5, at 238–42 (discussing these four typical requirements).

[38] For example, following the passage of the Trade Promotion Authority Act of 2002, US negotiators were given a set of negotiating objectives for international free trade agreements that required seeking environmental and labor protections. US negotiators, therefore, sought provisions prohibiting the reduction of existing laws that offer protection in those areas and requiring domestic enforcement. See LORAND BARTELS, *Social Issues: Labour, Environment and Human Rights, in* BILATERAL AND REGIONAL TRADE AGREEMENTS: COMMENTARY AND ANALYSIS, *supra* note 4, at 364, 377–78.

[39] For CAFTA, *see infra* notes 134–148. For KORUS, *see infra* notes 149–154.

[40] On International Monetary Fund conditionality in general, *see* QURESHI & ZIEGLER, *supra* note 5, at 275–305.

7 Special and Differential Treatment

Special and Differential Treatment, or S&D as it is often called, is the collective term for a basket of policies through which the trading system takes into account the special needs and challenges of developing and least developed countries.[41] S&D provisions also date back to the postcolonial period, as emerging states sought inclusion into an economic system designed by their former colonial parents, on terms that reflected their economic, social and political inequalities and challenges.[42] A key site for these early deliberations was the GATT treaty, and the text went through several rounds of amendment including the addition in 1964 of Part IV, the "development" part, and the adoption in 1979 of the so-called Enabling Clause.[43]

The core element of S&D is the principle of nonreciprocity. This allows, for example, the negotiation of market access provisions that give developing countries preferential access into developed country markets. In the WTO, it also allows market protection mechanisms, such as differential implementation periods, that make it possible for developing countries to protect their markets from premature liberalization.[44] Finally, nonreciprocity is accompanied by a commitment to technical assistance, involving the provision of expertise and related funding to increase trade capacity and trade infrastructure, with the understanding that this is a concomitant obligation on developed countries seeking better access through market liberalization.[45]

S&D is most often considered in the context of multilateral trade, where special treatment is sought for developing countries in a context of multilateral rules perhaps more appropriate for developed economies. There S&D can be criticized on a number of grounds, including

---

[41] See generally ROBERT E. HUDEC, DEVELOPING COUNTRIES IN THE GATT LEGAL SYSTEM (1987). For the normative context of S&D, see FRANK J. GARCIA, TRADE, INEQUALITY, AND JUSTICE (2003).

[42] See SONIA E. ROLLAND, DEVELOPMENT AT THE WTO 15–34 (2012).

[43] Id.

[44] However liberal this seems, it must be remembered that it reflects the WTO "single undertaking" approach, and replaces the earlier policy space developing countries enjoyed under the GATT by selectively joining, or not joining, earlier GATT side agreements on contentious subjects. See GARCIA, supra note 41.

[45] See ROLLAND, supra note 42.

adequacy (is it enough?),[46] effectiveness (is it working?)[47] and normative justifiability (is it fair?).[48] Nevertheless, it remains an important element in the multilateral trading system's response to problems of inequality and development.

Within a bilateral or regional trade agreement, it might be presumed that S&D would not be relevant, since the entire agreement could be seen to reflect the special situation of the developing country partner, or at least an opportunity for that to be directly considered in the negotiations. However, it is still useful to think in these terms when analyzing such a treaty, both to foreground how the treaty approaches certain key and predictable flash points (agricultural market access, for example), and also to identify where the treaty introduces some of the weaknesses endemic to multilateral S&D, such as hortatory language in the case of obligations key to the developing country party, versus binding language for developed country priorities.[49] Moreover, as will be seen, the special needs of the less developed partner may in fact not be addressed at all, but actively exploited during the negotiations. For this reason and others, S&D by itself cannot make up for fundamentally unfair agreements, or agreements that are not about trade at all but about something else.

With this brief survey of typical trade subjects in mind, we can now turn to the subject of consent in modern trade agreements.

II CONSENT AND OPPRESSION IN CONTEMPORARY TRADE AGREEMENTS

With a basic understanding of the kinds of provisions characteristic of a modern free trade agreement, we can now undertake an evaluation of the degree to which in these agreements we are dealing with trade, or

---

[46] *See* Alex Ansong, *The Adequacy of Special and Differential Treatment Provisions for Developing Countries in the WTO*, 2 GHANA INST. MGMT. PUB. ADMIN. L. REV. 91, 115 (2016).

[47] JEFFREY L. DUNOFF, *Dysfunction, Diversion and the Debate Over Preferences: (How) Do Preferential Trade Policies Work?*, *in* DEVELOPING COUNTRIES IN THE WTO LEGAL SYSTEM 45 (Chantal Thomas & Joel P. Trachtman eds. 2009).

[48] GARCIA, *supra* note 41, at 147–92.

[49] On the issue of hortatory language, *see* HUDEC, *supra* note 41; Frank J. Garcia, *Beyond Special and Differential Treatment*, 27 B.C. INT'L & COMP. L. REV. 291 (2004).

something predatory, coercive or exploitative. It is useful to remember as well that this is not necessarily a binary exercise. The same agreement may contain elements of trade and elements of coercion, predation or exploitation, or it may be that the agreement is so marked by one or more of these pathologies that we can't really call it a trade agreement at all – we will have to see.

A Evaluating the Modern Free Trade Agreement

The discussion that follows is organized around a subset of the issues and substantive provisions that regularly come up in trade agreement negotiations, those which are often flash points and which may therefore offer good litmus tests for the way power and consent are at play in the relationships and negotiations in question. These are: (1) market access and associated rule of origin issues, especially around agriculture and textiles; (2) trade remedies such as safeguards and AD/CVD; (3) dispute resolution and (4) law reform.[50]

In terms of the consent dynamics of trade agreements, I will be looking for examples of what is ostensibly free trade, but in fact may be a form of coercion (no free bargaining), exploitation (unfair advantage taking) or predation (no consent at all). This is of course intimately tied in with the way such agreements are negotiated, but I hope to try first in this chapter to look for evidence of trade or otherwise in the substantive provisions themselves, and then, insofar as non-trade patterns emerge, explore how they may have come about in Chapter 3.

As subjects, I will be relying on two hemispheric trade agreements – one regional and one bilateral – between the United States and a range of smaller parties, specifically the DR-CAFTA trade agreement between the United States and the Central American

---

[50] While I consider investment a crucial area in which to investigate the health of consensual economic relations in the global economy, it is sufficiently distinct from trade in its socioeconomic context that I believe it merits a study of its own. However, I will offer a few preliminary reflections in the concluding chapter.

states (including the Dominican Republic),[51] and the US–Colombia Trade Promotion Agreement (CTPA).[52] The Central American states that negotiated CAFTA with the United States are among the poorest in the hemisphere, with a combined GDP as a group that is dwarfed by that of the United States.[53] Colombia, while a more advanced economy than any of the CAFTA countries, is nevertheless still a developing country with significant economic challenges, not to mention security challenges.[54] I am focusing on the United States not because US trade practice is uniquely egregious (though I consider it to be egregious in many respects), but because it is the context I know best, and the asymmetries of economic power among the participants are quite marked in this context. For these reasons, I have reason to hope that whatever is latent can be surfaced most effectively here.[55]

As a contrast, I will also take a look at the US–Korea FTA (KORUS).[56] While the US economy clearly dwarfs the size of the Korean economy as well, Korea is a developed country that ranks as

---

[51] *CAFTA-DR (Dominican Republic–Central America FTA)*, OFFICE OF THE US TRADE REPRESENTATIVE, https://ustr.gov/trade-agreements/free-trade-agreements/cafta-dr-dominican-republic-central-america-fta (last accessed Feb. 22, 2018).

[52] United States–Colombia Trade Promotion Agreement, Colom.–US, OFFICE OF THE US TRADE REPRESENTATIVE, https://ustr.gov/trade-agreements/free-trade-agreements/colombia-fta/final-text (last accessed Nov. 22, 2006, hereinafter CTPA).

[53] The combined GDP of the CAFTA-DR countries in 2002 was less than one percent of the US GDP. US DEPT. OF LABOR, UNITED STATES EMPLOYMENT IMPACT REVIEW OF THE DOMINICAN REPUBLIC–CENTRAL AMERICA–UNITED STATES FREE TRADE AGREEMENT 9 (2005). In fact, a Congressional Research Service report found that the employment growth effects on the US economy of the CAFTA are essentially negligible. *Id.* at 45–48.

[54] Colombia is the third-largest economy in Latin America, and is twenty-second on the list of US trading partners ranked by US exports, twenty-fifth by US imports, according to US Commerce Department statistics for 2016. US Dept. of Commerce, *Top U.S. Trade Partners*, http://trade.gov/mas/ian/build/groups/public/@tg_ian/documents/webcontent/tg_ian_003364.pdf.

[55] Examples of similar dynamics from other regions include critiques of EU partnership agreements with developing countries. *See* Patrick Gomes, *Reshaping an Asymmetrical Partnership: ACP–EU Relations from an ACP Perspective*, 25 J. INT'L DEV. 714 (2013); Tony Heron, *Asymmetric Bargaining and Development Trade-Offs in the CARIFORUM-European Union Economic Partnership Agreement*, 18 REV. INT'L POL. ECON. 328 (2010).

[56] Office of the US Trade Representative, *Free Trade Agreement Between the United States of America and the Republic of Korea* (June 30, 2007), https://ustr.gov/trade-agreements/free-trade-agreements/korus-fta/final-text (hereinafter KORUS).

the seventh largest US trading partner (the United States is Korea's third largest trading partner).[57] This is still asymmetry, but not on the CAFTA or even Colombia scale. Moreover the "social history," if you will, of KORUS presents an interesting contrast to CAFTA and the CTPA. To begin with, the colonial history is different in significant ways, Korea being concerned primarily with Japanese and Chinese ambitions in the region more than European or American.[58] In this context the United States does not enter the negotiations as the traditional regional hegemon, but is in fact seen as a balancing force against the region's historic hegemons.[59] However, offsetting this, the United States as the postwar superpower plays a major role in Korean security, with potential repercussions for the negotiations, as we shall see.[60]

I will conclude the analysis with a look at select aspects of the WTO treaty system. While the WTO is a massive treaty system in itself and is not the primary subject of this study, it nevertheless offers an instructive comparison to the kinds of regional or bilateral negotiations to be discussed, and is therefore a useful counterpoint. In a multilateral context the large economies with the power to drive unbalanced agreements in other contexts (the United States and the EU would be the leading examples), can be counterbalanced in the WTO context, first by each other, and second by coalitions among other medium-sized and smaller WTO members.[61] This sets up the interesting possibility of a different dynamic in some areas, such as agriculture trade where there is a distribution of power among large and medium-sized states.[62] Whether or not this turns out to be the case will have to be seen.

---

[57] Lee et al., *supra* note 3, at 116.

[58] *See Korea*, ENCYCLOPÆDIA BRITANNICA, www.britannica.com/place/Korea (last accessed July 20, 2017).

[59] *See* Lee et al., supra note 3, at 119 (United States to negotiating FTA with Korea to serve as a check on China in the region).

[60] *Id.* at 153 (for Korea, an unbalanced agreement may not be sufficient reason not to conclude an FTA with the United States, given its essential security role).

[61] *See generally* Sonia E. Rolland, *Developing Country Coalitions at the WTO: In Search of Legal Support*, 48 HARV. INT´L L.J. 483 (2007).

[62] The Cairns Group, which pushes for liberalization of trade in agricultural exports, is composed of nineteen agricultural exporting countries across five continents, including developed and developing countries. *About the Cairns Group*, THE CAIRNS GROUP, http://cairnsgroup.org/Pages/Introduction.aspx (last accessed Feb. 20, 2018).

B Substantive Provisions

So, let us begin and take a look at the agreements themselves. I want to first examine the structure and timing of market access as negotiated for each party, since this can reveal something fundamental about the balance of opportunities and concessions each country has had to make in the negotiation process. Market access can take us right into the question of good bargains, bad bargains and, possibly, coercion or exploitation.

Second, I will look at trade remedies such as safeguards and AD/CVD issues, since these can often be arranged or manipulated to offer a convenient back door out of what are otherwise ostensibly liberalizing commitments. If a party has been able to neutralize a concession or unilaterally insist on an escape valve when concessions start to bite, that may be important. Then we will turn to the treaty's dispute resolution mechanism, since inequalities in power, and what is done about them, are at the heart of any system of resolving disputes and can represent either a check against oppressive behavior, or further oppression.

I will conclude with an examination of the extent and nature of domestic law reform mandated by the treaty. The degree of involvement one state is willing to tolerate on the part of another state into its domestic legal policy could be an important indicator of underlying dynamics such as coercion or exploitation.

1 Market Access

Market access provisions are a key – and relatively transparent – treaty element that allows us to assess the balance of opportunities and protections asymmetric parties have been able to negotiate. The terms and timing of market access can speak volumes about a weaker party's capacity to protect its markets from external competition, which can often be destructive if local industry isn't ready or adjustment measures are not in place. Correspondingly, improved market access into a large wealthy market is often the most important objective a smaller economy may have when negotiating with a larger economy.[63] When we look at which sectors are excluded and by whom, we can get a more complete picture of the weaker party's ability to bargain, or not, for

[63] On the importance of this relative market size, see GARCIA, *supra* note 41, at 148–50.

what it wanted and needed. Market access provisions are thus a handy litmus test for the health of a treaty as a whole.

The market access provisions in many US regional and bilateral trade agreements reveal a pattern of selective liberalization and protection strongly favoring US interests, with little to no corresponding success on the part of US negotiating partners. To take the CAFTA agriculture sector as an example, the treaty mandates broad duty-free access for US agriculture exports.[64] This eliminates the protections in place throughout Central America for regional small-scale farmers and agricultural workers in several key sectors such as rice and yellow corn, exposing them to immediate competition from highly subsidized US agricultural products.[65]

In return for these concessions, the CAFTA states appear to have achieved very little. In particular, sectors in which CAFTA agricultural exports might have a comparative advantage, access was either blocked or neutralized. The United States maintained its protective barriers to sugar imports, one of its most sensitive and highly subsidized sectors and of particular interest to Central American exporters, who have a comparative advantage in that sector.[66] Although tariff rate quotas (TRQs) for CAFTA sugar exports were raised slightly, and will eventually be phased out by 2020, in the meantime CAFTA states will have opened their markets to a broad spectrum of US agricultural exports. Thus the United States established a pattern of successfully offering higher quotas in its sensitive sectors, in exchange for achieving full liberalization in its partners' sensitive sectors, an example of

[64] See CAFTA, *supra* note 34, at annex 3.3. *See generally* Office of the US Trade Representative, *CAFTA-DR – Agriculture: Specific Fact Sheet* (2005), https://ustr.gov/archive/assets/Trade_Agreements/Regional/CAFTA/Briefing_Book/asset_upload_file119_7211.pdf.

[65] *Id.; see also* CARLOS GALIAN, *CAFTA: The Nail in the Coffin of Central American Agriculture, in* WHY WE SAY NO TO CAFTA 4 (Alliance for Responsible Trade 2004).

[66] *See* Office of the US Trade Representative, *CAFTA Facts – Textiles in CAFTA-DR* 9 (2005) (hereinafter CAFTA Facts), https://ustr.gov/archive/assets/Trade_Agreements/Regional/CAFTA/Briefing_Book/asset_upload_file551_7185.pdf; Annex 3.3, Schedule of the United States–CAFTA Treaty, https://ustr.gov/sites/default/files/uploads/agreements/cafta/asset_upload_file412_3952.pdf; *see* GALIAN, *supra* note 65; *see also* Elizabeth Becker, *Costa Rica to Be 5th Country in New Trade Pact with U.S.,* N.Y. TIMES, Jan. 26, 2004, at A6 (reporting that the United States won its demand for opening the Central American agriculture market to its exports while maintaining protection for sugar industry, of interest to the region).

asymmetric outcomes due to asymmetric power that will recur in other negotiations, as we shall see below with respect to agriculture in the US–Colombia FTA negotiations.

Moreover, in sensitive US sectors where it would appear some market access goals of the CAFTA states were achieved in principle, such as textiles, actual improved access was effectively blocked in other ways, such as by the negotiation of special safeguard mechanisms for US textiles, which I will discuss further in the second subsection, or the deployment of sanitary or phytosanitary measures against agricultural imports.[67] Here too this pattern – the successful blocking of effective market access through safeguards and nontariff barriers – will be seen as a pattern characteristic of US negotiations. Even in sugar, the value to the Central American states of modest interim success in TRQ liberalization is offset by a special sugar compensation mechanism. This mechanism, available only to US producers against CAFTA sugar exports and not CAFTA producers against other US imports, allows the United States to elect to pay CAFTA sugar exporters rather than honor its sugar access commitments.[68] This mechanism gives the United States an immediate unilateral option out of its duty-free sugar imports, at a price borne by US taxpayers, not the sugar producers. Once again, this pattern of seeking unilateral escape clauses or other unilateral concessions will surface again in other negotiations.

It is also important to note that although CAFTA governments announced success in reducing US tariffs across agricultural sectors, their exports had already enjoyed duty-free access under the US trade preference programs, so there was essentially no further liberalization in exchange for the market access commitments CAFTA states made themselves.[69] Certainly, to shift duty-free access from a discretionary

---

[67] Dwi Susanto et al., *Agriculture Trade in the CAFTA-DR Agreement: An Applied General Equilibrium Approach* 2 (2007), http://cnas.tamu.edu/Publications/Cafta.pdf; GALIAN, *supra* note 65, at 6 ("for example, much of the region's tropical fruit products are plagued by the Mediterranean fruit fly and, therefore, cannot be exported to the United States"). I will have more to say about this in the Trade Remedies section.

[68] CAFTA, *supra* note 34, at art. 3.16. This curious mechanism gives the United States, at its discretion, the option to pay cash compensation to CAFTA sugar exporters for lost exports, rather than accord them duty-free treatment per the tariff rate quota agreed by the United States. *Id.*

[69] *See* Mechel S. Paggi, P. Lynn Kennedy, Fumiko Yamazaki & Tim Josling, Regional Trade Agreements and Implications for US Agriculture: The Case of CAFTA-DR, 2nd Quarter CHOICES 139 (2005); GALIAN, *supra* note 65, at 6.

GSP-style program to a treaty commitment is an important step toward a more stable and bilateral footing. However, as I have written elsewhere, the US preferential trade program is highly coercive in how it is applied, conditioning discretionary access on compliance with a range of US policy goals.[70] I think this may put the CAFTA states' announcement in a different light, suggesting that what they achieved in fact was to get out of a highly coercive context into a possibly less coercive context (we shall have to see how the overall agreement stands up), but at a high price in terms of new concessions demanded by the United States – suggesting a possibly even more coercive negotiation dynamic, as I will discuss in the next chapter. The fact that this was touted by the CAFTA states as a market access success has suggested to some a political attempt to save face, while not in fact being able to advance national liberalization priorities at all.[71]

A very similar pattern seems to have played itself out in the US–Colombia FTA (CTPA) negotiations, with some small variations perhaps attributable to Colombia's larger size, market power or negotiation ability. Overall, however, the US–Colombia negotiations have been elsewhere characterized as a clear case of asymmetric outcomes flowing from asymmetric bargaining, to Colombia's detriment.[72]

To begin with, as with CAFTA, due to overall low US tariffs and the special preferences already in place through the Andean Trade Preference Program, essentially all Colombian agricultural exports to the United States already entered duty-free, with the exception of sugar.[73] The United States thus had very little to swallow in the form of effective tariff concessions.

The CTPA "builds" on these unilateral preferences that favor Colombia, by requiring Colombia to grant reciprocal and immediate

---

[70] GARCIA, *supra* note 41, at 156–68 (problems with GSP).

[71] GALIAN, *supra* note 65, at 6.

[72] LOUIS JORGE GARAY ET AL., *Negotiating the Colombia–US FTA: A Colombian Perspective*, in ASYMMETRIC TRADE NEGOTIATIONS 137 (Sanoussi Bilal et al., eds. 2011).

[73] LUIS JORGE GARAY SALAMANCA ET AL., IMPACT OF THE US–COLOMBIA FTA ON THE SMALL FARM ECONOMY IN COLOMBIA (2016), www.oxfamamerica.org/static/media/files/colombia-fta-impact-on-small-farmers-final-english.pdf. For example, prior to the CPTA, the US average tariff on Colombian goods was three percent and in 2010 about ninety percent of Colombian exports to the United States "entered duty-free under trade preference programs or through normal trade relations." M. ANGELES VILLAREAL, CONG. RES. SERV., RL34470, THE US–COLOMBIA FTA: BACKGROUND AND ISSUES 2 (2014).

duty-free access for the bulk of US agricultural exports in exchange for making the preferences into binding tariff commitments.[74] While rendering these preferences permanent was an important goal for Colombia, it was achieved at great cost to the agricultural sector, perhaps as much as 4.4 percent of agricultural GDP, and over predictably strong opposition from the Colombian agricultural sector.[75] As a result of the treaty, as with CAFTA, producers in the sensitive Colombian rice and corn sectors now face increased US competition but without any compensating additional trade benefits, since they already enjoyed duty-free access to the United States, other than the shift from a highly coercive discretionary regime toward a possibly less coercive treaty one.

For its part, the United States was again able to preserve in substance its protective domestic sugar policies, despite granting Colombia an increased duty-free import quota.[76] This "concession" is disappointing and chimerical, given that the United States did not allow Colombia a single across-the-board product exclusion for its part, and the larger quota share is still only in line with the quotas of the other major sugar exporters of the region.[77] Moreover, the United States included same special sugar compensation mechanism it had negotiated in CAFTA, allowing the United States to elect at its discretion to pay Colombian sugar exporters rather than honor its sugar access commitments.[78] As with CAFTA, this mechanism gives the United States a unilateral option out of its duty-free sugar imports at a price borne by US taxpayers, not the sugar producers, an example of a below-the-table uncompensated wealth transfer from taxpayers to sugar producers, which also has the result of maintaining higher domestic US sugar prices.

---

[74] Overall, the agreement provides for immediate duty-free access for seventy-seven percent of all US agricultural exports, including high-priority items such as beef, cotton, wheat and soybeans, with the elimination of most other tariffs on agricultural products within 15 years. VILLAREAL, *supra* note 73, at 4.

[75] Kevin J. Fandl, *Bilateral Agreements and Fair Trade Practices: A Policy Analysis of the Colombia–US Free Trade Agreement (2006)*, 10 YALE HUM. RTS. DEV. L.J. 78, 80 (2007); GARAY et al., *supra* note 72, at 154.

[76] GARAY et al., *supra* note 72, at 152.

[77] *Id.*

[78] CTPA, *supra* note 52, at art. 2.19.

In contrast, regarding the poultry sector, a key part of domestic Colombian agriculture, Colombia was only able to negotiate a ninth-year consultation on the impact of the agreement's duty free access by US poultry into Colombia.[79] However, by its nature an agreement to consult does not guarantee any particular result or modification of the treaty at all in the event of a problem, particularly where the parties are highly asymmetric, and is an example of soft-law-style hortatory statements that typify commitments in other areas such as S&D.[80] The contrast is particularly noteworthy when compared to the US special sugar compensation mechanism. Colombian poultry importers were not so fortunate in securing a similar escape option on their behalf, let alone an exclusion – in any event, such a compensation measure would most likely be fiscally and politically impossible for the Colombian government.[81]

Such one-sided bargains are evidence of the disparity in bargaining power that characterizes these treaties.[82] What, in the end, did Central America and Colombia get in return for granting duty-free access to US agricultural exports in return for essentially maintaining their prior duty-free access into the US market under GSP-style programs? Very little, it would seem. What are we to make of the shape of such a bargain? Of the fact that at least in international law terms, Colombia and the CAFTA states formally consented to this bargain?

In order to understand the consent by Colombia or the Central American governments to such lopsided provisions, it may be helpful to work with the concepts of coercion and exploitation introduced in

---

[79] *Id.* art. 2.20.

[80] *See supra* Section I.B.7.

[81] Where maintaining the freedom to offer domestic transfer payments or subsidies is contemplated, a country's effective fiscal capacity to make such payments must be taken into account in order to assess if it is a valuable concession or not. For example, while Colombia could in principle maintain a similar domestic agriculture subsidies program to the United States, it cannot afford to do so and this is well-known to the United States. GARAY et al., *supra* note 72, at 151.

[82] Editorial, *Harvesting Poverty: A New Trade Deal,* N.Y. TIMES, Dec. 22, 2003, at A30 (asserting CAFTA's terms reflect asymmetry in negotiating power between the United States and the Central American region). Such allegations have also been raised about the WTO agreements and the Uruguay Round. *See* J. Michael Finger & Julio J. Nogués, *The Unbalanced Uruguay Round Outcome: The New Areas in Future WTO Negotiations* 3–4 (World Bank Policy Research, Working Paper No. 2732, 2001).

Chapter 1. The one-sided nature of the market access provisions in agriculture are evidence that in these respects the treaties may have been shaped by dynamics that are more coercive or exploitative than they are about trade, understood as mutually beneficial and consensual exchanges of roughly equal value. Treaty parties appear to be accepting bargains that would not be in their self-interest, in an overall agreement that similarly fails to yield much in return for difficult concessions. This may be a result of the leverage afforded the United States as a function of the deep asymmetry between the parties, as well as the leverage afforded it by Latin American states not wanting to settle for the GSP-style status quo. In any event, we would want to know more about the negotiation dynamics between the parties, which I will explore in the next chapter.[83] Nevertheless, the pattern is both suggestive and disturbing.

In the case of the KORUS, we see a slightly different pattern of outcomes, but underlying dynamics that seem quite similar. Gaining better access to Korean agriculture was a top priority for the United States, given its comparative advantage in agriculture.[84] However, and equally importantly, maintaining the viability of an admittedly less efficient agriculture sector was key to the Korean government, for reasons of rural unemployment, orderly adjustment, food sufficiency and social stability.[85]

In this area the United States achieved its objective, securing commitments liberalizing access in virtually all Korean agricultural sectors.[86] The exception was rice, long considered a national security and cultural

---

[83] However, we may never know the full details of the negotiations, despite the efforts of the media and civil society, since as has been pointed out all members of the CAFTA negotiations signed confidentiality agreements. See Catholic Relief Services, *Transparency and Participation in the CAFTA Negotiations*, FAIR TRADE OR FREE TRADE? UNDERSTANDING CAFTA 5, 5 www.citizen.org/sites/default/files/caftabriefingpacket.pdf (last accessed Mar. 17, 2007).

[84] Key US goals necessary for Congressional consent included agriculture liberalization, addressing the imbalance in Korean auto exports into the United States, and the special treatment of Korea's outward processing zone or OP with North Korea, the Kaesong Industrial Complex. Lee et al., *supra* note 3, at 115; *see supra* note 9 and accompanying text.

[85] Lee et al., *supra* note 3, at 135.

[86] *Id.* at 135–36.

identity product and therefore a unique product in Korean society.[87] This certainly represents an important success for Korea. However, for our purposes here, the key issue may be not so much that Korea managed to maintain its rice industry protections while CAFTA states and Colombia could not (although that is noteworthy), but whether Korean producers, even in other sectors, got equivalent benefits in return for the rest of the liberalization commitments. It is always about the balance.

Unfortunately, Korea did not achieve that balance. One of the most controversial and high-profile US successes was in the beef sector, long a bone of contention. Following liberalization of the Korean beef sector to foreign competition as a result of the 1989 GATT case brought against Korea by the United States and other major beef exporters,[88] never had grown by 2003 to be the third-largest export market for US beef producers, accounting for half of all beef consumed in Korea.[89] When mad cow disease (bovine spongiform encephalopathy, or BSE) hit the United States, Korea acted swiftly to ban a majority of US beef imports.[90] After mutual consultations, Korea began expanding US market access subject to quotas and quarantines, which provoked massive public protests and some retrenchment.[91] Further liberalizing the Korean market to US beef became a key negotiating objective, and the United States succeeded in securing a commitment on the part of Korea to eliminate all tariffs on US beef imports over a fifteen-year period.[92] Because of this, by 2017 US beef exports to Korea had recovered their pre-BSE levels, leading the US cattle industry to tout KORUS as creating an "ideal environment" for US beef in Korea.[93]

---

[87] Multifunctionality refers to the idea that agriculture is more than just food, and can create non-commodity outputs. *Multifunctionality, or Multifunctional Agriculture*, OECD (Mar. 23, 2003), https://stats.oecd.org/glossary/detail.asp?ID=1699.

[88] *See generally* Report of the Panel, *Republic of Korea – Restriction on Imports of Beef – Complaint by the United States*, L/6503 (Nov. 7, 1989).

[89] REMY JURENAS & MARK E. MANYIN, CONG. RESEARCH SERV., CRS 7–5700, US–SOUTH KOREA BEEF DISPUTE: ISSUES AND STATUS 1–2 (2010).

[90] *Id.* at 3–4.

[91] Reuters, *Anti-U.S. Beef Protest Draws 100,000 S. Koreans*, REUTERS (May 31, 2008), www.reuters.com/article/us-korea-protest/anti-u-s-beef-protest-draws-100000-s-koreans-idUSSEO21734120080531.

[92] JURENAS & MANYIN, *supra* note 89, at 5–8.

[93] Jane Chung, *U.S. Regains Status as Top Beef Exporter to South Korea*, REUTERS (Jan. 15, 2018), www.reuters.com/article/us-southkorea-usa-beef/u-s-regains-status-as-top-beef-exporter-to-south-korea-idUSKBN1F40OW; Press Release, *Nat'l Cattlemen's Beef Ass'n*,

In addition to food security, key Korean goals entering the negotiations included reform of trade remedies, increased access to working visas for Korean executives and professionals, access to the US coastal shipping services market and addressing rule of origin concerns regarding textiles.[94] Korea largely failed to achieve any of these goals, suggesting that in the overall negotiation it gave a great deal in exchange for comparatively little.

In textiles, the key goal for Korea was reform of the US textiles rules of origin, which embody a "yarn-forward" approach to the origin of a textile that would require everything from yarn forward to be Korean in order for the finished good to qualify as Korean in origin, hence entitled to duty-free treatment under KORUS. Since Korea imports many of its textiles for assembly and finishing in Korea as textile products, relaxation of this rule would be key to Korea enjoying any meaningful tariff reductions at all. For its part, the United States sought a special safeguard mechanism for textile products, allowing it to protect US textiles producers from import surges anticipated due to the textile tariff reductions to be negotiated.

At the end of the day, despite an apparently balanced outcome, it would seem that, when one gets down to the details, Korea settled for a bad bargain. Although the parties did agree to the phased elimination of all textile tariffs between the two countries, the United States successfully maintained its yarn-forward origin rule, though with a few specific product exceptions in Korea's favor.[95] Moreover, Korea agreed to the US safeguard mechanism. Taken together, this means that, despite the appearance of improved access for Korea, in reality most Korean textile producers will not qualify for these benefits due to

---

U.S. Beef Industry Highlights Success of Korea Free Trade Agreement, NATIONAL CATTLE-MEN'S BEEF ASSOCIATION (July 27, 2017), www.beefusa.org/newsreleases1.aspx? NewsID=6377.

[94] Lee et al., *supra* note 3, at 134; *see also* Jeffrey Schott et al., *Negotiating the Korea–United States Free Trade Agreement* (2006), https://piie.com/sites/default/files/publications/pb/pb06–4.pdf (United States would have to reform long-standing trade barriers against Korean exports and resolve the visa issue to create a Korean FTA).

[95] Lee et al., *supra* note 3, at 136. It is interesting that Korea was able to secure some exceptions to the yarn-forward rule for certain products in its interest, suggesting (when compared to CAFTA) that when a negotiation is less drastically asymmetric, some exceptions to onerous rules can be negotiated, even if more balanced rules themselves cannot be. I shall have more to say about this later in the chapter. *See infra* Section II.B.5.

the yarn-forward rule, and if, through a change in the Korean textile industry, more do, they will then run into the US safeguard against increased textile imports.[96]

A similar pattern played out in the area of services liberalization, a sector in which the United States enjoys a significant comparative advantage against every economy other than the EU. Korea entered the negotiations with several specific services-related negotiation objectives (relaxed visa rules for professionals and access to the US coastal shipping services market),[97] and concerns over the larger systemic and social effects of premature liberalization on its the services sector, one in which Korea has real competitive potential but not yet at the level of the United States.[98] The United States, for its part and not unpredictably, entered the negotiations asking for broad liberalization of the services sector and the dismantling of key barriers in Korean domestic law to US service providers.[99] The end result was that the United States made substantial progress in its requests in the areas of financial services, broadcasting, telecommunications and services-related technical standards, whereas Korea failed to achieve any of its substantive services goals.[100] It would seem that Korea's "success" consists of resisting wholesale services liberalization while securing none for itself in return.

This im-balance reflects the overall and disappointing reality, from a Korean perspective, of how few concrete market access goals Korea did manage to accomplish in the context of these negotiations. In addition to losing on the textiles origin issue, losing on the work visa issue, losing on coastal shipping services and losing on the related trade remedies issue, as I will discuss in the next subsection,[101] Korea also failed to achieve its desired special origin rule for goods produced in the Kaesong outward processing zone it maintains with North Korea.

---

[96] Lee et al., *supra* note 3, at 136.
[97] *Id.* at 134.
[98] *Id.* at 126–32. Colombia and the CAFTA countries lack any globally competitive services industries, so the story there is simply one of the erosion of local protections against US service providers, raising both the possibility of welfare gains to consumers but also the loss of any future competitive indigenous service providers, as a serious concern for any growing middle-income country. *See* Fandl, *supra* note 75, at 78, 85.
[99] Lee et al., *supra* note 3, at 137.
[100] *Id.* at 137–39.
[101] Lee et al., *supra* note 3, at 155–56.

The Kaesong outward processing zone, or OP, had been a key element in security relations and cooperation between the two Koreas, and the South Korean government went into the KORUS negotiation determined to maintain the economic momentum of this project by ensuring that OP products would qualify as South Korean in origin, which it had been able to achieve in its FTAs with Singapore, EFTA and ASEAN.[102] The outcome in KORUS was a special joint commission to meet annually to evaluate whether any Korean export zones were suitable for special origin treatment, and imposing a series of security and other conditions necessary to achieve that decision, but no special treatment for OP products at present.[103]

Overall, what we see in the KORUS is not that markedly different from what we see in the CAFTA and CTPA, despite the latter parties being more highly asymmetric when compared to the United States than Korea. Despite its greater economic power, and the increased leverage one might presume from that, in the end Korea was forced to surrender key market protection goals without securing compensating export benefits, as were Colombia and the CAFTA states. One has to ask what would account for such a lopsided outcome? I will return to this question in the following sections and in the next chapter.

2 Trade Remedies

As has already been discussed, even those market access provisions that may at first appear to be US concessions can on closer inspection prove otherwise. Either the "concessions" are in areas the United States already allowed duty-free entry on a preferential basis, as is the case with agriculture, CAFTA and the CTPA, with the additional coercive dynamics described earlier in the chapter; or, what has been granted as a concession is undermined elsewhere through, for example, trade remedy provisions such as safeguards.

One consistent example throughout the treaties examined here concerns textiles, long a sensitive subject in US trade policy.[104]

---

[102] Suk Hi Kim, *The Korea–US Free Trade Agreement, the Kaesong Industrial Complex, and US–Korea Relations*, 5 no. 2 ASIA-PAC. J. (Feb. 2, 2007).

[103] *Id.*

[104] From 1974 until 1994, the Multifibre Arrangement governed textiles and – contrary to the general preference for tariffs rather than quotas – set quotas for imports into

In the CAFTA, concessions on textiles were widely trumpeted as one of the premier benefits conferred by CAFTA on the Central American economies.[105] However, the CAFTA textiles rules include safeguard provisions allowing the United States to unilaterally impose tariffs if there is a surge of textile imports that have the potential to hurt domestic manufacturing.[106] Such safeguards were also negotiated in the KORUS agreement.

By itself there is nothing necessarily coercive about safeguards measures, which can play an important part in orderly trade adjustment. Much will depend on the rigor and transparency of the standards to be met for invoking the safeguard, and how it is in fact deployed. However, whether such measures are unilateral or bilateral can in certain cases say something about the mutuality of the bargain. It can be of concern simply that a special safeguard is negotiated for the dominant party wherever there is a concession made to the weaker party. Whether that concern is born out in practice would then depend on how the provision is used.

In this respect there is reason for concern about the use of safeguards in US trade practice. In the case of CAFTA, the United States appears to have already used the threat of invoking this safeguard in an attempt to renegotiate a CAFTA provision, raising questions about the use of the mechanism before it is even deployed, and the real reasons it was negotiated in the first place.[107] Shortly after entry into force, at the behest of the textile lobby, the United States demanded either the delay of duty-free importation of socks from CAFTA states or, alternatively, the modification of the relevant rule of origin requirements in order to protect the US sock manufacturing industry.[108] Thus under

---

countries suffering from increasing imports. *Textiles: Back in the Mainstream*, WTO, www.wto.org/english/thewto_e/whatis_e/tif_e/agrm5_e.htm (last accessed Nov. 9, 2017).

[105] CENT. AM. DEPT. AND OFFICE OF THE CHIEF ECONOMIST, LATIN AM. AND CARIBBEAN REGION, DR-CAFTA: CHALLENGES AND OPPORTUNITIES FOR CENTRAL AMERICA 4 (2005).

[106] *See* CAFTA Facts, *supra* note 66.

[107] *See Pension Bill Including Trade Provisions Faces Uncertain Path in Senate*, INSIDE U.S. TRADE, Aug. 4, 2006.

[108] *Id.* Apparently, the US threat was made in order to fulfill an eleventh-hour promise to a US Representative to seek a treaty modification, as a condition of securing his support for the treaty. *See* Eliza Brinkmeyer & Chris Slevin, *Rep. Robert Aderholt's CAFTA Flip-Flop Basis of Empty Sock Promise Will Leave Him Wearing Nothing But*, PUBLIC CITIZEN

special-interest-based Congressional pressure, the George W. Bush administration raised the spectre of a trade remedy, without going through the process of invoking the measure and satisfying the criteria of the mechanism, as a threat in order to attempt to force a change in the terms of a previously negotiated agreement.

Such an attempt to force the renegotiation of a previously negotiated agreement using the threat of a trade remedy is an example of coercion, and illustrates the manner in which safeguard provisions can jeopardize consent. If this were a case in private law, any modifications resulting from such tactics would most likely be held invalid under traditional contracts doctrine, as a modification made under threat or duress.[109] The nature and presence of such a threat, whether or not it is ever carried out in practice, has disturbing implications about the way problems in the US politics of trade at home are eased by threats of coercion abroad.

It is interesting to pause here for a moment and consider contract law more broadly as a proxy for domestic notions of fairness in protecting bargained-for agreements. Looking at contract modification norms under US contract law may offer a useful exercise to measure US negotiation practice by standards it can't easily claim as alien. The Restatement Second of Contracts states that "[a] promise modifying a duty under a contract not fully performed on either side is binding if the modification is fair and equitable in view of the circumstances not anticipated by the parties when the contract was made."[110] In this case, a modification made under threat would not be considered fair, and the circumstances invoked – that CAFTA could lead to an influx of imported socks – hardly unanticipated (indeed, that is the purpose of negotiating a safeguards clause in the first place). Therefore, on this standard, any modification to CAFTA made on this premise would be

---

(Aug. 4, 2005), www.citizen.org/sites/default/files/aderholt_post_cafta_deals_090905_final.pdf.

[109] *See generally* Daniel A. Graham & Ellen R. Pierce, *Contract Modification: An Economic Analysis of the Hold-Up Game*, 52 LAW & CONTEMP. PROBS. 9 (1989) (invoking Corbin's term for such modifications under threat as the "hold-up game," and offering a law and economics account of why, even under an efficient breach theory, modifications made under certain threats should not be enforced).

[110] RESTATEMENT (SECOND) OF CONTRACTS §89(a) (AM. LAW INST. 1981).

invalid and would not be sustained in court, independently of the element of duress mentioned already.

Although a private law example does not of course directly map onto the case of an international treaty, it offers another lens into how the law protects consensual exchanges in ways that resonate within the trade context, and how US trade policy is not always consistent with the values inherent in its own domestic private law. Stated differently, the rules at home are not the same as the rules abroad.[111]

Trade remedies were also an issue in the KORUS negotiations, where Korea sought reform to US AD/CVD policy in the face of what it considered protectionist applications favoring US industries at the cost of Korean exporters. Economic studies have suggested that the real barriers to Korean access into US markets have been protectionist trade remedies, not tariff levels.[112] The USTR responded that this was not in the purview of the USTR, but rather reflected standards and priorities in US law, which is up to Congress.[113]

However correct that may be as a matter of formal US separation of powers doctrine, it is naïve in terms of the protectionist use of trade remedies, and disingenuous with respect to the scope of options available to willing negotiators in a context of greater equality. When Canada, a much closer match to US economic power than Korea, raised similar concerns in the context of the US–Canada FTA and then its successor NAFTA, it succeeded in creating a special binational panel review mechanism, named Chapter Nineteen, solely devoted to countering perceived nationalist trends in the administration of US trade remedy law.[114]

The United States has not created any similar mechanisms in other FTAs, and as of this writing has stated its intention to eliminate this mechanism from the NAFTA in the current renegotiation.[115] Whether

---

[111] I am indebted to Daniel Blanchard for his elaboration of this point.

[112] Lee et al., *supra* note 3, at 132; *see also* Schott et al., *supra* note 94 (United States would have to reform long-standing trade barriers against Korean exports and resolve the visa issue to create a Korean FTA).

[113] Lee et al., *supra* note 3, at 149.

[114] NAFTA, *supra* note 10, at art. 19.

[115] Ana Swanson, *Trump Administration Unveils Goals in Renegotiating NAFTA*, WASH. POST (July 17, 2017), www.washingtonpost.com/news/wonk/wp/2017/07/17/trump-administration-outlines-goals-for-nafta-rewrite.

that succeeds or not, it is unlikely the United States will create Chapter Nineteen panels in any other FTAs, but this is a political decision and not a structural implication of our Constitution. This leaves complaining parties like Korea in a quandary: refuse the FTA on offer, or accept the possibility that US exporters will gain genuine market access advantages into the Korean market, while any purported trade advantages to Korean exporters will face neutralization by the same old nontariff barriers.[116]

As with CAFTA, Korea has also discovered that the coercive dilemmas around trade remedies do not end when the agreement is signed. At the time of this writing, the United States has just announced that it has successfully renegotiation key provisions of KORUS that it felt unfairly burdened US manufacturers,[117] after earlier signaling its desire to renegotiated what the Administration felt was a "horrible" trade deal.[118] In a manner reminiscent of the CAFTA sock threat, the Administration was able to do so after threatening to group South Korea into the steel and aluminum tariffs the United States planned to impose predominantly on China.[119]

By doing so, the Administration succeeded in reducing Korean auto exports into the United States while securing larger import quotas

---

[116] Lee et al., *supra* note 3, at 133.

[117] *President Donald J. Trump Is Fulfilling His Promise on the U.S.–Korea Free Agreement and on National Security*, WHITE HOUSE FACT SHEETS (Mar. 28, 2018), www.whitehouse.gov/briefings-statements/president-donald-j-trump-fulfilling-promise-u-s-korea-free-trade-agreement-national-security/.

[118] *South Korea Eases Cap on Auto Imports in Return for U.S. Steel Tariff Exemption*, THE JAPAN TIMES (Mar. 26, 2018), www.japantimes.co.jp/news/2018/03/26/business/economy-business/u-s-south-korea-reach-agreement-trade-steel-tariffs/. The United States indicated that the approximately seventy percent increase in trade in goods deficit and overall trade deficit between the United States and South Korea since KORUS went into effect was the main impetus for renegotiating the provisions of KORUS. WHITE HOUSE FACT SHEETS, *supra* note 117, at 17.

[119] Alan Rappeport & Jim Tankersley, *Trump Gets First Major Trade Deal as South Korea Looks to Avoid Tariffs*, N.Y. TIMES, Mar. 27, 2018, at A7, www.nytimes.com/2018/03/26/business/south-korea-us-tariffs.html. Despite the threat to impose steel and aluminum tariffs on South Korea, there is some indication that South Korea would have been exempt from these tariffs, as the United States cited national security concerns as the basis for imposing the tariffs, and South Korea had previously been granted exemptions from national security concerns. John Brinkley, *U.S.–S. Korea Trade Pact Revision Is Full of Holes*, FORBES (Mar. 27, 2018), www.forbes.com/sites/johnbrinkley/2018/03/27/us-korea-fta-revision-is-full-of-holes/.

into Korea for US cars, a US goal in the initial negotiations for KORUS.[120] Thus through this most recent coercive action, the United States was able to revisit negotiations and secure concessions that Korea had resisted in the first place. In return, the United States promised to exempt South Korea from the steel tariffs targeted at China.[121]

Thus in the area of trade remedies we can also see coercive dynamics at work, and the consensual nature of trade undermined. Safeguard actions are used as threats to force renegotiation, rather than as orderly adjustment mechanisms. Special safeguards are created, and existing trade remedies applied, to block increased market access for the weaker party, while actual market access is demanded by the stronger party, undermining the mutuality of agreed market access commitments. None of this is surprising when viewed as part of power politics between nations (though it may still be disappointing), but when viewed through the lens of consent, it suggests something other than trade is going on.

3 Dispute Resolution

Another revealing aspect of trade agreements is the manner in which their dispute resolution provisions are structured. Informal nonbinding consultations, while apparently neutral, favor the more powerful party because the outcome is not determined by law but by power.[122]

---

[120] The KORUS revisions extended US tariffs on South Korean pickup trucks for twenty years, increased the quantity of US automobile imports from twenty-five thousand to fifty thousand vehicles and cut South Korean steel exports by thirty percent. Simon Lester, *The First Trump Trade Deal: The KORUS Renegotiation May Be Complete*, INT'L ECON. L. & POL. BLOG http://worldtradelaw.typepad.com/ielpblog/2018/03/the-first-trump-trade-deal-the-korus-renegotiation-may-be-complete.html (last accessed Mar. 29, 2018). The United States has indicated that the revisions also include an elimination or simplification of regulations in the automobile and pharmaceutical industries as well as a simplification of South Korean customs procedures. WHITE HOUSE FACT SHEETS, *supra* note 117. There has been some suggestion that though these revisions do alter the provisions of KORUS they do not practically alter the trade relationship between the United States and South Korea as US automakers have not exported more than the twenty-five thousand automobile quantity provided for under KORUS originally and the other revisions may not have an appreciable effect on the trade deficit. *See* Brinkley, *supra* note 119.

[121] Rappeport & Tankersley, *supra* note 119.

[122] *See* JOHN H. JACKSON, THE JURISPRUDENCE OF GATT & THE WTO: INSIGHTS ON TREATY LAW AND ECONOMIC RELATIONS 278 (2000). On the norm creation side, this was the genesis of the critique of the GATT "Green Room" process whereby small

The development of binding international dispute settlement under the rule of law in the WTO context represents an important step and a major contribution to the international rule of law.[123] Thus it is of concern that, while the WTO's binding dispute settlement process has been key to several victories by developing countries, in regional and bilateral treaties such as NAFTA, CAFTA, the CTPA and KORUS the United States has structured the dispute resolution provisions to allow room for the disparities in economic power to influence outcomes.

When the dispute resolution provisions of CAFTA are examined closely, it can be seen that the provisions echo the NAFTA-style preference on the part of the United States for nonbinding dispute resolution.[124] Article 20.15 of the treaty states that "[o]n receipt of the final report of a panel, the disputing Parties shall agree on the resolution of the dispute, which *normally* shall conform with the determinations and recommendations, if any, of the panel [emphasis added]."[125] In other words, the arbitral panel's final report is not implemented as a binding legal decision; rather, it is the basis for a settlement by the parties, which technically need not track or implement the panel report at all.[126] The CTPA and KORUS dispute

---

invited groups of powerful states would work out trade policy compromises with the GATT Director General, that would then be presented to the Contracting Parties as fait accompli. *See* Kent Jones, Green Room Politics and the WTO's Crisis of Representation, 9 PROGRESS DEV. STUD. 349 (2009); Dan Zoll, *Developing Nations Complain of Being Shut Out of Ministerial Planning Process*, WORLD TRADE OBSERVER (Nov. 24, 1999), https://depts.washington.edu/wtohist/World_Trade_Obs/issue1/devnations.htm.

[123] For John H. Jackson's influential distinction between rule-oriented and power-oriented diplomacy, *see* JOHN H. JACKSON, THE WORLD TRADING SYSTEM: LAW AND POLICY OF INTERNATIONAL ECONOMIC RELATIONS 110–11 (2d ed. 1989).

[124] *See generally* Frank J. Garcia, *Decisionmaking and Dispute Resolution in the Free Trade Area of the Americas: An Essay in Trade Governance*, 18 MICH. J. INT'L L. 357, 378–83 (1997) (analyzing NAFTA dispute resolution mechanism). This practice has roots in the GATT and the carryover of that approach into the US–Canada Free Trade Agreement. David A. Gantz, *Settlement of Disputes Under the Central American–Dominican Republic–United States Free Trade Agreement*, 30 B.C. INT'L & COMP. L. REV. 331, 387 (2007). Although the GATT's nonbinding system was replaced by the creation of the WTO's binding procedure under the DSU, US bilateral and regional practice did not follow suit.

[125] CAFTA, *supra* note 34, at art. 20.15.

[126] *See* Gantz, *supra* note 124, at 400–01 (in the face of the panel report, parties retain flexibility to work out an arrangement). It is true that the parties can elect to pursue a claim in the WTO instead in cases where they have overlapping rights, but this is of no help where the rights are unique to CAFTA, and in any event does not alter the essentially nonbinding nature of CAFTA dispute settlement per se.

resolution mechanisms also carry forward the same political "escape clause" that the CAFTA mechanism offers.[127]

The word "normal" in this context can be misleadingly neutral in appearance. As many government representatives and commentators have indicated across a range of contexts, for smaller states there is nothing "normal" about entering into dispute settlement proceedings against a superpower, for reasons that make negotiations in such a context similarly fraught, as will be discussed in the next chapter.[128] When the power differentials are so great, one cannot assume "normal" outcomes and assumptions will apply, particularly when the rules themselves create wiggle room for the play of such differentials.[129]

In such a context, rules like these raise the possibility that dispute resolution will be subject to the coercive dynamics we have been tracking in other areas of treaty practice. It can be coercive, first, because there will be pressure brought to bear against the weaker state's initiating a formal dispute settlement process in the first place, as has been already seen in other contexts.[130] Second, even if the dispute panel itself is independent and unbiased, their report does not settle the dispute, but only adds a further input into what is essentially a negotiation between unequal parties about a trade conflict, leaving the door open to resolution by power and coercive tactics and not by law.

However the dispute settlement process concludes, there is the final step of compliance and enforcement, and the mechanism agreed in all of these treaties lends itself to exploitation by the United States. Should

---

[127] CTPA, *supra* note 52, at art. 21.15; KORUS, *supra* note 56, at art. 22.12.

[128] JAMES H. CASSING, *Trade Dispute Diversion: The Economics of Conflicting Dispute Settlement Procedures Between Regional Trade Agreements and the WTO*, *in* FRONTIERS OF ECONOMICS AND GLOBALIZATION: TRADE DISPUTES AND THE DISPUTE SETTLEMENT UNDERSTANDING OF THE WTO 303, 310–12 (James C. Hartigan ed. 2009).

[129] Fandl, *supra* note 75, at 81–82.

[130] *See* CASSING, *supra* note 128, at 310–12; *see also* Gantz, *supra* note 124, at 389–90 (a dispute settlement mechanism's effects on informal consultations and settlements is a key element in assessing its effectiveness, but hard to determine with publicly available information); World Health Org., *Access to AIDS Medicines Stumbles on Trade Rules*, BULLETIN OF THE WORLD HEALTH ORGANIZATION (May 2006), www.who.int/bulletin/volumes/84/5/news10506/en/; *The Separate Doha Declaration Explained*, WORLD TRADE ORG., www.wto.org/english/tratop_e/trips_e/healthdeclexpln_e.htm (last accessed Nov. 10, 2017).

a losing party make an unsatisfactory final settlement offer that falls short of full implementation, or fail to honor its implementation commitments once agreed, these treaties all provide that the prevailing party's only recourse would then be suspension of equivalent benefits.[131] At first reading, this might seem effective and evenhanded, and satisfy any concern over possibly coercive outcomes. However, it is well documented that such suspensions are particularly inadequate in agreements between states with great economic disparities, because the markets of small economies are simply too small for such measures to create any real economic incentive on the part of a country like the United States to change its policies.[132] Moreover, the danger of economic harm to the prevailing country in the face of its own sanctions is real, since these economies tend to be so import dependent in general and, thanks to the FTA, even more dependent on imports from the more powerful losing party!

This kind of enforcement system creates conditions that the United States, or any party in a similar situation, could exploit to its advantage. In other words, it opens the possibility that the United States will take unfair advantage of the structural impediments against real enforcement, to act in ways that would subject it to the risk of dispute settlement actions that, but for the nature of these provisions, could result in real consequences for the United States. Whether or not that has happened or will ever happen, it seems unwise to build a dispute settlement system that could so easily lead to exploitation, if one is purportedly aiming to build a treaty protecting mutually beneficial consensual exchanges.

When considered in light of the current US administration's intentions to renegotiate NAFTA's dispute settlement provisions to make them even more explicitly advisory, one is also left with the sad impression that the United States, long a champion of the rule of law in many contexts around the world, has opted in its most intimate trade agreements to create an archaic power-oriented dispute

---

[131] CAFTA, *supra* note 34, at art. 20.16, pt. 2.

[132] Report of the Panel, *United States – Measures Affecting the Cross-Border Supply of Gambling and Betting Services*, WT/DS285/RW (Mar. 30, 2007). *See generally* Gregory Shaffer, *The Challenges of WTO Law: Strategies for Developing Country Adaptation*, 5 WORLD TRADE REV. 177 (2006) (surveying challenges to developing countries in dispute resolution).

settlement mechanism, despite the prevailing trends toward increased rule-oriented dispute settlement.[133]

4 Domestic Law Reform

As part of investigating consent in trade agreements, we need to also take a close look at those aspects of these agreements that mandate non-trade law reform in order to determine who benefits from these reforms and how they were agreed. With respect to domestic commercial law, the CAFTA treaty tells a particularly egregious story, though unfortunately not a unique one, which merits an extended examination.

The CAFTA services chapter requires Costa Rica, for example, to undertake significant substantive revisions of its domestic agency and distribution law.[134] Agency and distribution laws typically offer enhanced, judicial supervised protections for agents and distributors in the event of termination, as they are generally understood to be the weaker parties in such contracts and hence subject to exploitation.[135] The United States had identified these rules, a source of frustration to US business, as a key goal for CAFTA reform.[136] The US aim was to weaken these protections for the benefit of foreign – in this case United States – principals.

First, the treaty requires Costa Rica to enact new laws that will not presume that such commercial relationships are exclusive, whereas, under Law No. 6209, such contracts were impliedly exclusive.[137]

---

[133] Megan Cassela, *USTR Considers Non-Binding Dispute Settlement Mechanism in NAFTA*, POLITICO (Sept. 21, 2017), www.politico.com/tipsheets/morning-trade/2017/09/21/ustr-considers-non-binding-dispute-settlement-mechanism-in-nafta-222412; *see generally* JACKSON, *supra* note 123.

[134] *See* CAFTA, *supra* note 34, at annex 11.13, §A, pts. 1–6 (mandating changes to Costa Rica's Law No. 6209, "Law for the Protection of the Representative of Foreign Companies").

[135] Pilar Perales Viscales, *The Good, the Bad and the Ugly in Distribution Contracts: Limitations of Party Autonomy in Arbitration?*, 4 PENN ST. J.L. & INT'L AFF. 213, 219 (2015).

[136] Office of the US Trade Representative, *Free Trade with Central America: Summary of the U.S.–Central American Free Trade Agreement (2003)*, https://ustr.gov/archive/Document_Library/Fact_Sheets/2003/Free_Trade_with_Central_America_Summary_of_the_US-Central_America_Free_Trade_Agreement.html (discusses dismantling distribution barriers that locked US firms into distributor arrangements).

[137] US COM. SERV., US DEPT. OF COMMERCE, DOING BUSINESS IN COSTA RICA 10 (2006).

The treaty also requires new laws that mandate that termination with notice – but absent any breach of obligation – is nevertheless to be considered termination for just cause, thus waiving all rights of the agent or distributor to indemnification. Under the old law, Costa Rican representatives had been broadly protected against termination, subject only to narrow grounds for "just cause."[138] Finally, all such contracts will now be deemed subject to private arbitration unless expressly subject to litigation, even though, under Law No. 6209, access to Costa Rican courts could not be waived by contract, even with explicit arbitration clauses.[139]

It is worth taking a closer look at the arbitration aspects of this audacious case of extraterritorial private law reform, as it offers what is perhaps the most consent-undermining aspect of any measure studied thus far. The treaty requires what is in essence a retroactive modification of any agency and distribution contracts then currently in force to submit the parties to arbitration, by creating the rebuttable presumption that where the contract is silent as to judicial settlement of disputes, such silence indicates an intention to settle any disputes by arbitration.[140] Given the fact that the Costa Rican agency law in force prior to CAFTA expressly required judicial supervision of disputes and prohibited alternative methods, it would not be unusual to find agreements that lacked express choice of forum clauses. The CAFTA provision not only retroactively amends the Costa Rican statute by creating a presumption that expressly contradicts the terms of the law then in force, but it does so in a way that contradicts what are likely to have been the reasonable assumptions of the contracting parties themselves under that regime.[141] Such a modification would under contract law be unenforceable as an example of duress, and which works a kind of theft against the party losing valuable rights without its consent.[142]

---

[138] See David R. Martinez, *At Termination, Independent Sales Reps Are Anything But*, 7 LATIN AM. L. & BUS. REP. 19 (1999).

[139] *Id.*

[140] CAFTA, *supra* note 34, at annex 11.13, §A, pt. 3.

[141] As one author puts it, the Costa Rican case reveals that even "mandatory" laws aimed at protecting the weaker party in such contracts are not enough, as they are not truly mandatory under the effects of the trade regime. Viscales, *supra* note 135, at 239–41.

[142] See CAFTA, *supra* note 34, at annex 11.13, §A, pt. 4.

Although Costa Rican law may have been in some respects more protective than other developing-country agency laws,[143] these changes go beyond simply conforming Costa Rican law to contemporary standards.[144] These changes soften provisions found particularly onerous by US firms, such as restrictions on their freedom to terminate agreements without cost, and they limit important rights previously enjoyed by Costa Rican citizens, such as access to the courts.

This imposition of arbitration is particularly noteworthy for two reasons. First, it appears quite self-serving, given that the United States already influenced Costa Rica toward adopting a US-style arbitration code through its key role in the 1997 overhaul of Costa Rica's arbitration system.[145] Second, in the context of an asymmetric treaty negotiation, such US actions seem opportunistic and unprincipled, given that under US domestic law the imposition of arbitration through contracts of adhesion is one ground for their unenforceability.[146] In other words, one of the places where private firms exercise their unequal bargaining power over consumers is by imposing arbitration instead of litigation,

---

[143] Interview with Prof. F. E. Guerra-Pujol, Univ. Cent. Fla., in Bogotá, Colom. (May 19, 2006); *see also* Salli A. Swartz, *International Sales Transactions: Agency, Distribution and Franchise Agreements, in* NEGOTIATING AND STRUCTURING INTERNATIONAL COMMERCIAL TRANSACTIONS 15–19 (Mark R. Sandstrom & David N. Goldsweig eds., 2d ed. 2003).

[144] In any event, the idea of "contemporary," less protective standards must itself be evaluated in the current neoliberal economic context, since there is nothing necessarily "neutral" about the contemporary.

[145] US AGENCY FOR INT'L DEV., TRADE AND COMMERCIAL LAW ASSESSMENT: COSTA RICA VII-4 (2004) (USAID was influential in the passing of 1997 Costa Rican ADR law); *see also* Elizabeth Thomas, Commercial Arbitration in Costa Rica (2005) (unpublished manuscript) (on file with author) (documenting the US role in reforming Costa Rican arbitration law to its own way of thinking, arguably giving US parties an advantage).

[146] Although the Federal Arbitration Act favors the enforcement of arbitration agreements, they are still subject to challenges under state law principles of unconscionability. Generally, to be unenforceable a contract of adhesion must be both substantively and procedurally unconscionable. Given that, under CAFTA, arbitration may be implied by law, those agreements are arguably already procedurally unconscionable. Thus, if these were US contracts, absent the unique imprimatur of federal law, their enforceability would depend solely on the ability of their substantive terms to withstand strict scrutiny. *See generally* Thomas H. Oehmke & Joan M. Brovins, *The Arbitration Contract – Making It and Breaking It*, 83 AM. JUR. PROOF FACTS 1 (3d ed. 2005).

and US contract law typically rejects such provisions. It is ironic that the United States is using a highly unequal treaty negotiation process to impose such measures on Costa Rican parties *as a class*, acting as an agent of the US manufacturers *as a class*, provisions that US courts themselves would be reluctant to enforce in parallel private law circumstances at home.

When viewed in this light, the fact that the Costa Rican government would agree to strip protections from agents and distributors, and to impose US-style arbitration on a class of private parties through treaty law, may be evidence of coercion at the state level, which results in duress or even theft (understood as the nonconsensual stripping of a private party's valuable legal rights) with respect to private parties.[147] Thus in the area of law reform, CAFTA fails both aspects of free trade. As an agreement, it does not preserve the bargained-for exchanges among private parties, and with respect to law reform it does not seem to be a voluntarily bargained-for exchange between negotiating states. While the CAFTA states of course formally consented to the treaty through the ratification process, once again we have to weigh the degree to which they would in fact jeopardize the core trade benefits they are urgently seeking in such a treaty, for the domestic law reforms imposed on them as a price. In this sense, CAFTA might be considered an adhesion treaty, a point I will return to in the next chapter.[148]

We find echoes of this same story in the case of the KORUS. Here, the United States also entered the negotiations with a long list of changes it sought to domestic Korean laws, reaching deep into Korean economic, social and cultural policies.[149] The overall goal was to "adopt a comprehensive FTA that requires Korean laws and practices to conform to US standards in areas where US trade interests are affected."[150] This

---

[147] As a further irony, were a state to engage in such a taking with regard to a foreign private party, it would almost certainly amount to a compensable expropriation under international investment law.

[148] *See* ARTHUR LINTON CORBIN, CORBIN ON CONTRACTS §1.4 (rev. ed. 1993) (noting the origin of the term "adhesion contract" was the international law term for a treaty which states must accept or reject despite having no voice in formulating its provisions).

[149] Lee et al., *supra* note 3, at 124 (quoting a US government source).

[150] *Id.* at 118.

meant seeking changes in domestic law areas as diverse as screen quotas for Korean film, affecting the viability of a Korean film industry; and Korea's universal health care system, a key social policy with important affordability goals.[151]

Overall, the United States achieved its goal of substantial reforms of Korean law according to US models,[152] leading commentators to characterize this as part of a larger trend toward legal harmonization to US standards through FTAs.[153] US law reform efforts in CAFTA would certainly fit this characterization as well, which raises a disturbing question. Given that this is a high-stakes, take-it-or-leave-it way of doing law reform, when key market access and other benefits are put into the balance, the United States seems to once again have opted for coercive or exploitative methods to change other countries' laws under the guise of negotiating trade agreements.

Such dynamics have led commentators to charge that the KORUS (and presumably any agreement like it) is an exercise beyond trade liberalization and toward asymmetric economic integration, in which "one country's regulatory scheme for legitimate public policy objectives had to be abandoned to satisfy the interests of its trading partner."[154] If so, we have moved far away from agreements consisting of freely bargained mutually beneficial exchanges, toward something else.

We shall have to see in the next section if negotiations in a multilateral context that includes some parties that are rough equals can produce meaningfully different outcomes.

---

[151] *Id.* at 125. The United States sought abolition of screen time quotas mandating a minimum number of days for screening Korean films (though not limiting film imports), and changes to the drug pricing policies employed by Korea's universal health care system to keep consumer drug prices affordable. *Id.*

[152] The United States succeeded in negotiating key reforms in the intellectual property law, legal services market and telecommunications industry. *Id.* at 138–40.

[153] *Id.* at 144–47 (quoting Australian Professor Ross Buckley on the US approach to FTA negotiation). For example, screen time quotas were abolished, and Korea agreed that drug reimbursement policies would proceed according to competitive market-driven prices, threatening the Korean health care system with significant additional costs. *Id.* Altogether, the Korean legislature had to pass twenty-five statutes altering domestic law in order to conform with the FTA prior to its ratification. *Id.* at 149.

[154] *Id.* at 147.

C Consent in a Multilateral Context

Bilateral and regional agreements illustrate quite dramatically the dynamics of both consent and oppression due to their small size and the kinds of leverage possible due to the asymmetries among the parties. One could imagine that a multilateral agreement could neutralize some of these advantages, given its larger membership and the fact that its membership includes a number of large and midsized powers.

However, the dynamics of consent and oppression also turn out to be present in multilateral trade agreements as well. This should not be surprising, given Weil's point about the structural relationship between oppression and socioeconomic institutions of all kinds. It would indeed be surprising *not* to find these processes at work in the analysis that follows. In discussing the WTO, I am going to highlight the same four areas: market access, remedies, dispute resolution and law reform.

1 WTO, Market Access, Coercion and Exploitation

A core function of the WTO system is to organize the process of multilateral negotiations around the reduction of tariff and nontariff barriers, toward increased market access for members and progressive market liberalization. This was the essential function of the GATT Treaty of 1947 and its associated negotiation "Round" process, which has carried over into the WTO's complex treaty structure in which the GATT Treaty (now GATT 1994) constitutes a major part of "Annex 1," the trade rules annex to the WTO Agreement.[155]

The political philosopher Richard Miller has identified elements of coercion and exploitation in the ways the WTO system accomplishes this core goal. This is important in its own right, given the centrality of

---

[155] Marrakesh Agreement Establishing the World Trade Organization, Apr. 15, 1994, 1867 U.N.T.S. 154. The other Annex 1 agreements are the General Agreement on Trade in Services, or GATS, and the or TRIPS (I shall have more to say about this agreement in Section 4). Annex 2 consists of the Dispute Settlement Understanding or DSU (I shall have more to say about this in Section 3). Annexes 3 and 4 contain a trade policy review mechanism, and smaller agreements that not all WTO members are party to.

market access (now including both goods and services) to most economies, particularly developing ones. It is of particular concern when we
recall that the WTO is much more than the GATT – as Miller points
out, it is a global framework agreement creating a global regulatory
institution. Opting out is not an option – for any serious economy with
development goals, there is simply no other game in town. Thus, it
matters a great deal how this institution accomplishes its regulatory
purposes, through its own behavior and through the behavior its rules
and norms facilitate in its powerful members.

Miller analyzes the way major developed countries "take advantage" of the urgent need of developing countries for market access, to
negotiate unbalanced agreements through what he deems "bullying."[156] He cites numerous examples of US behavior during the
Uruguay Round negotiations that consisted of flamboyant threats of
trade disputes, or threats to create alternative and exclusive regional or
bilateral trade deals, if the United States did not get its way.[157] The
result, in his view, is a framework that is seriously unbalanced against
developing countries, both in specific areas such as market
liberalization, which is uneven due to a toxic combination of developed
country agricultural subsidies and high tariffs against competitive
exports from developing countries;[158] and in overall structural patterns
such as the lack of free movement of labor (unskilled and semiskilled
labor is a comparative advantage of many developing countries) when
compared to goods and services.[159]

Miller's account of US behavior against weaker states in a multilateral setting closely tracking the idea of coercion, and the concept of
taking unfair advantage at the heart of our account of exploitation.[160]
If an agreement is reached on the basis of "threats of exclusion and
discrimination," that would be an example of coercion, not trade.
Similarly, Miller characterizes a trade regime achieved on the basis of

---

[156] RICHARD W. MILLER, GLOBALIZING JUSTICE 70 (2010).
[157] Id. at 70.
[158] Id. at 81. Such a combination can be disastrous, as when the Philippines opened its corn
    sector to increased foreign imports to comply with Uruguay Round commitments,
    leading to the loss of thousands of jobs and serious social dislocation in a country that
    could ill afford it, while US and European agricultural subsidies remained intact. Id.
[159] Id. at 77–79.
[160] Id. at 70.

concessions that countries would only make under conditions of need, as a case of "the strong taking advantage of the weak," which we would call here exploitation. State behavior can certainly combine elements of both, in the sense that a powerful state can seek to take unfair advantage of problematic background conditions such as the legacy of colonialism (exploitation), through bullying tactics that would count in themselves as coercion.

The alternative to such tactics, Miller writes, is instead to engage in "reasonable deliberations." Put in the terms of this study, I take Miller to mean that the alternative to exploitation and coercion in multilateral trade negotiations is to engage in negotiations toward a consensual agreement, what he calls "the willing acceptance of a shared commitment by all."[161] This is a theme that I will return to in Chapter 3.

2 WTO, Trade Remedies and Exploitation

WTO rulemaking in the area of trade remedies – safeguards is a good example – tells a somewhat more nuanced story when compared to how remedies seem to play out in a regional/bilateral context, which I think has a lot to do with the benefits of multilateralism. However, even in the WTO context there is evidence of the dynamics we are studying here when it comes to rules on subsidies, a pernicious area in the WTO as elsewhere.

The WTO Agreement on Safeguards regulates how and under what circumstances parties can have recourse to domestic safeguards actions under Article XIX of the GATT.[162] Article XIX had been roundly criticized prior to the creation of the WTO, for reasons including overly broad language, protectionist abuse biased in particular against developing country exports and the use of safeguard actions as a poorly disciplined escape clause against tariff liberalization commitments (a story familiar to us already from the US hemispheric context).[163] Unsuccessful reform efforts during the Tokyo Round of GATT negotiations centered on "Group of Seven" meetings aimed at

---

[161] Id. at 70–71.
[162] General Agreement on Tariffs and Trade art. XIX, Oct. 30, 1947, 61 Stat. A-11, 55 U.N.T.S. 194.
[163] See, e.g., Jorge Perez-Lopez, GATT Safeguards: A Critical Review of Article XIX, and Its Implementation in Select Countries, 23 CASE WEST. RES. J. INT´L L. 519 (1991).

disciplining safeguards actions with the concerns of developed countries in mind.[164] However, developing countries also made important progress, as part of the overall Tokyo Round North–South dialogue, achieving a declaration reinforcing their right to have recourse to the more permissive safeguards rules under Article XVIII, contained in the so-called development part of the GATT, Part IV.[165]

These efforts culminated in the WTO Agreement on Safeguards, which substantially improves multilateral disciplines on safeguard actions, while preserving differential treatment for developing countries.[166] With respect to the issues plaguing safeguards actions at the regional or bilateral level, the Agreement eliminates for WTO members some of the potentially abusive laxity and unilateralism that characterize the special safeguards actions the United States negotiates at the regional or bilateral level. Thus we can say that, in the area of safeguards, the multilateral system offers something of a success story with respect to the abuses documented at the regional or bilateral level. Why is that?

I think there are a couple of reasons, both of which are relevant to the approaches to consent issues that we will consider in the next chapter. First of all, the larger set of negotiating partners in the multilateral context, and the fact that this set includes a broader range of larger powers, means that more evenhanded safeguards rules can be negotiated among a subset of rough equals, each with the reciprocal goal of reducing each other's abusive practices, which developing countries can then piggyback onto.[167] Second, the earlier modest Tokyo Round successes of developing countries in this area, preserved in the Agreement, came about at a time when the political threat posed by postcolonial nationalism and the general ferment around North–South issues in the GATT and elsewhere, meant that there was

---

[164] *Id.* at 536–37 (the group consisted of the United States, the then-EEC, Japan, Australia, Canada, Switzerland and the Nordic countries).

[165] *Id.*; *see* World Trade Organization, *Safeguard Actions for Development Purposes*, L/4897 (Nov. 28, 1979). *See generally* ROLLAND, *supra* note 42.

[166] *See* Yong-Shik Lee, *The WTO Agreement on Safeguards: Improvement on the GATT Article XIX?*, 14 INT'L TRADE J. 283 (2000). *But see* Chad P. Bown & Rachel McCulloch, *Nondiscrimination and the WTO Agreement on Safeguards*, 2 WORLD TRADE REV. 327 (2003).

[167] *See* Lee, *supra* note 161; *see also* Perez-Lopez, *supra* note 163 (role of Group of Seven at the Tokyo Round).

political will among developed country members, albeit limited, to recognize some of the concerns of smaller and weaker economies as long as it did not seriously derail their efforts aimed at disciplining each other. Thus developing countries were poised to gain a bit of policy space, while freeriding on the broader rule-of-law gains developed countries achieved for everyone because of their specific concerns about each other. This is a classic case of the benefits that multilateralism can under the right conditions offer for weaker members.

Unfortunately, when we turn to the question of subsidies, the story is not as positive, in ways that illustrate both the limits of multilateralism, and some of the same dynamics of coercion and exploitation we are studying here. The WTO Agreement on Subsidies and Countervailing Measures, or SCM,[168] does contain some improvements in the rule of law regarding subsidies and countervailing measures when compared to the prior Tokyo Round code and the GATT rules.[169] However, it nevertheless contains serious defects, allowing developed countries to subsidize widely, due in part to the unresolved battle between developed countries over agricultural subsidies.[170]

On a global structural level this deficit works to the detriment of everyone, but is particularly costly to developing countries. While the SCM agreement (and the related Agreement on Agriculture) have allowed developing countries to nevertheless score a few noteworthy successes against developed country subsidies in the dispute settlement system,[171] this is nevertheless no substitute for the deep structural reform

---

[168] Agreement on Subsidies and Countervailing Measures, Apr. 15, 1994, Marrakesh Agreement Establishing the World Trade Organization, Annex 1A, 1869 U.N.T.S. 14.

[169] See PEGGY A. CLARKE ET AL., *WTO Dispute Settlement Practice Relating to Subsidies and Countervailing Measures, in* THE WTO DISPUTE SETTLEMENT SYSTEM 1995–2003 379 (2004), www.wilmerhale.com/uploadedFiles/WilmerHale_Shared_Content/Files/Editorial/Publication/Horlick%20WTO%20Dispute%20Settlement%20re%20Subsidies%20and%20Countervailing%20Measures.pdf.

[170] See Lorand Bartels, *The Relationship Between the WTO Agreement on Agriculture and the SCM Agreement: An Analysis of the Hierarchy Rules in the WTO Legal System* (International Trade, Working Paper No. 2016/15, 2016).

[171] Notification of Mutually Agreed Solution, *United States – Subsidies on Upland Cotton,* WTO Doc. WT/DS267 (Oct. 23, 2014); Understanding between Brazil and the European Communities, *European Communities – Export Subsidies on Sugar,* WTO Doc. WT/DS266/36 (June 9, 2006).

necessary in order to truly eliminate the distorting subsidy practices of developed countries, reform they are successfully blocking.[172]

In addition to the macroeconomic and development problems that developed country subsidies cause for developing countries, the relatively undisciplined nature of subsidy practice today creates the kind of background condition that developed countries then can then exploit, in the terms of the present study. We see evidence of this in the WTO context when powerful states are negotiating multilateral market access concessions against a background of subsidization, as Richard Miller points out; and in the regional and bilateral agreements we have been studying here.

With respect to both KORUS[173] and the US hemispheric agreements,[174] when the United States uses its substantial leverage to insist on broad agricultural concessions, yet refuses reform of its own domestic agricultural subsidies, it is exploiting a background condition of its own making (poorly constrained domestic subsidies) to force what will in economic terms be unbalanced concessions. In the terms we have been using here, this is a classic case of unfair advantage taking. Through these tactics, the heavily subsidized agricultural sector of a major economic power will be competing on newly improved terms against the unsubsidized (or weakly subsidized) sectors of much smaller economies, that will also continue to face the specter of trade remedies where they manage to make any inroads. While liberalization in such a regime can seem facially neutral, in practice it is anything but.

These dynamics also illustrate the weakness of the free-rider position many developing countries find themselves in within a multilateral treaty system. When the bigger powers hammer out a fairer system for and against each other, then everyone benefits (i.e., safeguards). However, as long as the bigger powers have yet to work out their disagreements, the smaller powers are left to endure what they must and make what progress they can at the margins (i.e., subsidies). The few high-profile dispute resolution successes in the subsidy area do, however, illustrate both the strengths and the weaknesses of the

---

[172] Shaffer, *supra* note 132.
[173] Lee et al., *supra* note 3, at 135.
[174] *See, e.g.*, Fandl, *supra* note 75, at 79–80.

WTO DSM from a developing country perspective, and it is to the DSM that we now turn.

3 *WTO Dispute Settlement and Exploitation*

The WTO Dispute Settlement Understanding (DSU) governs the adjudication of disputes on alleged noncompliance and, if necessary, enforces obligations through an arbitral panel process that results, in the case of noncompliance, in the authorized application of unilateral sanctions (called the suspension of concessions).[175] One of the most widely recognized shortcomings of the system, from the perspective of developing countries, is the time, money and human resources neces- sary to mount or defend against WTO cases.[176] When developing countries win cases they bring against developed country members, it is widely recognized as a significant achievement and a vindication, at least in part, of the strength of the dispute settlement system.[177] However, what is perhaps less readily visible, and certainly more common, is the pressure developing countries face to settle cases they bring or cases they are subject to, often simply because of resource constraints independent of the merits of the case.[178]

An even more subtle, and perhaps even more damaging, shortcom- ing in the DSU system is the fact that it depends ultimately on the effectiveness of trade sanctions, which in turn depend on the relative market size of the sanctioning and sanctioned states and their respect- ive capacities to absorb the economic effects of sanctions, which are felt by both the sanctioning and sanctioned states.[179] An authorized

---

[175] *See generally How Does the WTO Settle Disputes?*, WORLD TRADE ORG., www.wto.org/ english/thewto_e/whatis_e/tif_e/disp1_e.htm.

[176] *See* Shaffer, *supra* note 132, at 1. For this reason, the WTO Advisory Centre for Dispute Resolution, a kind of state-funded Legal Aid for developing countries, is a key element in helping lessen the effects of unequal background conditions on WTO dispute resolution. *See, e.g.*, Roderick Abbott, *Are Developing Countries Deterred from Using the WTO Dispute Settlement System: Participation of Developing Countries in the DSM in the years 1995–2005* (ECIPE, Working Paper No. 01/2007, 2007).

[177] *See* Stephen J. Powell & Andrew Schmitz, *The Cotton and Sugar Subsidies Decisions: WTO's Dispute Settlement System Rebalances the Agreement on Agriculture*, 10 DRAKE J. AGRIC. L. 287, 288–90 (2005).

[178] Shaffer, *supra* note 132, at 2.

[179] *See, e.g.*, CHENG-YAN TUNG, CROSS-STRAIT ECONOMIC RELATIONS IN THE ERA OF GLOBALIZATION: CHINA'S LEVERAGE AND TAIWAN'S VULNERABILITY (2007);

suspension of concessions is generally effective in bringing a party into compliance with its WTO obligation in cases brought by developed countries, with large markets that are significant to the sanctioned state and which can themselves absorb the effects of the higher costs of the sanctioned goods to domestic industry and consumers.

However, the same mechanism is not as effective when a developing country, with its small and highly trade-dependent market, is awarded the right to suspend concessions against a larger noncomplying state. This is so because, first, its consumers can ill afford the higher costs of the sanctioned goods, and second, the volume of trade with the noncomplying state is simply too small from that state's point of view for the sanctions to make any appreciable impact.

In the view of Chi Carmody and others, this is a structurally unfair result, because it represents a frustration of member expectations based in the agreements themselves, through a means of dispute settlement that is effective for some members more than others.[180] As Carmody points out, the WTO agreements establish a series of rights and obligations for WTO members, and create a series of expectations in these members, based on their formal equality. Fairness in the WTO "is ... about maintaining the distribution of expectations, which is equal; the ethos is justice-as-equality."[181]

The asymmetric nature of the effectiveness of the WTO remedy suggests that at least in certain respects, the WTO DSU can also be said to facilitate exploitative behavior. In a system whose substantive principles operate on the basis of formal equality between parties, the dispute settlement system in practice achieves unequal outcomes due to background conditions of a structural nature: a sanctions-based remedy works unequally in practice when small economies are

Philip I. Levy, *Sanctions on South Africa: What Did They Do?* (Yale Univ. Econ. Growth Ctr., Discussion Paper No. 796, 1999), www.econ.yale.edu/growth_pdf/cdp796.pdf. Brazil was recently authorized to cross-retaliate against the United States as part of the long-running cotton case, but the two sides have suspended that course in order to further negotiations. *See* RANDY SCHNEPF, CONG. RES. SERV., R43336, STATUS OF THE WTO BRAZIL–U.S. COTTON CASE 3 (2013); *DS267: United States – Subsidies on Upland Cotton*, WORLD TRADE ORG., www.wto.org/english/tratop_e/dispu_e/cases_e/ds267_e.htm (last accessed Feb. 22, 2018).

[180] Chios Carmody, *A Theory of WTO Law*, 11 J. INT'L. ECON. L. 527 (2008).

[181] *Id.* at 542.

involved, and developing countries are not equally staffed or resourced when it comes to mounting or defending these cases.[182]

Therefore, when a developed country pushes hard for seemingly balanced concessions (remember Miller), such concessions will not be truly reciprocal, insofar as they will not be equally enforceable by both sides against each other. Similarly, when a developed country violates existing agreements with respect to a developing country, it is doing so in a context in which the target state will often lack an effective remedy.[183] In either case, it can be said that the DSU is allowing developed WTO members to exploit unfair background conditions.

4 TRIPS, Domestic Law Reform and Coercion

Perhaps the most widely cited example of alleged dynamics of coercion coming out of the multilateral context involves the debate surrounding the WTO TRIPS Agreement.[184] The TRIPS Agreement sets out minimum standards on IP protection to which all WTO members must conform, or else face WTO dispute settlement action. These minimum standards include the types of IP that must be protected under domestic law and for how long; and the legal mechanisms that must be available in domestic law to protect these rights.[185]

While at first glance such an agreement might seem unobjectionable, TRIPS represents the conclusion of an underlying, long-running, urgent and passionately argued debate over the proper role of IP protection in a postcolonial development process.[186] In this debate, the most advanced economies, holding the bulk of the world's IP then

---

[182] See Shaffer, *supra* note 132, at 1. For this reason, the WTO Advisory Centre for Dispute Resolution, a kind of state-funded legal aid for developing countries, is a key element in helping lessen the effects of unequal background conditions on WTO dispute resolution. See Abbott, *supra* note 176.

[183] It is not possible for a small developing country to effectively enforce a judgment against a large advanced economy in a sanctions-based regime, absent some creative alternatives. See Asim Imdad Ali, *Non-Compliance and Ultimate Remedies under the WTO Dispute Resolution System*, 14 J. PUB. & INT'L AFF., Spring 2003; Shaffer, *supra* note 132.

[184] Agreement on Trade-Related Aspect of Intellectual Property Rights, Apr. 15, 1994, Marrakesh Agreement Establishing the World Trade Organization, Annex 1C, 1869 U.N.T.S. 299 (hereinafter TRIPS).

[185] See *supra* note 184.

[186] See generally Danielle Tully, *Prospects for Progress: The TRIPS Agreement and Developing Countries After the Doha Conference*, 26 B.C. INT'L & COMP. L. REV 129 (2003) (reviewing history of IP and developing countries).

and now (and, not coincidentally, also the former colonial powers), argued not surprisingly for strong IP protection, whereas the developing countries argued on development and postcolonial justice grounds for looser standards.[187] Moreover, the issue (and negotiations) came to a head during the global HIV/AIDS pandemic, in which pharmaceuticals were a critical weapon, and which illustrated painfully and dramatically the nature of the inequalities in both IP holdings and wealth (in the form of social safety nets and health care resources). This all occurred in a context (Africa) that had felt and continues to represent the full brunt of colonialism at its worst.[188]

The fact that we have a TRIPS Agreement clearly represents the victory of the developed country IP holders in this debate, which in itself would have assured enduring controversy around the agreement. However, and even more to the point for the purposes of this study, many scholars consider the manner in which TRIPS was adopted to have been highly coercive.[189] Thus the TRIPS Agreement is an important site in which to evaluate how domestic law reform efforts (in this case, of developing country IP laws) are handled and mishandled when included in a multilateral trade negotiation.

Within the complex tangle of the Uruguay Round negotiations that led to the creation of the WTO (and the TRIPS Agreement), two elements stand out that are relevant to the coercive aspect of these negotiations. First, in the background of the negotiations we have the United States aggressively pursuing a policy of unilateral IP enforcement actions under Section 301 of its domestic trade law[190] against individual high-profile developing countries, in order to enforce its more aggressive stance on IP rights.[191] These actions, perfectly legal under pre-WTO law but deeply resented both in the context of the global IP debate and for their unilateralism, could lead to US trade sanctions that developing countries could not afford or effectively counter, and deliberately

---

[187] *Id.*

[188] *See* Abbott, *supra* note 176.

[189] Donald P. Harris, *Carrying a Good Joke Too Far: TRIPS and Treaties of Adhesion,* 27 U. PENN. J. INT'L ECON. L. 681, 732 n.205 (2006).

[190] Trade Act of 1974, Pub. L. No. 93–618, §301, 88 Stat. 2041, 2041–43 (codified as amended at 19 U.S.C. §2411).

[191] Harris, *supra* note 188, at 732–36.

intensified during the TRIPS negotiation period.[192] Second, we have the decision in 1993 by the so-called Quad Countries (United States, EU, Canada and Japan – again, not coincidentally including the major IP holding states) that the WTO should be launched as a "single undertaking," in other words as a package of treaty obligations that every country had to accept *in toto* to become a WTO member.[193]

Together, these two elements combined to create a highly coercive dynamic for developing countries in the IP area: accept the deeply resented TRIPS Agreement, representing as it does the triumph of the developed country side of the IP debate, or face exclusion from the WTO (unthinkable in 1994 and even more so now), and the prospect of continued unilateral US sanctions over IP policy. This illustrates precisely the same dynamic surrounding domestic law reform and trade negotiations that we saw in US regional and bilateral trade agreements, with the same coercive effects. There seems to be little chance that a developing country will refuse a trade agreement with vital market access and other benefits, in order to resist even as deeply unpalatable a domestic law reform as the TRIPS Agreement.

For such reasons, D. P. Harris has made the interesting argument that TRIPS should be considered an adhesion treaty, under principles drawn from the private law of adhesion contracts.[194] Harris cites the characteristics of a treaty that render adhesion theory relevant as follows: (1) one state, generally a developed country, had superior bargaining power; (2) the agreement has aspects or characteristics of a form or preformulated contract and was presented on a take it or leave it basis; (3) the receiving state, generally a developing country, lacked sufficient bargaining power to modify or reject the terms and (4) the imposed terms are onerous or unfavorable and offend norms of distributive fairness.[195] In Harris's view TRIPS meets those criteria,

---

[192] *Id.* at 735.

[193] *See* Andrew L. Stoler, *Breaking the Impasse: A Critical Mass Approach to Multilateral Trade Negotiations* (2008), https://iit.adelaide.edu.au/docs/critical_mass_speech_final .pdf; Robert Wolfe, *The WTO Single Undertaking as Negotiating Technique and Constitutive Metaphor*, 12 J. INT'L ECON. L. 835 (2009).

[194] Harris, *supra* note 188.

[195] *Id.* at 724–38. The TRIPS negotiations meet all of these criteria, as many elements of the earlier regional and bilateral negotiations profiled in this chapter, which I will explore in greater detail in Chapter 3.

but his larger goal is to argue for private law concepts of adhesion to be available to international tribunals as a general principle of law under Article 38 of the ICJ Statute, justifying an interpretation *contra proferentem*, or against the party responsible for the drafting, in favor of developing states.[196] I shall have more to say about this interesting suggestion in the next chapter.

5 *Conclusion*

Thus, multilateralism by itself is no panacea to the risks that weaker states encounter when they set out to negotiate trade agreements with powerful states, and then often find themselves in the middle of negotiating something quite different. However, multilateralism can nevertheless play a key role in addressing trade's pathologies, as we shall see in the following chapter.

III DRAWING THE STRANDS TOGETHER

What have we learned about the state of consent in contemporary trade practice? While this has not been a comprehensive study, I believe the examples chosen are both representative and indicative, highlighting several substantive and procedural issues of concern. Most importantly, it would seem that looking at trade agreements through the lens of consent, and with dynamics such as predation, coercion and exploitation in mind, offers a useful way to begin to get at the dynamics of power that are deeply worked into the nature of negotiations among unequal parties.

Looking at market access, it seems that unless checked by other roughly equal parties or an effective coalition, as sometimes happens in the WTO context, powerful parties are free to use their leverage to coerce market opening on the part of the less powerful states, while successfully maintaining market protections on their own sensitive areas. While S&D concepts such as nonreciprocity protect weaker

---

[196] This principle of interpretation *contra proferentem* has been recognized by the European Principles of Contract Law, the UNIDROIT Principles, and the Restatement, 2nd, of Contracts, lending weight to Harris's argument. Harris, *supra* note 188.

states in a multilateral context up to a point, such concepts are by definition absent from an FTA, with its complete liberalization agenda, thus further reinforcing the potential for destructively unequal outcomes.

In the regional and bilateral context, trade remedies appear to have become convenient tools for creating the appearance of concessions by more powerful states, while opening back doors out of these concessions when their predictable effects are felt. In certain cases developing countries were also successful in securing special safeguards, but that is not the norm. Instead, the CTPA example of Colombia's securing only a ninth-year review of its poultry concessions, when compared to the US special safeguard for sugar in the same agreement, seems more typical.

When it comes to dispute resolution, the contrast between multilateral and regional/bilateral outcomes is perhaps most pronounced. Whereas the WTO's truly binding dispute resolution mechanism is widely touted – rightly in my view – as key to its success and a genuine step forward in the international rule of law (despite its exploitative element, as Carmody profiles), the DSMs that typify at least US regional/bilateral practice are examples of powerful parties maintaining the freedom to do what they will, and using law to bury this discretion deeply in the details.

Finally, law reform offers perhaps the most powerful examples of how asymmetric agreements can result in substantive provisions that reach right into the consensual basis of private transactions themselves. There is perhaps no more powerful illustration of this, even when we consider the controversial TRIPS Agreement, than when the United States uses the CAFTA negotiations to rewrite not only Costa Rican agency and distribution law, but retroactively amend agency and distribution contracts between private parties then in force under the old regime.

This all implies a need for change in our approach to trade negotiations and to the social costs of agreements that work through coercive or exploitative dynamics instead of consensual trade. If trade is indeed about voluntary bargained-for exchanges, then this has to be kept in the foreground when states negotiate the trade agreements that set the terms of their economic relationships, and that regulate the space within which private parties trade. If the rules governing trade aren't themselves the fruit of consensual bargaining, and don't preserve the possibility of bargained-for exchanges among private parties, they have failed as law and undermined that which they sought to regulate.

Meeting this regulatory objective is a challenge. If we are to build trade agreements that are truly about trade, then we need to first allow ourselves to truly re-envision what trade is all about, and then allow that to change how we negotiate trade agreements, and the kinds of provisions we include, or do not include. A consent approach would alter the way we understand the bargaining process itself, and how we evaluate (and reform) the fruits of that bargaining. That will be the subject of Chapter 3.

3 (RE)BUILDING TRADE AGREEMENTS

We've now taken a look at contemporary trade practice when it comes to consent, and to the pathologies of trade, including exploitation and coercion. Agreements such as CAFTA, KORUS and the CTPA contain provisions that are significantly unbalanced in terms of the rights, interests and goals of the various negotiating parties, and their ratification points toward problems in the consent of the weaker states. We have also seen that the WTO agreements are not free from these dynamics either, particularly when the interests of the powerful states align against those of the less powerful.

This leads us to ask two necessary questions: how were such agreements ever agreed to? And if we have reasons to care about consent, whatever our views of justice or even basic fairness, which I have argued we do, then what can be done about this, both for future trade negotiations and with the agreements we now have?

Understanding how we got here requires that we take a closer look at how inequalities affect the negotiation dynamics between unequal parties, both generally and in the specific contexts discussed in the last chapter. The examples drawn from US treaty practice and the WTO, while only a sampling, are consistent with the (unsurprising) view that inequality tends to produce unbalanced agreements, and the more inequality, the more the unbalance. Perhaps more surprisingly, the specific examples also fit patterns of predation, coercion and exploitation that both illustrate the utility of a consent analysis, and – more importantly – caution us against allowing inequalities to run unchecked in trade negotiations if we are in fact interested in negotiating trade, and not something else.

Framing a response to these dynamics should include at least the following four moves. First, it means changing our expectations of trade agreements, once we've absorbed what we've understood about trade as consensual exchange and considered carefully our reasons for caring about consent. Second, it means determining which kinds of agreements – and provisions – we should be aiming at if we intend to create trade, and which to avoid. Third, it requires a look at how we might change trade negotiations, even between highly unequal parties, to take this new understanding into account when we negotiate new agreements. Finally, it will mean determining our options concerning the problematic agreements that will likely remain in force.

I HOW DID WE GET HERE?

A Negotiation Among Unequal Parties

This study has underscored the importance of understanding how economic asymmetry in negotiations among trade partners can lead to agreements that seem to be about trade but operate as something else. The negotiation process is where inequalities manifest themselves most forcefully, skewing substantive provisions away from trade and toward predation, coercion or exploitation.

In this section I want to look first more generally at what patterns we can discern from these examples of negotiating outcomes and dynamics when the negotiating states are unequal. Then I want to look more closely at these particular examples, and see how those dynamics fit the patterns of predation, coercion or exploitation identified in Chapter 1 as the pathologies of trade.

1 Asymmetry and Regional or Bilateral Trade Agreements

Chapter 2 offered us a selective introduction to key aspects of contemporary trade agreements, in a context (principally US regional and bilateral trade policy) that gives maximum scope for bargaining between very unequal parties. These treaties afforded us some fairly clear examples of the kinds of provisions that can result from such dynamics across a range of situations.

Although my sample set is small, it may be useful to try to mark the differences in degrees of asymmetry between different countries in different agreements, and see if this is potentially significant in evalu-ating how consent works in the resulting agreements. Given the par-ticular regions looked at in Chapter 2 and the patterns that emerged, we could organize the question of asymmetry along two dimensions: regional or bilateral agreements between highly asymmetric partners; and regional or bilateral agreements between moderately asymmetric partners. We could then bring in the WTO as a third dimension, multilateral agreements whose negotiations include both the dynamics of asymmetry among unequal partners, and negotiations among rough equals, as a comparison to both. We would expect to see that the more unequal the bargaining power, the more the substance of the agree-ment would tend toward one-sidedness as well, and the treaties seem to bear that out.

On this model, CAFTA can stand for the set of agreements between highly asymmetric partners. As mentioned before, the CAFTA states are among the poorest in the hemisphere, with a combined GDP dwarfed by that of the United States.[1] In terms of the effects of this degree of asymmetry on the resulting treaty, we can take market access as an example. It is perhaps not surprising then that CAFTA states were unable to make any real progress, for example losing at least for now on sugar, yet giving everything away on rice, beans and corn.[2]

The CTPA is also a highly asymmetric agreement, though not to the same degree as CAFTA. Colombia, while a more advanced econ-omy than any of the CAFTA countries, is nevertheless still a develop-ing country with significant economic challenges, not to mention security challenges, and is nothing like a roughly equal partner to the United States.[3] In market access, Colombia enjoyed small victories at

---

[1] US Dept. of Labor, United States Employment Impact Review of the Dominican Republic–Central America–United States Free Trade Agree-ment 9 (2005). In fact, a Congressional Research Service report found that the growth effects on the US economy of the CAFTA are essentially negligible.

[2] Sugar TRQs were increased and are on a schedule to phase out over fifteen years, whereas CAFTA agriculture sectors are liberalized on a much faster timetable. Office of the US Trade Representative, *CAFTA-DR – Agriculture: Specific Fact Sheet* 1, 9 (2005), https://ustr.gov/archive/assets/Trade_Agreements/Regional/CAFTA/Briefing_Book/asset_upload_file119_7211.pdf.

[3] *See* US Dept. of Commerce, *Top U.S. Trade Partners*, http://trade.gov/mas/ian/build/groups/public/@tg_ian/documents/webcontent/tg_ian_003364.pdf, *supra* Chapter 2, note 54.

least on paper, such as securing a ninth-year review mechanism for its poultry sector where the CAFTA states failed. Could such a marginal improvement, to the degree it is one, be attributable to slightly less asymmetry in the relationship? We would need a larger study to be sure, but it is an interesting possibility.

The KORUS offers a useful contrast to these two agreements. While the US economy clearly dwarfs the size of the Korean economy as well, Korea is a developed country that ranks as the seventh-largest US trading partner (the United States is Korea's third-largest trading partner).[4] This is still asymmetry, but nothing like on the CAFTA or even Colombia scales. Korea did manage to keep its key rice sector protected, something neither Colombia nor the CAFTA states could do, which it is tempting to ascribe to the less unequal relationship between Korea and the United States.

However, the overall results of the KORUS negotiations are nevertheless skewed in favor of the United States to a degree that I think cannot be completely explained according to relative economic size. The relationship between Korea and the United States can be characterized as only moderately asymmetric in terms of their respective economic size and importance to each other as markets. And yet, on important metrics such as services and trade remedies, the negotiation outcomes in the KORUS were not significantly less asymmetric than in CAFTA or the CTPA, where the economic asymmetries are much more marked. What could account for this?

Commentators suggest that in the end, the essential US role in Korean security, and increasing security pressures in the region, meant that Korea was not going to reject any trade bargain, no matter how lopsided.[5] This suggests that political asymmetry may matter as much as economic asymmetry, at least in certain trade negotiation contexts. Perhaps in this case security concerns converted what is ostensibly a moderately asymmetric negotiation in terms of economic size into a highly asymmetric negotiation when security is factored in, with predictable results.

---

[4] Young-Shik Lee et al., *The United States–Korea Free Trade Agreement: Path to Common Economic Prosperity or False Promise*, 6 U. PA. E. ASIA L. REV. 111, 116 (2011).
[5] *Id.*

What makes the WTO a useful comparison to the regional and bilateral negotiations mentioned thus far is not that WTO members are rough equals – as the TRIPS section of the last chapter illustrates, far from it. Rather, it is helpful because traditionally dominant actors such as the US and the EU, whose asymmetric power can distort agreements away from trade in other contexts, can be counterbalanced in the WTO context, first by each other, and second by coalitions among other medium-sized and smaller WTO members.[6]

This sets up the possibility of a different negotiation dynamic in some areas. We have seen some evidence of this inure to the benefit of weaker states at the dispute settlement level. Developing countries have won important victories through a dispute settlement mechanism that, while having unbalanced elements in terms of resources and effective remedies that could lead to exploitation as discussed in Chapter 2, does set a basic rule of law and was the fruit of a coalition of developed and developing states in the Uruguay Round.[7]

In terms of substantive rules, we see this dynamic benefitting developing countries in areas such as safeguard actions, in which the developed countries essentially checkmated each other, in the process negotiating rules that can benefit everyone. We also see it in agriculture trade, though less beneficially, where there is an interesting distribution of power among large and medium-sized states that has allowed developing countries to block progress in the Doha Round due to unresolved agricultural subsidy and special safeguards issues.[8]

However, even in a multilateral context we see examples of trade's pathologies in evidence. This is particularly so when negotiations involve issues of importance to the WTO's most powerful developed members acting in concert, such as TRIPS. Here the resulting agreement closely resembled the earlier agreed position among the Quad

---

[6] See World Trade Organization, Ministerial Declaration of 18 December 2005, WTO Doc. WT/MIN(05)/DEC; Rolland, supra note 58.

[7] See Stephen J. Powell & Andrew Schmitz, The Cotton and Sugar Subsidies Decisions: WTO's Dispute Settlement System Rebalances the Agreement on Agriculture, 10 DRAKE J. AGRIC. L. 287, 288–90 (2005); SYLVIA OSTRY, THE URUGUAY ROUND NORTH–SOUTH GRAND BARGAIN: IMPLICATIONS FOR FUTURE NEGOTIATIONS 6 (2000), http://sites.utoronto .ca/cis/ostry/docs_pdf/Minnesota.pdf.

[8] Jonathan Lynn, Efforts Begin to Salvage WTO Deal, N.Y. TIMES (Aug. 7, 2008), www.nytimes.com/2008/08/07/business/worldbusiness/07iht-trade.4.15091703.html.

Countries, and represents the oppressive possibilities that arise when the strongest developed countries speak as one voice *against* the interests of developing states. We also saw systematic evidence of this in Miller's analysis of market access negotiations when taken as a whole.

While a much broader study would need to be carried out to fully validate these intuitions, the patterns identified in the above section, and in the preceding chapter, reflect common sense about the role of power in negotiations, and are at a minimum highly suggestive. As will be seen in this chapter, more nuanced ideas of predation, coercion and exploitation can help us move beyond a simple calculation of relative bargaining power, and gain insight into the specific ways such asymmetries manifest themselves in provisions that undercut consent and therefore trade, which at the end of the day is what these agreements are at least ostensibly about.

B Theft, Coercion, Exploitation and Trade Negotiation Dynamics

As we have also seen in the preceding chapter, there are many points throughout a trade negotiation at which dynamics other than mutual consensual bargaining can enter into the process. Our concepts of exploitation, coercion and predation can be helpful in understanding these dynamics, and their implications for the larger trade project. Common to all these situations is that the powerful state, when behaving in a predatory, coercive or exploitative manner, mistakes in the process its own long-term interests, and the repeat-game nature of trade, foregoing the long-term benefits of a thriving mutually beneficial economy in exchange for immediate economic or political gains or gratifications. That, in my view, is the essence of a bad bargain.

1 Exploitation, Background Conditions and Genuine Alternatives

To begin with, there is a risk of exploitation whenever there may be problematic background conditions, including the very inequality itself and its complex causal matrix, which a powerful party can use to its advantage in securing a more one-sided deal than the exploited party would have agreed to, absent the problematic background conditions.

Some conditions may be of the powerful state's making, others not, but both kinds can equally be exploited to its advantage. Whatever the cause, exploitation on the part of more powerful states within the context of a trade negotiation is a generally recognized threat that smaller countries are uniquely vulnerable to.[9]

One kind of risk factor for exploitation in negotiations concerns the presence or absence of viable alternatives for any country negotiating trade with a powerful partner such as the United States. To the extent that any one party lacks such alternatives, this contributes dramatically to the other party's bargaining power, which in the case of the United States is already significantly greater due to its many advantages of scale.[10] This inequality in bargaining power can itself be deployed coercively, as will be discussed in the next section. However, in the case of the Americas, it can also be understood through the kind of exploitation highlighted by Steiner. Insofar as the United States can be said to have influenced the relative absence of other states in the region that are able to offer more attractive terms in the "auction," it has taken advantage of that situation to press for highly unbalanced agreements favoring itself.[11]

A constant spectre throughout all of the hemispheric negotiations discussed here was the primacy of the United States as each country's largest export market.[12] During the CAFTA negotiations, for example, it was often mentioned by the Nicaraguan government that the country

---

[9] EMILY JONES, NEGOTIATING AGAINST THE ODDS 86 (2013).

[10] See Editorial, Harvesting Poverty: A New Trade Deal, N.Y. TIMES, Dec. 22, 2003, at A30 (asserting CAFTA's terms reflect asymmetry in negotiating power between the United States and the Central American region).

[11] This despite recent increased efforts by Latin American states to diversify their trade portfolio and negotiate with as many other countries as possible. See infra note 23 on the importance of BATNA in asymmetric negotiations. In the case of the CTPA, this was definitely a factor in US industry support for concluding an agreement. See M. ANGELES VILLARREAL, CONG. RES. SERV., RL34470, THE US–COLOMBIA FTA: BACKGROUND AND ISSUES 26–28 (2014) (U.S. exporters concerned that they were losing market share in the Colombian market due to Colombia–Canada FTA). It will be interesting to see how the recently increasing Chinese presence in Latin America will affect such negotiations and their outcomes. This theory would predict more balanced agreements as a result, but it will be very difficult to reopen treaties such as CAFTA for adjustment, and the United States is rapidly sewing up the entire region in a network of bilateral and regional agreements, presenting future regional leaders with a fait accompli.

[12] See, e.g., LOUIS JORGE GARAY et al., Negotiating the Colombia–US FTA: A Colombian Perspective, in ASYMMETRIC TRADE NEGOTIATIONS 137, 137–45 (Sanoussi Bilal et al., eds. 2011).

did not have a real alternative to the treaty (and this was a revolutionary Sandinista government), due to the dominant US role in the Nicaraguan economy as the principal source of capital and markets.[13] Similar sentiments were expressed by the Colombian government during the CTPA negotiation process.[14]

However, this is not simply the logic of deepening economic ties with one's "natural" trading partners – there is little that is natural about trade patterns in the American hemisphere, to take the example closest to hand.[15] The United States exercised its role as regional hegemon during the last century by restricting regional and other states' opportunities in the hemisphere, which has continuing economic effects today.[16] Given this history of external domination of the southern hemisphere by the United States, both colonially and postcolonially, there is a genuine risk that other states in the region and elsewhere – states that might have offered more attractive alternative markets and sources of capital than the United States – may not have been able to do so to the fullest degree possible. Thus, to the extent that deepening ties with the United States would seem "logical" to weaker states in the hemisphere, it is a manipulated logic, not a natural one.

Expressed in the terms of a consent analysis, this raises the possibility that a treaty negotiated in such an environment will be exploitative. The risk here is that the United States will exploit the fact that in this trade negotiation "auction," to use Steiner's metaphor, its bid is the highest bid because other parties outside the region have not been able to develop ties – levels of commerce and investments – to match the levels of the United States, given its role as regional hegemon. Central American and Colombian negotiators were thus faced with

---

[13] Author interviews with Nicaraguan trade officials on background, Managua, Nicaragua, 2004.

[14] GARAY et al., *supra* note 12, at 138–44.

[15] This is not to say that deepening trade and economic integration in the Americas violates the economic logic of trade–only to say that trade patterns in this hemisphere, as elsewhere, have been deeply marked by political and social forces as much as by "natural" patterns of exchange and production.

[16] THOMAS E. SKIDMORE & PETER H. SMITH, MODERN LATIN AMERICA 5–7 (2d ed. 1989) (asserting that historic external domination has both threatened sovereignty and restricted available policy choices).

the prospect of this deal, or no deal, within a dearth of options that the US' historically hegemonic hemispheric policies have clearly contributed to.[17]

Such exploitation will influence the course of negotiations in several predictable ways. The chief risk, of course, is that the exploited party will accept suboptimal bargains since, on account of the exploitation, those are the best bargains on the table. In the previous chapter we saw many examples of outcomes and behavior that would seem to fit this pattern. This is compounded when the parties already operate from a distinct inequality in bargaining power, as is the case in multilateral, bilateral and regional trade negotiations involving developed and developing countries.[18] Moreover, these bad bargains have an intertemporal effect as well. Disadvantageous present negotiations impede better deals in the future, as the rules agreed in an unequal regional trade agreement become the baseline for that relationship in the future, even if politics at the multilateral level might have allowed for a better deal in principle.[19]

Latin American states have recognized this risk and sought to diversify their options by quickly negotiating a range of agreements with their other major trading partners besides the United States, such as Canada,[20] the EU[21] and Asia.[22] This is a key way for Latin American states to

[17] See GARAY et al., *supra* note 12, at 137–45.

[18] See John S. Odell, *Negotiating from Weakness in International Trade Relations*, 44 J. WORLD TRADE 545, 546–51 (2010) (cataloging this inequality among trade negotiating states).

[19] I am indebted to Sonia Rolland for pointing this out.

[20] Since the late 1990s and following the NAFTA with Mexico, Canada has negotiated FTAs with Chile, Colombia, Costa Rica, Peru, Panama and Honduras, and is exploring or negotiating trade agreements with MERCOSUR and a handful of other countries in the region. *Trade Agreements–Latin America and the Caribbean*, GOVERNMENT OF CANADA (July 7, 2017), www.agr.gc.ca/eng/industry-markets-and-trade/international-agri-food-market-intelligence/latin-america-and-the-caribbean/trade-agreements/?id=1466518583919.

[21] Since CAFTA entered into force in 2006, nine Latin American countries have negotiated trade agreements with the EU, bringing the total number of states in such agreements with the EU to eleven, in addition to the Caribbean states, which signed a new agreement in 2008. ENRIQUE GOMEZ RAMIREZ et al., Eur. Parl. Research Serv., *EU–Latin America Trade Relations*, E.U. Doc. PE 579.086 (Mar. 2016), www.europarl.europa.eu/RegData/etudes/IDAN/2016/579086/EPRS_IDA%282016%29579086_EN.pdf.

[22] In the last fifteen years, Latin American has concluded twenty-two trade agreements with Asian states, three of them with China. *See* Carol Wise, *Playing Both Sides of the Pacific: Latin America's Free Trade Agreements with China*, 89 PAC. AFF. 75 (2016). On the trade patterns between Latin America and China, *see* ROBERT DEVLIN & THEODORE KAHN,

improve their BATNA,[23] as will be discussed later in the chapter, but they are playing a game of catch up. Moreover, here we see the geographic logic of trade intersect with its social history: while non-hemispheric parties may increasingly be able to offer relevant trade and investment opportunities, their markets all lie at a considerable distance from Latin America, whereas the US market has tremendously significant advantages of proximity which cannot easily be matched by anyone else.

For Latin American states, the failure to conclude a deal would also have meant a perpetuation of trade under the lopsided, conditional and entirely discretionary trade preference programs already mentioned.[24] This suggests another kind of exploitation, implicit in the shift from preferential trade to bound trade, in two ways. First, the United States has had a direct role in creating and applying its own GSP-style regional trade preference schemes in an arguably coercive manner, creating a problematic background condition to the negotiations. In addition, the negotiations (and the GSP-style programs) take place against a second set of problematic background conditions, the overall market disparities and development challenges facing Latin American states, which at least echo if not embody colonial patterns and historical injustices of a structural nature, and which help explain why a coercive preferential trade scheme would be attractive at all in the first place.

When the United States then uses these background conditions to leverage essentially complete duty-free market access *for itself* as the price for its partners of getting out of that earlier coercive GSP situation, and of also potentially helping them ameliorate the structural background issues through trade, we could say that it was exploiting Colombia and the CAFTA states. In other words, the United States has taken advantage of problematic background conditions, some of its own

---

Latin American Trade with India and China: The Region Needs a Business Plan, in LATIN AMERICA AND THE ASIAN GIANTS 133, 151–53 (Riordan Roett & Guadalupe Paz eds., 2016).

[23] In negotiating theory, the latter is referred to as a party's BATNA, or "best alternative to a negotiated agreement." If a party has no BATNA, it is in a very weak position. FISHER & URY, *supra* note 11, at 104 (BATNA "is the only standard which can protect you both from accepting terms that are too unfavorable and from rejecting terms it would be in your interest to accept").

[24] *See* Chapter 2 65–66; *see generally* Frank J. Garcia, *Trade and Inequality: Economic Justice and the Developing World,* 21 MICH. J. INT'L L. 975 (2000)

making, to press for further advantages to itself at further cost to the already disadvantaged states, a clear case of unfair advantage taking.

The KORUS story is an interesting variation on this theme, affording us a second example of the exploitative possibilities presented to a powerful state because of problematic background conditions. As discussed earlier, the relationship between Korea and the United States can be characterized as only moderately asymmetric in economic terms, and yet the KORUS is in many ways as unbalanced as hemispheric agreements. Insofar as the essential US role in Korean security meant that Korea was not going to reject even a bad bargain, the United States was arguably exploiting the security situation as a background condition. Moreover, insofar as the United States in fact did have a role in both creating the Cold War and in setting the terms of the Korean armistice, it is also (as with GSP) exploiting security risks it had a hand in creating when it uses its role as regional security guarantor to negotiate unbalanced agreements.

Whether or not weaker states can effectively counterbalance such negotiating advantages remains to be seen, and options will be discussed later in this chapter. However, even if they can, that would not eliminate the underlying problem. When these negotiation dynamics are considered through the consent analysis employed in this study, they can be understood to illustrate a broader problem endemic in trade negotiations today.[25] Rather than being simply a (repeated) case of hard bargaining, trade negotiations carried out under conditions of such unequal bargaining power and against troubling background conditions have a built-in potential for exploitation. When these exploitative possibilities are acted on by stronger states, weaker states are compelled to negotiate bilateral and regional trade agreements that are inherently redistributive, further shifting power and resources from weaker states to stronger states.[26]

One troubling conclusion that could be drawn from this analysis, particularly in the political context at the time of its writing, is that powerful states seem unlikely to forego such exploitative opportunities,

[25] Joseph Stiglitz also highlights such dynamics as contributing to the problems facing globalization today. JOSEPH STIGLITZ, MAKING GLOBALIZATION WORK 96 (2007).

[26] THOMAS HALE ET AL., GRIDLOCK: WHY GLOBAL COOPERATION IS FAILING WHEN WE NEED IT MOST 162 (2013)

particularly as long as such exploitation is still considered "trade." This brings us directly to the question of coercion.

2 Coercion

In the preceding chapter we touched on many instances of what could be considered coercive behavior in the negotiation of CAFTA, the CTPA, KORUS and even the WTO. I want to return to them here briefly to consider them as a group, allowing us to step back and look at coercion itself as it has influenced such negotiations. Even where there is no history of background conditions that would create an exploitative environment, weaker parties often sign out of fear of losing what they have or of facing worse alternatives, a factor clearly understood and played up by more powerful states.

Inequalities in power can be directly employed to pressure or intimidate a party toward consent to disadvantageous agreements, which in contract law we call coercion and not simply "hard bargaining." These power inequalities may arise from factors intrinsic to the economic relationship, such as differences in economic size or wealth or levels of development. Alternatively, they may arise from factors extrinsic to the economic relationship, such as a state's role in addressing regional security concerns, that nevertheless give this state a power advantage it can deploy in a coercive manner to force its economic agenda through in the negotiation against the interests of the weaker state.

To begin with market access, the fact that such unbalanced market access provisions were agreed to by the weaker parties in the US agreements we have studied thus far suggests a coercive aspect to the negotiation. One form of coercion would be for the US to rely on the vast inequality in power and market size between itself and Central America or Colombia to keep certain options (such as liberalization of the sugar market) off the table, while pressing ahead for the concessions it wanted in other sectors equally sensitive to the Colombians and Central Americans, such as rice, beans, corn and poultry.[27] Since

---

[27] See James C. McKinley, Jr., *U.S. Trade Pact Divides the Central Americans, with Farmers and Others Fearful*, N.Y. TIMES Aug. 21, 2005, at A18, www.nytimes.com/2005/08/21/world/americas/us-trade-pact-divides-the-central-americans-with-farmers-and.html (reporting that Central American negotiators lacked sufficient leverage to

smaller economies in the hemisphere cannot afford to ignore the possibility of *any* increased market access into their most important trading partner, they are likely to accept such unbalanced terms.

Some might argue this is in fact what is meant by "hard bargaining" rather than coercion, but given the extreme power differential, and taken in the overall context of the negotiations as a whole, I believe this goes further. In fact, our willingness to consider this as a reasonable approach suggests to me instead that such tactics are so familiar in unequal negotiations that we have grown accustomed to thinking this is just "the way things are."[28]

Moreover, such structural inequalities and the leverage they create are only the beginning of the inquiry into coercive aspects of these negotiations. The shift from preferential trade under the US GSP program, to bound trade under a treaty, suggests a further, compounding and more explicitly coercive element. In my view, one of the more subtle yet pernicious examples of coercive behavior comes out of the interaction between market access negotiations in the western hemisphere and the background conditions set by the US GSP program, and related regional preference programs like the Andean Trade Preferences Act. If we consider the US program as applied to be coercive in itself, as I have argued elsewhere and in the last chapter, then it seems clear that the US used the threat of its partners' remaining in a coercive situation in the absence of a trade agreement, as leverage to press for further concessions for *itself* in order to secure that agreement, thus compounding the coercion. This suggests that Colombia and the CAFTA states merely "succeeded" in getting out of a highly coercive context (US GSP) into a possibly less coercive context (more stable treaty-based commitments), but through an even more coercive negotiation process that exacted a high price from them in terms of new concessions demanded by the United States.

Such behavior does not need a bilateral or regional context in which to play itself out. As we have seen with Richard Miller's study of the

extract needed concessions from the United States, and faced implicit threat of loss of trade preferences).

[28] This echoes all the way back to Thucydides' famous recitation of the Athenian debates on the fate of the Melians: "the strong do what they will, and the weak suffer what they must." THE HISTORY OF THE PELOPONNESIAN WAR (1972).

WTO negotiations, even a multilateral framework allows ample space for coercive behavior in market access negotiations, both by powerful individual states and by developed states as a whole. Miller cites numerous examples of US "bullying" behavior during the Uruguay Round negotiations that consisted of flamboyant threats of trade disputes, or threats to create alternative and exclusive regional or bilateral trade deals if the United States did not get its way.[29] His account of US conduct against weaker states in a multilateral setting closely tracks the idea of coercion.[30] If an agreement is reached on the basis of "threats of exclusion and discrimination," that agreement would represent coercion, as the law defines it, not trade.

Indeed, it is the WTO context that furnishes us with perhaps the most blatant example of negotiation through coercive behavior, the TRIPS agreement. Two elements of the TRIPS negotiations stand out in this regard for their coercive effects. First, recall that in the background of the negotiations we have the US aggressively pursuing a policy of unilateral IP enforcement actions under Section 301 of its domestic trade law[31] against individual high-profile developing countries, in order to enforce its more aggressive stance on IP rights.[32] These actions are coercive in themselves, in that they implied the threat of US trade sanctions that developing countries could not afford or effectively counter. However, they also deliberately intensified during the TRIPS negotiation period, introducing a further coercive element.[33] Taken together with the Quad States' decision that the WTO should be launched as a "single undertaking," these elements combined to create a highly coercive dynamic for developing countries in the IP area: accept the deeply resented TRIPS agreement, or face exclusion from the WTO, and the prospect of continued US unilateralism policy.

---

[29] RICHARD W. MILLER, GLOBALIZING JUSTICE 70 (2010).

[30] Id.

[31] Trade Act of 1974, Pub. L. No. 93–618, §301, 88 Stat. 2041, 2041–43 (codified as amended at 19 U.S.C. §2411 (2012)).

[32] Donald P. Harris, Carrying a Good Joke Too Far: TRIPS and Treaties of Adhesion, 27 U. PA. J. INT'L ECON. L. 681, 732–36 (2006).

[33] Id. at 735.

Finally, coercive opportunities do not end once an agreement is implemented, as the CAFTA textiles example vividly illustrates. Recall that the CAFTA textiles rules include safeguard provisions allowing the United States to unilaterally impose tariffs if there is a surge of textile imports that have the potential to hurt domestic manufacturing.[34] Such safeguards were also negotiated in the KORUS agreement. By itself there is nothing necessarily coercive about safeguard measures, which can play an important part in orderly trade adjustment. However, whether such measures are unilateral or bilateral can in certain cases say something about the mutuality of the bargain, and their coercive potential would then depend on how the provision is used. When the US used the threat of invoking this safeguard in an attempt to renegotiate a CAFTA provision, we are faced with a clear case of how safeguard provisions can be used as coercive tools and jeopardize consent.

The recent coercive tactics utilized by the United States against Korea to renegotiate KORUS may be even more troubling than those employed earlier with the CAFTA states. Unlike the threatened use of the safeguard measures in CAFTA, which were provided for by the agreement but are still undoubtedly coercive as employed, there is widespread concern that both the initial steel and aluminum tariffs[35] and the steel quotas South Korea voluntarily acceded to in the KORUS revisions[36] are potentially illegal under domestic and international law. By "successfully" renegotiating the KORUS this way, the United States is utilizing the threat of measures that in the long run may be

---

[34] *See* Office of the US Trade Representative, *CAFTA Facts – Textiles in CAFTA-DR* (2005), https://ustr.gov/archive/assets/Trade_Agreements/Regional/CAFTA/Briefing_Book/asset_upload_file551_7185.pdf.

[35] Simon Lester, *The Section 232 Tariffs in U.S. Court*, INT'L ECON. L. & POL. BLOG (Mar. 25, 2018), http://worldtradelaw.typepad.com/ielpblog/2018/03/the-section-232-tariffs-in-us-court.html. The first legal challenge to the steel and aluminum tariffs was filed in the US Court of International Trade on Mar. 22, 2018. Complaint, *Severstal Export GMBH v. United States*, No. 1:18-cv-00057 (US Ct. Int'l Trade Mar. 22, 2018), www.courthousenews.com/wp-content/uploads/2018/03/steel.pdf.

[36] Simon Lester, Will Anyone File a WTO Complaint Against the KORUS Steel Quotas?, Int'l Econ. L. & Pol. Blog (Mar. 28, 2018), http://worldtradelaw.typepad.com/ielpblog/2018/03/will-anyone-file-a-wto-complaint-against-the-korus-steel-quotas.html; John Brinkley, *U.S.–S. Korea Trade Pact Revision Is Full Of Holes*, FORBES (Mar. 27, 2018), www.forbes.com/sites/johnbrinkley/2018/03/27/us-korea-fta-revision-is-full-of-holes/#1f6edc9c20a3.

proven to be illegal, to coerce lasting changes to what is ostensibly a trade agreement.[37]

As discussed in the last chapter, if such a pattern of behavior was reviewed in a contract case under private law, any modifications resulting from such tactics would most likely be held invalid under traditional contracts doctrine, as a modification made under threat or duress.[38] The deployment of such threats has disturbing implications about the way problems in the US politics of trade at home are eased by coercive threats abroad.

When put side by side, the many instances of coercive behavior in bilateral, regional and multilateral negotiations speak volumes about the temptations of power in any negotiation, the unbalanced agreements that can result when those temptations are surrendered to and the problems this can lead to. For example, unbalanced agreements can in a repeat game damage the prospects for successful future bargains, and provoke resentment, hostility and even violence on a social and political scale as word of their imbalance spreads, and the effects on local economies become clearer, as will happen inevitably in the age of global social media.[39] In my view, this illustrates the costs of short-term thinking, driven equally by the ballot cycle as by the quarterly return cycle, as we have seen both domestically and globally in financial crises large and small throughout economic history.

This all cries out for a fresh look at the dynamics of trade negotiation once these costs are more clearly understood, and their link to the role of consent in trade brought to the forefront. However, before we can turn to this, we have to consider one more example of how dynamics other than trade enter into the negotiation of these agreements.

---

[37] Alan Rappeport & Jim Tankersley, *Trump Gets First Major Trade Deal as South Korea Looks to Avoid Tariffs*, N.Y. TIMES, Mar. 27, 2018, at A7.

[38] *See generally* Daniel A. Graham & Ellen R. Pierce, *Contract Modification: An Economic Analysis of the Hold-Up Game*, 52 LAW & CONTEMP. PROBS. 9 (1989) (invoking Corbin's term for such modifications under threat as the "hold-up game, and offering a law and economics account of why even under an efficient breach theory, modifications made under certain threats should not be enforced).

[39] *See, e.g.*, STIGLITZ, *supra* note 25, at 97 (discussing coercion in the context of globalization and citing CAFTA as an example).

3 Theft and Lack of Representation

No negotiation process is perfect in terms of equality and freedom, yet one can nevertheless highlight key issues that pose significant risks to consensual agreement, and I have been aiming to do that. In order for an agreement to be an expression of freedom, there must be consent at some meaningful level, beyond mere recognition of the formal sovereign independence of states, the formal legitimacy of governments and the formalities of ratification. As Beyleveld and Brownsword warn us, legal systems are prone to fictionalizing consent.[40]

We have already seen one kind of problem arising from a lack of voice when states make treaty commitments altering legal rights at the private party level. Recall our discussion in Chapter 2 of the domestic legal changes Costa Rica was required to make as a condition of CAFTA trade benefits, retroactively creating in agency and distribution contracts already in force a presumption in favor of arbitration. Not only does this presumption expressly contradict the law then in force, but this kind of *ex post* contract modification contradicts what are likely to have been the reasonable assumptions of any contracting parties not including an express choice of forum clause in the context of the law in force at the time. Such a modification works a kind of theft against Costa Rican agents and distributors, the parties to such contracts that lose valuable rights and see their likely contractual intentions subverted without any voice in the matter at all.

This kind of theft as the absence of voice finds its political analogue in the question of representation in the treaty negotiation process. Nowhere is the issue of voice more complex yet critical than when it comes to the exercise of political voice in trade, or the consent of the citizens of a country negotiating a trade agreement. This is an issue of concern not just to the government in question, but to any party negotiating a trade agreement with an underrepresentative government. The current controversy surrounding trade, and the widespread public perception that agreements have been negotiated without the consent, and against the interests, of major sections of society,

[40] *See* DERYCK BEYLEVELD & ROGER BROWNSWORD, CONSENT IN THE LAW 337–38 (2007).

illustrates the risks that come from even the perception of nonconsensual economic treaty making.

All of this requires us to delve into difficult questions, such as whether a negotiating government speaks for the full range of affected citizens, whether it speaks for its people at all and what a trading partner should do if it doesn't. While daunting, if we fail to consider such issues, we risk, as Weil warns us, mistaking or accepting a mere form of consent for actual consent.[41]

We cannot assume even in Europe or the United States, let alone most developing countries, that the government speaks for all affected sectors of society. This issue is of special concern in the case of developing countries, such as throughout the Central American region, where governments have a history of capture by elites.[42] More generally, the problem of representation is a systemic issue in liberal theory, and is the reason Rawls wrestles with the dilemma of liberal states in international relations with hierarchical states: how can we best take the absence of democratic representation within other states into account in our economic relationships with them, given our liberal commitments and our political necessities?[43]

Here our concerns are less philosophical and more pragmatic, since the lack of representation affects consent when fundamental economic decisions are being made. This issue arose in the CAFTA negotiations in the context of the problem of underrepresented groups. In Nicaragua, for example, during the CAFTA negotiations, local and international NGOSs and opponents to the treaty alleged widespread ignorance among most affected groups regarding what CAFTA would do, and a campaign of disinformation on the part of the government.[44]

---

[41] Similarly, Weil writes that in looking purely at the fact of voting, democratic theory mistakes true consent for a form of consent, which can easily, like any other form, be mere form. SIMONE WEIL, *Justice and Human Society, in* SIMONE WEIL 123, 126 (Eric O. Springsted ed., 1998).

[42] This problem has a long-standing history in Latin America. *See, e.g.,* SKIDMORE & SMITH, *supra* note 16, at 46 (discussing exercise of political power by or for elites endemic to region); *see generally* DECLINING INEQUALITY IN LATIN AMERICA: A DECADE OF PROGRESS? (Luis F. López-Calva & Nora Lustig eds., 2010).

[43] JOHN RAWLS, THE LAW OF PEOPLES (1999).

[44] Author interviews on background with Nicaraguan NGO and civil society representatives, Managua, Nicaragua 2004.

Many sectors of society were concerned that the new government only spoke for and negotiated on behalf of the moneyed interests (not unique in Latin America, despite a recent history of social revolution).[45]

Similar patterns have affected the domestic politics of other more recent US negotiating partners. In the case of the CTPA, the Colombian government was widely criticized for publishing misleading analyses of its "success" in the CTPA negotiations, prepared by consulting firms closely tied to the government, against a background of widespread public, academic and civil society criticism of its unbalanced concessions in key areas such as agriculture.[46] In Korea, the signing of the KORUS, and its subsequent introduction into Parliament for ratification, provoked huge public protests and much criticism of the government, including an opposition MP igniting a tear gas canister on the floor of Parliament to highlight widespread and vociferous opposition to the deal and to delay ratification.[47]

Such dynamics do not pose merely abstract problems in political theory – they raise the existential risk that, for these underrepresented or voiceless sectors, the treaty and its resulting economic activity are neither mutual nor voluntary. In other words, these stakeholders are not agreeing to trade – something is being taken from them. In the terms of a consent analysis, the risk is that the treaty does not create trade between the two states, but a form of theft or extraction by one sector against another, as much as from one state to another. In other words, the ruling elites are secure in the expectation that the "trade" agreement they negotiate will bring economic advantages to them and the economic sectors they control, at a cost to other constituencies within their own country.

---

[45] *See, e.g.,* GINGER THOMSON & STEVEN R. WEISMAN, *U.S. Suspends Military Aid to Nicaragua*, N.Y. TIMES Mar. 21, 2005, at A3 (US-backed conservative governments have historically failed to address extreme poverty and been widely perceived as corrupt).

[46] *See* VILLARREAL, *supra* note 11; GARAY et al., *supra* note 12; Kevin J. Fandl, *Bilateral Agreements and Fair Trade Practices: A Policy Analysis of the Colombia–U.S. Free Trade Agreement (2006)*, 10 YALE HUM. RTS. & DEV. L.J. 78 (2007).

[47] Haroon Siddique, *South Korean MP Lets Off Tear Gas in Parliament*, THE GUARDIAN (Nov. 22, 2011, 8:51 AM), www.theguardian.com/world/2011/nov/22/south-korean-mp-lets-off-teargas

This suggests that the consensual nature of a trade agreement can be undercut just as much when important constituencies – that a state should be negotiating on behalf of – do not get a fair bargain, as it can when the state as a whole does not get a fair bargain due to dynamics between itself and its negotiating partner.[48] Here too the waters are deep, but if we fail to consider such questions, we again risk the consequences of mistaking or accepting the presence of formal consent for actual consent. We may find ourselves facilitating uncompensated and unjustified wealth transfers among constituencies in our "trading" partners, facilitated by a "trade" agreement that functions as an enabling device for kleptocratic elites, and which was negotiated and implemented with our help and complicity.

II HOW DO WE MOVE FROM HERE TOWARD CONSENSUAL TRADE?

"If you look at the head of the nail, you'll hit it."

Anonymous

If we want to move away from this pattern and instead move toward consensual trade, the most important change we can make, in my view, is to let our understanding of trade return to trade's roots in consensual exchange. Asymmetric and exploitative agreements can be negotiated in part because we have come to accept that this is what trade and trade negotiations are all about. Moreover, even if one remains unconvinced that consensual trade should be the object of our negotiations, or is even central to what makes trade *trade*, there are important pragmatic reasons to take consent seriously if we aim to construct the working market that we ourselves will depend on to sell our wares. Whatever way we get there, a new understanding of the role of consent in trade opens many new possibilities, and will require something of all of us, not just trade negotiators.

---

[48] I shall have more to say about this in Chapter 4.

A Taking Seriously What We Know About Consensual Exchanges

Fundamentally, insofar as we have found ourselves immersed in agreements that seem to have more to do with exploitation or coercion than consensual bargaining, we have lost sight of what trade is really all about. Not to put this too harshly, but we are here because we have collectively let ourselves be brought here. We have done so, I believe, because of confusion over what trade really *is*, what it means to engage in trade, and why we have so consistently valued trade throughout our human experience.

Of course, most everyone reading this book could justifiably object that they have nothing whatsoever to do, in practical terms, with the negotiation of trade agreements, and neither does the author. So, what can I mean by saying we are here because *we* have lost sight of trade?

I mean, fundamentally, that we have asked too little of our leaders and often ourselves when it comes to the "trade" agreements they have negotiated ostensibly on our behalf, and that we have collectively supported, and we have accepted too much of something other than trade as a result. We have done so because of a lack of clarity in some cases about what trade is really all about, or a lack of transparency about the true nature of the negotiations, or even in some cases because we have been misled about this. And yet, curiously, the business people I have spoken with about trade understand intuitively what consensual bargaining is, and why if they want to succeed long-term in business, they must take consent seriously, whatever their personal ethics. This means in many cases not doing everything you can get away with simply because you *can* – what goes around, comes around. Everyone reading this book, I suspect, knows intimately the difference between a consensual exchange and a coercion, an exploitation or a theft, often from personal experience, and the relational consequences that follow from such behavior in and out of economic situations.

So, what has happened such that in the aggregate we behave as if we don't know what trade really is, when in our daily lives we do? The answers are of course complex, touching as they do on deep issues in human nature, the nature of representative government, the political process itself and the complexity of modern society, all with their inevitable and cumulative tendency to diffuse responsibility and obscure facts, motives, effects. There is obviously nothing simple or easily remedied about any of this, but the good news is that we need not worry that in order to address the problems with trade agreements today, we must fundamentally alter politics or society, let alone human nature. Not only is that not possible, even if it were thought desirable, but it isn't actually necessary.

The key, first of all, is to wake up. I mean, step back and simply take a look. Pay attention to what we already know about bargains, and consent, and its opposites, and take that seriously. Let ourselves come to know what we already know: a kind of remembering, if you will. Watch that we don't let ourselves get confused by the differences in scale and scope between the private exchanges of a personal or commercial nature that we know well, and the agreements our governments purport to negotiate on our behalf that are often distant and inscrutable. A market, even a global market, is at the end of the day a constructed set of conditions for exchanges of many kinds, and trade agreements are a major way those conditions are established and monitored. It is all about exchange.

B Remembering Why We Care About Consent

Even after some consideration one may reject the view that trade is about consent, or that the proper object of trade agreements is to consensually establish a framework for consensual exchanges. There remain powerful reasons, reasons that lie in the nature of markets and the human response to perceptions of unfairness, for why one should nevertheless be concerned about the state of consent in trade agreements today. I began our consideration of these reasons in Chapter 2, and it is worth returning to them again now.

1 Trade Is a Repeat Game

Consensual trade makes a kind of purely pragmatic sense, if one properly evaluates the kind of game that trade is. Recall that the key insight from applying the literature of game theory to trade is that *trade is a repeat game*, in which partners must contemplate a series of ongoing exchanges with no clearly determined end point.[49] The self-interested calculation of what strategies and tactics to employ changes when one contemplates a repeat game, as opposed to a single iteration. Approaches that may seem attractive for their short-term gains in a one-shot game seem less attractive if they depend on exploitation, coercion or manipulation, which can all poison the well for future iterations of the game. Over time, the oppressive nature of such agreements becomes clearer, and their consequently diminishing returns as well.

Respecting consent can therefore simply mean limiting the use of one's power in one's own long-term self-interest. If we correctly understand trade as a repeat game, then we will favor pro-consensual strategies as rational self-interested strategies. Just because you have the power to drive home an unfair deal, doesn't mean it is always smart to do so. There is a difference between making a killing and making a living, and the two terms are evocative in many ways – markets that survive and thrive over time have to be careful that they promote the latter and regulate the former. Economic frameworks that restrict or abrogate consent, invite people who are drawn to the former, and then gone again tomorrow to make another killing somewhere else, leaving damage and resentment in their wake. There is nothing stable about the business environment that creates, which has more in common with speculation than growth, as we all learned to our dismay in the global financial crisis. Businesses that survive and thrive learn that how you behave in the market will have long-term consequences either for or against your own self-interest.

This is no more, and no less, than what a consent theory of trade seeks to bring home at the level of treaty, policy and politics. If you ignore consent, you undermine the basis for future bargains, since trade is a repeat game embedded in a complex set of structural relations. We have concrete self-interested reasons to care how we

---

[49] This can alter the incentives of the players toward cooperation. *See* George Norman & Joel P. Trachtman, *The Customary International Law Game*, 99 Am. J. Int'l. L. 541, 559–60 (2005); Jeffrey L. Dunoff & Joel P. Trachtman, *Economic Analysis of International Law*, 24 Yale J. Int'l L. 1 (1990). *See generally* George J. Mailath & Larry Samuelson, Repeated Games and Reputations (2007).

are structuring such games and relationships through our "trade" agreements. To powerful market actors such as the US, the urge is simply to say, "You don't have to be good, whatever that means, just be *smart!*"

2 The Social Costs of Provoking Resentment

To the extent that we engage in predation, coercion or exploitation, we not only may lose potential partners for future beneficial transactions, we certainly increase the social costs of making and enforcing such bargains. It can't be overstated that whatever we think of the fairness of what we are doing, and even (especially!) if we don't particularly care whether we are being fair or not, it has to be kept in mind that the people we are engaging with will be registering perceptions of the fairness or unfairness of what we do, and registering them strongly. Recall that social psychology research into justice has found that our responses to a perception of injustice involve the strongest emotions we are capable of, including indignation, resentment, outrage and hostility, reactions that can set in motion social and economic dynamics with high personal, political and social costs.[50]

When considered in light of the kinds of treaties we have profiled in the previous chapter, it seems obvious that being subject to dynamics of coercion or exploitation in a variety of ways – being forced to accept either bad bargains or an outright theft – are going to be too easily and widely perceived in this social media world as the injustices that they may in fact be, and certainly as the coercive or exploitative agreements they seem to be, and provoke civil conflict, instability and even violent counterreaction.[51] In the present environment of this writing, with its surge of rightist authoritarianism around the world, it is hard to escape the conclusion that in its economic populist manifestations[52] we are

---

[50] *See generally* KJELL TORNBLOOM, *The Social Psychology of Justice, in* JUSTICE: INTERDISCIPLINARY PERSPECTIVES 177 (Klaus R. Scherer ed., 1992).

[51] *See* Garcia, *supra* note 45, at 78.

[52] *See* Kenneth Himes, *The State of Our Union*, 78 THEOLOGICAL STUD. 1 (2017) (analyzing contemporary populist reactions into their economic and nativist elements).

seeing the long-term fruits of ignoring consent in how we have built globalization and its current "trade" patterns, and how we have redistributed, externalized or ignored its costs.

For such reasons, whether we are engaged in trade or something else matters, not only to those of us concerned as citizens or progressive market participants, but also to those who may be concerned only with the reduction of social friction toward optimal performance of a transnational market.[53] If trade agreements are negotiated under circumstances in which our partners have no real possibility of consent, and significant sectors of their domestic societies have no way of expressing their consent or lack of consent, such treaties are not going to promote an effective trading environment over the long term. Instead, they promote overreaching and instability, and provoke resentment and unrest. Perhaps even more pernicious, and certainly more subtle and harder to quantify, is the long-term failure to thrive – for want of a better term – that an economic relationship subject to these forces will manifest.[54]

So, what should states be negotiating instead? It would seem that even for purely pragmatic and self-interested reasons, powerful states and the powerful actors within them that disproportionately impact trade policy should consider negotiating truly consensual bargains, as a way to maximize their own returns in the long run under conditions of a stable and thriving market. But understanding this has implications not just for states and their individual negotiating objectives – how do these objectives fit within the larger framework of international trade law and its goals?

---

[53] *See generally id.*

[54] Of course, a thriving market needs more than individual agency – it needs sound regulation to deal with market failures and to align short and long-term incentives, and private incentives with social aims. But the foundation is agency as expressed in consensual exchange. I am indebted to Sonia Rolland for pointing this out.

C Remembering What We Should We Be Aiming for in Trade Negotiations

As is the case with negotiation, so with regulation: it must begin with the clearest possible understanding of the goal. What is our regulatory objective? What are we trying to ensure? What are we trying to prevent? What are we hoping to safeguard?

International trade law is no different in this respect. Once we understand the consensual nature of trade, then it follows that the policy goal of international trade law should be more than simply liberalizing commercial flows by eliminating economically distorting domestic legislation. The goal should be to maintain an environment in which *trade* can take place and flourish, much as the goal of economic regulation in a domestic setting is to protect and promote a healthy and thriving market, which means recognizing, protecting and promoting consent at all levels. Put another way, promoting and protecting a healthy and thriving global market requires more than simply reducing or eliminating protectionist regulation. A consent analysis of trade thus alters what in international law is called the "object and purpose" of a trade agreement: building a *trading* system and not a disguised system for predation, coercion or exploitation.

1 Revisiting the Object and Purpose of a Trade Treaty

The canons of interpretation for international law give a central role to the "object and purpose" of a treaty when one aims to interpret the ordinary meaning of the treaty's terms in their context.[55] Since the end of the Second World War, the ostensible goal of international trade law has been to liberalize trade by reducing national barriers to transnational economic flows, in the pursuit of efficiency gains and economic growth. Consider this quote from the Preamble to GATT 1947, in which the Contracting Parties:

> Recognizing that their relations in the field of trade and economic endeavor should be conducted with a view to raising standards of

[55] 1969 Vienna Convention on the Law of Treaties, art. 31, Jan. 27, 1980, 1155 U.N.T.S. 331 (hereinafter Vienna Convention). In full: "A treaty shall be interpreted in good faith in accordance with the ordinary meaning to be given to the terms of the treaty in their context and in the light of its object and purpose."

living, ensuring full employment and a large and steadily growing volume of real income and effective demand, developing the full use of the resources of the world and expanding the production and exchange of goods,

Being desirous of contributing to these objectives by entering into reciprocal *and mutually advantageous* arrangements directed to the substantial reduction of tariffs and other barriers to trade and to the elimination of discriminatory treatment in international commerce, have through their Representatives agreed as follows . . .[56]

A considerable body of economic theory backs this up, and a remarkable policy apparatus, including the WTO, has emerged to implement this goal.[57]

However, I would argue that in a fundamental way we have gotten it wrong. One way to understand the crisis over economic globalization is as evidence that we have missed the mark, that many among us are dissatisfied with the shape we've given to international trade law and with its effects in practice, particularly given its increasing influence in a global economy and globalizing world.

The consent analysis in Chapter 1 suggests that we have focused too much on the "free" part and not enough on the "trade" part. Most of us would not rally behind calls for open and unrestrained economic coercion, predation or exploitation, but that is what "free trade" has become in many instances, because we have misunderstood the nature of trade itself. When we ignore the role of consent in economic exchange, we risk facilitating coercion or exploitation, instead of promoting trade. The fact that in the process, our global deregulatory apparatus has progressively reduced tariffs and nontariff barriers – the domestic regulatory burden attendant to such transactions and the conventionally understood "free" part of trade – does not make the resulting transactions "trade," nor does it augment their intended social benefit or fulfill trade's larger social promise.

---

[56] General Agreement on Tariffs and Trade 1994, Apr. 15, 1993, Marrakesh Agreement Establishing the World Trade Organization, Annex 1A, 1867 U.N.T.S. 187 (emphasis supplied).

[57] *See, e.g., About The WTO*, WORLD TRADE ORG., www.wto.org/english/thewto_e/whatis_e/who_we_are_e.htm.

Instead, trade law should be about facilitating a thriving trading environment at all levels of this emerging global market. It is not simply about promoting economic exchanges of any kind, provided they are free of protectionist domestic regulation. That is not free *trade*. The problem arises when the methods we use to advance trade, so to speak, undercut trade itself because they undercut consent, both in the negotiations between nations about the rules, and in the transactions that the rules facilitate. This is really a new form of mercantilism – the view that trade law should be about "my market trouncing your market," with law playing a dual role: supporting and regulating my market at home, and deregulating markets abroad in order to facilitate my exploitation of other markets transnationally.[58] This is a disservice both to the economic opportunities that trade offers, and to law itself.

This makes it critically important that we understand what it is we are trying to regulate and protect. In this sense, the global economy has grown faster than our intelligent regulation of it. Some see in this the natural tendency for law to lag behind social facts; others see in it a deliberate attempt to create a particular vision of the global market: the under-regulated market of "robber baron" capitalism. It is probably a bit of both. But if we understand trade more accurately, we can create an environment that, over time, can make us all better off by truly promoting a market and not an open space for exploitation.

Both points can be illustrated in a different, contemporary context, namely the global financial crisis and its roots in the failures of domestic economic regulation.[59] Because of an impoverished view of the free market, certain financial actors were allowed, through a deregulatory process on top of accumulating market failures, to pursue strategies that had tremendous short-term yields for them, but within a framework allowing them to shift the tremendous risks onto other parties, allowing these actors take great personal advantage of their

---

[58] Indeed, Sonia Rolland has observed that the very negotiating modalities through which we negotiate trade agreements are themselves mercantilist, leading unsurprisingly to mercantilist outcomes. Sonia Rolland, *Redesigning the Negotiation Process at the WTO*, 13 J. INT'L ECON. L. 65 (2010).

[59] *See generally* KATHLEEN C. ENGEL & PATRICIA MCCOY, THE SUBPRIME VIRUS (2011); Brian Quinn, *The Failure of Private Ordering and the Financial Crisis of 2008*, 5 N.Y.U. J.L. & Bus. 549 (2009).

considerable insider knowledge of financial markets to the detriment of others (Wall Street versus Main Street).[60] When this collapsed, global society was left shouldering the costs.[61]

This illustrates the risks for us and for trade law when the conditions for a healthy market are misunderstood by the regulators or overridden by political forces, and key market actors are allowed to operate speculatively for the short-term, while rampantly externalizing costs and risks. I consider that counteracting the tendency for those with control to shift risk while securing profit to be – following the work of my teacher Joseph Vining – at the heart of the social purpose of economic regulation.[62] This means that trade agreements should not be allowed to become yet another means for risk shifting through law, at the cost of society as a whole.

All of this affects, or should affect, our understanding of what we are aiming for in trade agreements, what it takes to get there and what our expectations should be of our leaders and the agreements they make or fail to make. Armed with a clearer sense of trade's nature and requirements, there are important ways in which trade negotiations can be restructured, and important political steps we can take in our domestic politics and through global civil society to demand input into the negotiation and ratification processes for new agreements. At the end of the day, these are *our* agreements.

III BUILDING A LAW OF CONSENSUAL TRADE

A Reasoning by Analogy Toward Basic Legal Characterizations

The first step toward regulating a phenomenon through law is a conceptual one: we must identify or recognize that there is a problem

---

[60] *See* ENGEL & McCoy, *supra* note 59.

[61] Anup Shah, *Global Financial Crisis*, GLOBAL ISSUES (Mar. 24, 2013), www .globalissues.org/article/768/global-financial-crisis#.

[62] JOSEPH VINING, FROM NEWTON'S SLEEP 287–90 (1995); *see also* Larry D. Thompson, *The Responsible Corporation: Its Historical Roots and Continuing Promise*, 29 NOTRE DAME J.L. ETHICS & PUB. POL'Y 199 (2015) (citing the contributions of Joseph Vining toward our understanding of corporations in social life).

in our social relations that needs legal analysis and response. That is what I have sought to offer here with the analysis of dynamics such as coercion and exploitation that currently operate unregulated and often unrecognized within the space we have labeled "trade."

Second, we have to begin to think our way into the problem using the tools of legal analysis, toward a sort of legal characterization: what *kind* of legal problem is this? One such tool is reasoning by analogy, when the legal mind begins with one area of behavior which is legally well understood, then seeks by analogy to reason its way into a new one. I have offered such analogies to the law of contracts at key points when exploring the nature of coercion, adhesion and unconscionability, on the theory that contract is the most appropriate legal source for relevant analogies on the nature of consent and its defects in economic agreements.

One conclusion we can take from these analogies to the law of duress or adhesion is that dynamics such as coercion and exploitation are not new to us in the law – we understand something important in the law of contracts concerning how to distinguish between consensual exchanges and their pathologies, and something important about what to do about them. Simplifying greatly, the task in contract law – the private law of consensual exchange agreements – is to distinguish contracts that ought to be enforced, though consent may be imperfect, and contracts (or contract provisions) that ought not to be enforced, either because consent is so defective as to rise to the level of duress, or the provision or contract as a whole is so egregious as to be unconscionable. This much is clear from contracts law: we don't put the machinery of legal enforcement behind agreements or provisions arrived at by threats and illegitimate means.[63]

Extending the analogy to trade agreements – the public law of consensual exchange agreements – the question is therefore whether

---

[63] *See, e.g.,* RESTATEMENT (SECOND) CONTRACTS §§ 175, 176 (Am. Law Inst. 1981) (a contract is voidable if manifestation of assent reached by duress through "improper threat," defined as where "the resulting exchange is not on fair terms and (a) the threatened act would harm the recipient and would not significantly benefit the party making the threat, (b) the effectiveness of the threat in inducing the manifestation of assent is significantly increased by prior unfair dealing by the party making the threat or (c) what is threatened is otherwise a use of power for illegitimate ends."

we can determine if there are treaties or treaty provisions that ought not to be enforced, or at a minimum ought to be considered as illegitimate even if the legal question of their enforceability never presents itself as ripe for decision, for a host of reasons I will touch on in Section IV. We would want to be able to distinguish such treaties and provisions from other treaties or provisions that should be enforced, even when the latter might not in all respects be fully consensual, or fully embody the ideal bargain that a party might have sought under conditions of perfect freedom.

This is a profound and complex question, one that in the law of contracts we have spent many years thinking through. Moreover, in the common law of contracts it is a process that depends greatly on the facts of particular cases and requires the weighing and balancing of the relative power of the parties and the effects of upholding the contract on the weaker party; and one that has benefitted from the collective pragmatic wisdom of many judges sitting in many contract cases, and of many generations of legal scholars – here there are no simple bright-line rules. By comparison, while dynamics of predation, coercion and exploitation in economic relationships are old problems, understanding this as a *legal* problem in trade law with specific consequences is new. It would thus seem premature to aim for any kind of taxonomy of enforceable and unenforceable treaties, at least in the strong legal sense, let alone anything like a bright-line rule, even if such were possible.

It may nevertheless be useful to begin gesturing toward the general shape of the law in this area, as a subject for further development by jurists and scholars, and as guidance for the less technical – though equally important – court of public opinion. We can see from the analogies employed thus far in Chapters 1 and 2 that the law of contracts identifies two basic situations where consent is at stake. First, there are cases in which the law finds there to be no enforceable agreement, either because of duress, where the threat or coercion is such that there is no consent as the law recognizes it, or unconscionability, where the agreement itself is so egregious as to be one that no party would voluntarily agree to but for the conduct of the stronger party. Second, there are cases where the law finds the agreement as a whole enforceable but takes exception to specific provisions on grounds of adhesion or unconscionability.

I would suggest that, for the purposes of this study, the most useful approach at this stage in our understanding of a *consensual* trade law is to focus on the latter category, and seek to identify particularly egregious provisions or patterns of concession and obligation, and the context of dynamics of coercion and exploitation in treaty negotiations that might explain the appearance of consent. The more systemic question of how to identify entire treaties as void or illegitimate for reasons of duress or exploitation is best left to further research and more detailed analysis of individual treaties. In developing such further insights, we may be able to learn from how domestic courts have worked slowly in a fact-intensive way, and have focused on evaluating the relative power of the treaty parties and the effects of upholding the treaty on the weaker party. We are unlikely to find bright-line rules, but we may find helpful principles.

One such forensic principle could be to presume coercion or exploitation when nothing else can satisfactorily explain why the weaker party has entered into such a disadvantageous agreement. More generally, we may see a kind of inverse relationship between reciprocity and coercion or exploitation that may also have forensic value. The less reciprocal an agreement, the more we must be on the lookout for dynamics of coercion and exploitation that might explain the appearance of consent when the mutuality of the bargain gets thinner and thinner.

With this in mind and building on the discussion in preceding sections of the problematic dynamics of coercion and exploitation in trade negotiations, in the sections that follow I will identify a few of the most problematic kinds of provisions that come from such dynamics. I then conclude with a modest initial suggestion regarding problematic treaties currently in force, namely that we look for ways to blunt, through interpretive strategies, the most egregious provisions in the event that they do in fact come before an adjudicative body. In other words, whether or not we enforce imperfectly consensual agreements, there are ways to avoid enforcing egregious provisions which but for the coercion or exploitation would not have been included.

B Substantive Provisions to Aim or Watch Out For

Animated by a vision of what trade is and is not – in other words, by the object and purpose of a trade agreement – and armed with a preliminary understanding of the nature of the sorts of provisions and obligations we elsewhere judge as not meriting enforcement, we can turn in this penultimate section to consideration of some of the kinds of treaty provisions that should – and should not – be found in every true trade agreement. Economic relations take place within the framework of the substantive provisions that become law through the ratification and implementation of trade agreements. Therefore, ensuring that the rules themselves do not undercut consent, and instead support and enhance consent, is critical.

1 Guardrails and Third Rails: Provisions that Protect Consent

Consent is best protected through negotiations that allow parties to accept or reject bargains as they see fit, with a minimum of coercive or exploitative behavior. However, there are certain provisions that by their nature are so critical to protecting consent that they should be considered virtually de rigueur in any real trade agreement, and their absence should be considered a red flag in terms of consensual negotiations and their opposite.

a Dispute Resolution and the Rule of Law

Agreements that suffer from basic rule of law deficits do not serve anyone's long-term interests, even if in the short run they might appear to favor the stronger party. Chief among such deficits would be dispute resolution mechanisms that do not bind the parties automatically to the independent outcome of whatever kind of panel or body is convened under the agreement to resolve disputes.

For this reason, every trade agreement should have a fully binding dispute resolution mechanism that places the outcome of trade disputes in the hands of impartial third-party decision makers, rather than leaving them open to the coercive power politics that have undermined the agreement in the first place. One can still have a system that emphasizes the value of settlement, as the WTO DSU does. However, it should be a settlement negotiated under the shadow of binding independent dispute resolution, not under the shadow of essentially "advisory" opinions that may only result in a final post-judgment negotiation against a more powerful party, as the NAFTA-style system invites.

Given the asymmetries in enforcement capabilities discussed earlier when trade sanctions are the only authorized sanction, consideration should also be given to alternative means of enforcement when disputes arise between highly unequal parties. Cross retaliation across sectors should certainly be an option, such as for example in the WTO, in disputes in which Mexico, Brazil and Antigua have prevailed against much larger parties.[64] Consideration might also be given to the possibility of an assignment of claims to a larger state, in much the same way the Doha Declaration allows states with valid compulsory licensing privileges under TRIPS to seek fulfillment of those rights through the use of other states having a generic pharmaceutical capability.[65] Finally, we should not rule out lump-sum settlements, particularly if there can be an accountability mechanism to ensure the settlement works to the benefit of the sector or workers most affected by the violation.[66]

None of these suggestions are new – they have all been discussed and explored in the literature of economic law dispute resolution. What is important here is the opportunity to understand them in a new way: not simply as functional mechanisms to promote the rule of law, but as necessary elements for protecting mutually beneficial consensual bargains in a truly mutual manner, for keeping trade "trade."

---

[64] See Lucas E. F. A. Spadano, *Cross-Agreement Retaliation in the WTO Dispute Settlement System: An Important Enforcement Mechanism for Developing Countries?*, 7 WORLD TR. REV. 511 (2008); *see generally* Gregory Shaffer, *The Challenges of WTO Law: Strategies for Developing Country Adaptation*, 5 WORLD TRADE REV. 177 (2006) (surveying challenges to developing countries in dispute resolution).

[65] See Ellen 't Hoen, *TRIPS, Pharmaceutical Patents and Access to Essential Medicines: Seattle, Doha and Beyond*, 3 CHI. J. INT'L L. 27, 38–43 (2002); *The Separate Doha Declaration Explained*, WORLD TRADE ORG., www.wto.org/english/tratop_e/trips_e/healthdeclexpln_e.htm.

[66] See Marco Bronckers & Freya Baetens, *Reconsidering Financial Remedies in WTO Dispute Settlement*, 16 J. INT'L ECON. L. 281, 300–04 (2013); Nuno Limao & Kamal Saggi, *Tariff Retaliation Versus Financial Compensation in the Enforcement of International Trade Agreements* 10–13 (World Bank Policy Research, Working Paper No. 3873, 2006) (noting that fines may be more effective than tariffs, although fines must be paid by the violating state and retaliatory tariffs can be unilaterally imposed by the injured state).

b Market Access

It is more difficult to say at an appropriate level of generality how market access should be handled, given how unique each negotiation and set of market access needs and goals are to the parties involved. However, one can still examine market access provisions from an overall perspective, in order to assess whether the balance of opportunities and commitments bears some reasonable proportion to the needs and goals of each party, or not.

In particular, one should take a careful look when it seems the weaker party has failed to achieve its primary market access goals, while at the same time conceding to the stronger party market access in key sectors of economic or cultural significance. One important pattern suggesting the absence of meaningful consent involves agricultural market access in sectors that are culturally significant and are often critical to subsistence agriculture and traditional patterns of employment. It is illuminating in this respect to consider Mexico's experience under NAFTA with corn, in tandem with Central America's and Colombia's experiences under CAFTA and the CTPA with rice and corn, as well as Korea's under KORUS with beef. What we see in each case is the weaker party making important concessions in these key sectors with very little if anything to show for them in return, either in market access or elsewhere in the treaty. Under such circumstances we may be able to conclude that only dynamics such as coercion or exploitation can explain such unbalanced agreements.

Thus, we may in certain cases be able generalize as to a few of the kinds of provisions that might represent unbalanced market access outcomes, and a few that might suggest a more consensual exchange. One possible pattern that might *reinforce* consent in asymmetric situations comes out of regional experiences with US GSP-style programs. When preferential schemes are in the background, we can look for whether new concessions have come from the preference-granting state, rather than only from the weaker party, in exchange for surrendering the preferential scheme itself. Another possibility would be a presumption that where trade has been carried out under a GSP-style program, the first five years or so of the FTA's market access commitments simply make those concessions permanent, with no further reciprocal concessions asked for from the weaker state, until the relationships have settled in and the issue can be negotiated with more complete information. At a minimum, the weaker party receiving the preferences should not be expected to concede everything in order to make them permanent, and receive nothing in return except for coming out from under a coercively administered preference program.

More generally, one could also draw on the many studies of the market access needs of developing countries to assemble a list of what might be on the wish list of any developing country negotiating a trade agreement. Joseph Stiglitz, for example, advocates for two such measures: first, the elimination of tariff escalation structures that penalize manufactured and higher-value goods, thus perpetuating asymmetric economic development, and second, deeper liberalization in the low-skill services sector (part of the so-called Mode IV under the GATS) and looser rules on economic migration.[67] The degree to which any of these get into the final agreement may be one metric, however imprecise, through which to assess the degree of consent the agreement embodies.

c Safeguards

Safeguard provisions are an easy place for powerful parties to undo the appearance of market access concessions, and maintain an asymmetric advantage in the de facto economic regime created by the trade agreement, whatever the market access commitments state. Therefore, safeguard provisions should be negotiated in a way that is mutual in terms of availability, thresholds and duration, and that can be effectively policed through the dispute resolution mechanism in the agreement.

It would seem advisable to avoid negotiation of special unilateral safeguard measures available only to the dominant party, in areas of market access "concessions" that seem to favor the weaker party. In the cases profiled earlier, this creates at least the perception that in the event there is any genuine market access improvement for a key export sector for the developing country, the dominant party has a special safeguard unilaterally available to block, stall or force renegotiation of

---

[67] STIGLITZ, *supra* note 25, at 87–90. Non-tariff barriers such as technical standards and sanitary or phytosanitary measures are also often cited as barriers developing countries face when trying to gain access into wealthy markets. *Id.* at 94–95.

this provision. Whatever that is, it does not look like a balanced, mutually beneficial and freely negotiated agreement.

Alternatively, it may be wise in particularly asymmetric cases to shift safeguard and other trade remedy determinations to an impartial decision maker to avoid abuse.[68] This was the brilliance of Canada's successful demand in NAFTA for an international tribunal to hear appeals from domestic US AD/CVD cases. It is unfortunate that in the NAFTA renegotiation under way as of this writing, that mechanism is being repudiated by the United States – with what effect remains to be seen. For the reasons outlined here, it should instead be extended across all regional and bilateral FTAs.[69]

The overall theme here is simple: if the agreement is truly consensual, why would trading parties not choose balanced, equal standards and treatment? If they haven't, one must ask whether in fact the agreement reflects consensual trade, or something else.

d Law Reform in a Trade Agreement

When non-trade-related law reform is carried out through the mechanism of asymmetric trade negotiations, the potential for harm seems quite pronounced, and the trade rationale for inclusion quite weak.

- *Non-Trade Domestic Law*   Chief among provisions worth highlighting in this category are provisions aimed at reforming issues in a party's commercial or other domestic law that are not strictly trade related. As we saw earlier in the chapter in the CAFTA case, it is so easy for a powerful state to attempt through a trade negotiation to reach through a counterparty's sovereignty into aspects of its domestic law that constituencies in the powerful state find obnoxious, in the CAFTA case going so far as to reach into prior existing private contracts as well.

---

[68] *See id.* at 91. Stiglitz links such institutional reform to reform of the substantive standards, linking for example industry problems to the specific import surge, a causal link, and not just a correlation. Similarly, in the area of technical standards, Stiglitz advocates balanced internationally supervised TBT standards. *Id.*

[69] For similar reasons, Stiglitz advocates reforming dumping law to be more like domestic competition law, requiring proof of monopolization not simply a moment of LTFMV pricing under rigged price criteria. In fact, it may be better to unify unfair trade practices law in domestic and international settings, since the current bifurcation can work a kind of NT violation. *Id.*

Korea had its own examples, with the United States. expressly announcing its intention to remake Korean commercial law in its image through the KORUS. Finally, on the multilateral level, the TRIPS is most definitely an object lesson of the risks for the weaker parties of being boxed into law reform through coercive or exploitative tactics.

Whether or not there is a reasoned case to be made with respect to the wisdom of those domestic laws, law reform is best not done at the end of a gun. Conditioning urgently needed trade benefits on such changes is, in my view, a textbook case of coercive negotiation.

- Investment? Including an investment chapter in a trade agreement is a harder call. Certainly, there is a case to be made that investment and trade are closely intertwined, as I have argued elsewhere.[70] However, given the highly asymmetric and problematic nature of investment law today, it is hard to see how inclusion of investment chapters does not, at a minimum, extend the scope of such highly unbalanced rules into new economic zones of deepening interconnection, broadening their negative systemic impact. Conversely, it is hard to see how trade negotiations between unequal parties would offer a chance to redress such an asymmetry, except for the fact that rules in investment chapters work both ways, as more powerful parties such as the United States and Germany have discovered to their dismay when they experience the adverse domestic impact of asymmetric rules.[71]

For the time being, then, given investment rules as they are and bilateral or regional negotiations as they are, it might be wisest to forego inclusion of an investment chapter in a regional or bilateral agreement between unequal partners. Perhaps the best option given the growing

[70] Frank J. Garcia et al., *Reforming the International Investment Regime: Lessons from International Trade Law*, 18 J. INT'L ECON. L. 861; on reforming how we think of investment law in trade, see Chapter 4 173–77.

[71] *See* NATHALIE BERNASCONI, BACKGROUND PAPER ON VATTENFALL V. GERMANY ARBITRATION (2009), www.iisd.org/pdf/2009/background_vattenfall_vs_germany.pdf (background on Vattenfall arbitration); Garcia et al., *supra* note 70. In certain cases when a new and more inclusive treaty is being negotiated, such as appeared to be the case for a time with the investment chapter of the Trans Pacific Partnership, the asymmetry "blowback" lessons learned by a more powerful state (the US in this case), and the inclusion of many other states in the negotiation, might lead to the creation of a new forum for disputes in which some of the more egregious asymmetric grabs of the superseded forum can be addressed in the new negotiation. I am indebted to Sonia Rolland for pointing this out.

convergence of the two fields, is to do as Rolland suggests elsewhere and carry out trade and investment negotiations in parallel, independent tracks so that a dissatisfied party can reject the investment rules without jeopardizing the trade benefits.[72] Alternatively, it may be wisest to hold out and aim for a true multilateral agreement on investment, which has a greater chance of resolving some of the imbalance for the reasons discussed in this section.

C Changing How We Negotiate Our Trade Agreements

"While it is still true that the strong do what they will and the weak accept what they must, we have seen that both are subject to negotiation."

John S. Odell[73]

Of course, even the best provisions are useless if they do not make it into the final agreement – in other words, if they do not survive the negotiation process. Therefore, the process of substantive reform cannot be divorced from the negotiation reforms necessary to promote more consensual outcomes, and thus we end this section with a discussion of trade negotiations both functional and dysfunctional.

One need not be cynical about international relations or presume evil intent on the part of powerful states, to acknowledge the negotiating vulnerability small states face. In the world of trade negotiations, market access is often the primary goal, and reciprocity the coin of the realm. Small states need market access even more urgently than larger states, and have less to trade for it. By one estimate (using as benchmarks low to middle income and contributing less than one percent of world trade), almost two-thirds of WTO members find themselves in this predicament.[74]

As we have seen, such a situation can readily result in agreements that are not "trade" agreements but exploitation agreements or

---

[72] Rolland, *supra* note 58. This happened in the EU-Japan FTA. www.iisd.org/itn/2017/12/21/eu-japan-epa-negotiations-finalized-without-investment-eu-mexico-updated-fta-nears-completion/

[73] Odell, *supra* note 18.

[74] Odell, *supra* note 18, at 546–51.

agreements where consent has been coerced, which can also result in rules that due to their unbalanced nature reproduce at the private level a framework for exploitative commercial relationships among the private parties transacting within this framework.[75] What is then billed as a trade agreement liberalizing trade, results in fact in an exploitation framework enabling and enhancing predatory opportunities.

It is worth reemphasizing here that from a purely self-interested point of view an exploitative course of negotiations will damage even the exploiter's long-term prospects in a repeat game. One simply cannot afford to ignore the social costs of the resentment and conflict that such a pattern tends to create among one's "trade" partners, which if nothing else will damage the long-term business and investment climate. Reworking the negotiation process itself is therefore key to the long-term success of trade rather than its pathologies.

1 Changing the Negotiation Dynamics

A consent approach to trade law suggests that in matters of global rulemaking, which today means principally economic rulemaking through trade agreements, we should structure such negotiations to achieve and reflect the consent of their participants, aiming as well for substantive rules that protect and support consent at the private party level. We would want to do this not as a way of confining trade within a particular view of "fairness," but as a way to promote its flourishing through basic market principles (i.e., markets need healthy bargaining) across the widest possible spectrum of individuals, transactions and relationships. Powerful parties would do well to remember that while the immediate result of not taking consent seriously may seem like a better deal for them, game theory reminds us that insofar as trade is not a one-shot game, such behavior may well result in a poorer bargain over time, or no future bargains at all.

If we are to take consent seriously, we need to look at how consensual agreements can be reached within a context of steep asymmetries

[75] For an interesting series of reflections on the interrelationship between international commercial treaties and the facilitation, or frustration, of individual choice within the framework they create, *see* Anne-Marie Slaughter, *International Law in a World of Liberal States*, 6 EUR. J. INT'L L. 1, 19–20 (1995).

in power and negotiating capacity. Negotiations among unequal parties, whether they involve explicit coercion or exploitation, need not always result in bad bargains – it all depends on how the negotiations are managed.[76] Scholars analyzing trade negotiations note a variety of strategies both "away from the table" and "at the table," which weaker parties can in fact pursue to attempt to offset this disadvantage. While these strategies are far from perfect and the success stories are perhaps outnumbered by the failures, they are nevertheless a starting point toward consensual agreements.

a Strategies Away from the Table

Negotiation scholars have found that in asymmetric negotiations, working toward balanced agreements means taking full advantage of moves "away from the negotiating table," such as capacity building, coalition strategies and improving one's BATNA, as critical to the weaker party's efforts at improving outcomes. Once at the table, many of the parameters of the negotiation are already set.[77]

To begin with, small states face huge obstacles to effective negotiation in the form of information and capacity asymmetries in relation to their negotiation counterparties.[78] An important first step therefore is to build capacity, improve knowledge and reduce the strategic disadvantages of imperfect knowledge in trade negotiations. Capacity building has been an active focus for many international organizations for a number of years, including the WTO itself, UNCTAD, development banks and other special-purpose organizations such as the Commonwealth Secretariat.[79]

However, much of this capacity building is aimed at reinforcing the present system, rather than at strengthening a smaller state's negotiation skills toward different outcomes.[80] Trade- and development-focused NGOs like the South Centre exist to help bridge the expertise gap which smaller economies face in trade negotiations, but they are less

---

[76] Odell, *supra* note 18, at 545.
[77] Odell, *supra* note 18, at 552.
[78] *Id.*
[79] *Id.*
[80] I am indebted to Sonia Rolland for pointing this out.

adequately funded when compared to mainstream capacity efforts.[81] In any event, capacity building is essential, but by itself cannot fundamentally alter the negotiation dynamics in terms of interests and the risk/benefit analysis of powerful states. For this, negotiation theorists say we need to look at further "away from the table" strategies.

In this respect, it is critical that smaller states continue to take steps to improve their BATNA.[82] It is a fundamental tenet of negotiation strategy that the more that weaker parties have anticipated, studied and developed alternatives to a negotiated outcome, the stronger their hand even against powerful states.[83] The negotiation literature supports the importance and efficacy of this strategy in asymmetric trade negotiations. For example, Odell cites the example of Mexico's successful opposition to allowing US access into the oil sector during the NAFTA negotiations, which depended on a range of efforts Mexico made to make credible contingency plans should the negotiations fail over this issue.[84]

In the context of the hemispheric negotiations studied here, one way to read recent Latin American interest in trade agreements with Canada, the EU and China, to take three examples, is as a way to lessen the region's dependence on the US market, thereby improving its BATNA in any trade negotiations with the United States. This strategy seems to have been at least partially successful in the case of the CTPA, insofar as US industries pressured the US government to conclude the treaty in the face of Colombia's successful efforts to widen export markets elsewhere through an FTA with Canada.[85]

---

[81] *See, e.g.,* Carolyn Deere, *Changing the Power Balance at the WTO: Is the Capacity-Building Agenda Helping?*, 2005 Human Development Report Occasional Paper, UNDP, 2005 (reviewing funding and other shortcomings of trade related technical capacity building); GREGORY SHAFFER, *How To Make The WTO Dispute Settlement System Work For Developing Countries: Some Proactive Developing Country Strategies, in* TOWARDS A DEVELOPMENT-SUPPORTIVE DISPUTE SETTLEMENT SYSTEM IN THE WTO 29–33 (ICTSD Resource Paper No. 5, Mar. 2003) (discussing importance of cost-effective dispute resolution and role of Advisory Centre on WTO Law in narrowing capacity and resource gap).

[82] FISHER & URY, *supra* note 11, at 104.

[83] JONES, *supra* note 9; Odell, *supra* note 18, at 553.

[84] Odell, *supra* note 18, at 553.

[85] VILLAREAL, *supra* note 46, at 26 (discussing the concern of US exporters following Colombia signing an agreement with Canada); Trish Nixon, *Colombia Trade Deal May Give Canada Edge over U.S.*, REUTERS (Aug. 15, 2011), www.reuters.com/article/us-colombia/colombia-trade-deal-may-give-canada-edge-over-u-s-idUSTRE77E5SH20110815.

While this may have helped solidify US political will to ratify the agreement, whether that also strengthened Colombia's hand during the negotiations is more difficult to say, and the outcomes reviewed earlier are not encouraging. However, to take just one example from the CTPA market access negotiations, while Colombia did agree to duty free access to US textiles, it was able to secure a special textiles safeguard provision of its own.[86] When compared to CAFTA's total shut down in this regard, this may suggest that Colombia had at least enough leverage to secure a special exception from otherwise onerous rules, even where securing better rules was not possible.

The importance of coalition building as a pre-negotiation strategy for smaller states is also well-recognized.[87] Smaller states have been successful in using coalition strategies to improve their negotiation outcomes, both by using the coalition to mitigate capacity constraints and as a means to alter the incentive structure in multilateral negotiations, forcing larger players toward concessions they might not otherwise make.[88] Perhaps the most famous recent example is the coalition strategy used by smaller states at the WTO Seattle Ministerial in 1999 to block progress toward a Millennium Round of WTO negotiations until developing country concerns were addressed.[89] This coalition strategy was strong enough to force the inauguration of the Doha Development Round, ostensibly to address these concerns.

However, the demise of the Doha Round also illustrates the limits of coalition strategies – in this case, coalition states could block progress but not by themselves deliver outcomes.[90] Colombia's efforts to negotiate elements of the CTPA in tandem with Ecuador can be seen

---

[86] Fandl, *supra* note 46, at 78.

[87] Odell, *supra* note 18, at 553.

[88] *Id.* at 554.

[89] *See* Rolland, *supra* note 58.

[90] A more successful example is the coalition developed in the Doha negotiations over TRIPS and the HIV/AIDS crisis. Developing countries were also key to the recent successful negotiation of the WTO Trade Facilitation Agreement, which significantly cuts logistical barriers to effective access into wealthier markets. *See From Vision to Reality: Event Celebrates Success of the Trade Facilitation Agreement,* WORLD TRADE ORG. (June 2, 2017), www.wto.org/english/news_e/news17_e/fac_02jun17_e.htm; *WTO's Trade Facilitation Agreement Takes Effect,* INT'L CTR. FOR TRADE AND SUSTAINABLE DEV. (Feb. 27, 2017), www.ictsd.org/bridges-news/bridges-africa/news/wtos-trade-facilitation-agreement-takes-effect.

as an attempt to employ a coalition strategy to improve bargaining position on issues of IP law and agriculture.[91] However, the failure of this strategy in the CTPA negotiations also demonstrates how such efforts are not a panacea, in that the coalition must be stable and must be powerful enough to shift the balance, neither being true in this case.[92]

An interesting offshoot of this strategy is for weaker states to form temporary alliances with interest groups within the larger negotiating counterparty, who will act as an advocate from within, so to speak. Odell cites as examples Tunisia's cultivation of Germany as an advocate during negotiation of an EC association agreement, and – of particular interest in this context – Colombia's cultivation of US multinational companies as allies during its early bilateral negotiations with the United States.[93] Developing countries have also been successful in the WTO with the recent Trade Facilitation Agreement, promising reduced logistical barriers to entry into wealthier markets and a more development-led process of determining appropriate levels of obligation.[94] This has been the result of both concerted coalition building by developing and least developed countries within the WTO, and support from private sector interests including multinational and small and medium-sized enterprises eager to see goods move more freely across borders within given market access commitments.[95]

---

[91] See AG, IP Hobble Andean–US Free Trade Talks, Int'l Ctr. for Trade and Int'l Dev. (hereinafter Andean–US Talks), www.ictsd.org/ag-ip-hobble-andean-us-free-trade-talks (Ecuador, Peru and Bolivia had sought a coordinated approach to negotiations with the United States).

[92] Garay et al., supra note 12, at 163 (Colombia's negotiating position with the US weakened by Andean states' inability to effectively negotiate as a group); Andean–US Talks, supra note 91 (divergent positions on the part of the Andean states signaled breakdown in negotiations).

[93] Odell, supra note 18, at 554.

[94] Protocol Amending the Marrakesh Agreement Establishing the World Trade Organization, Nov. 28, 2014 (2014).

[95] Antoni Estevadeordal, Why Trade Facilitation Matters Now More than Ever (2017), www.brookings.edu/wp-content/uploads/2017/04/global_20170405_trade-facilitation.pdf. (citing the importance of public-private partnerships in this area); Azevedo Welcomes Efforts to Help Implement Trade Facilitation Agreement, World Trade Org. (Dec. 17, 2015), www.wto.org/english/news_e/news15_e/dgra_17dec15_e.htm.

Fourth, supporters of consensual trade can advocate for increased transparency about trade negotiations and the quality of domestic consultation mechanisms. Not only does transparency address information asymmetries, which it is important in itself, but it also offers an opportunity to directly reach global public opinion on trade negotiation matters. This can lead to increased public pressure on governments (ours and theirs) on the part of citizens who demand their government act in ways that reflect their own fundamental values.[96]

The citizenry within the EU has been very successful in this in relation to the recent TTIP negotiations and the role of ISDS in any EU trade agreements. The shift in Commission negotiation position from ISDS to a proposed permanent multilateral investment court and a true appellate mechanism was largely driven by public pressure channeled by citizens and NGOs into the European Parliament, thus underscoring the need for a representative body's input into the trade negotiation process.[97]

Moving into deeper waters, pressuring one's government to consider the degree (or absence) of political representation on the part of one's negotiation partner raises complicated issues of sovereignty, scope and manageability for a negotiating state. In this respect, one can see how the traditional international law approach of accepting formal legitimacy and accreditation of diplomats does simplify matters, though at the expense of substantive legitimacy. However, if we do not at least attempt to recognize and grapple with this problem, then a consent approach makes it clear that the cost to this simplification is to the very possibility of trade itself, versus theft or predation. Weil's admonition about the risks of mistaking formal for actual consent echoes here yet again.

We may be able to borrow a tool from traditional political theory in such cases. The importance Rawls places in *The Law of Peoples* on a domestic consultative mechanism for stakeholders even in non-liberal states could offer a useful guide for how to address this problem under

---

[96] Odell, *supra* note 18, at 554–55.
[97] Céline Lévesque, *The European Commission Proposal for an Investment Commission: Out with the Old, In with the New?* (Ctr. Int'l Governance Innovation, Investor-State Arbitration Series Paper No. 10, 2016).

a consent approach as well.[98] It may be that as an adjunct to trade negotiations with underrepresentative governments, developed states – urged on by civil society – demand of those governments that they form a special consultative mechanism for the purposes of that negotiation. Such a process could be run jointly by the two states, as a sort of joint public notice and comment period, and then both states would be jointly responsible for taking such feedback into account.[99]

In this context, the importance of such a mechanism lies not so much in reasons of political theory, but in order that the more powerful state safeguard for itself the possibility of creating genuine trade with the social benefits it may bring, and to minimize the risk of creating non-trade with its attendant social costs. This assumes, of course, that the more powerful government is interested in supporting consultation in its trading partners' governments, and not in taking advantage of its absence, under the misguided view that this is in the national interest. Here public pressure can play a role – citizens of liberal democracies should expect their governments to refrain from striking trade deals that are clearly not favored by the citizens of their trading partners, for principled as well as pragmatic reasons.

b Moves at the Table

Once "at the table" many aspects of the negotiation have already been set, but that does not mean that weaker states have no options. On the contrary, negotiation theorists teach that strategy during the negotiation itself can still be critical. Theorists organize strategic options at the table along a continuum between the purely distributive (strategies for claiming value and defending from losses) and the

---

[98] RAWLS, *supra* note 43, at 71–78. Such a mechanism must meet six criteria: (1) all domestic groups must be consulted; (2) each person must be a member of a group; (3) each group must be represented by a representative person or body; (4) the ultimate decision-maker must weigh the views and claims of each representative body of each group, and explain and justify the decision if asked; (5) the decision must reflect the special priorities of that people as a whole and (6) these priorities and the decision must fit into an overall cooperative scheme considered fair by that people. *Id.* These criteria create an interesting pattern when one maps them onto current civil society, and may also suggest what a treaty consultation mechanism could look like.

[99] I am indebted to Sonia Rolland for this suggestion.

purely integrative (shared problem solving along joint interest toward win-win outcomes).[100]

Although the efficacy of distributive versus integrative strategies for small states in the trade context has not been well studied, there are a few relevant examples. In a regional context, Odell cites the success of the African states in creating the 1963 Yaounde Association, in which these former colonies emerged with continued aid at a higher level than in their expiring arrangement, through a claim of moral obligation on the part of Europe and the threat of political instability.[101] This distributive strategy was doubtless aided by the context of ideological rivalry during the Cold War, making the threat more credible and politically salient. Far from limiting the relevance of the point, this illustrates instead the importance for small country negotiators of understanding the larger context of the negotiations, and the advantages it might offer them. Background conditions can be used just as skillfully to reduce asymmetries as to exploit them.

As did Odell, Jones also cites Mexico's exclusion of the oil sector in the NAFTA negotiations as a success, but for its effective use of defensive strategies (such as offsetting) in order to resist otherwise exploitative context of asymmetric bargaining power.[102] Mexico strategically offset US refusal to liberalize its maritime shipping sector, a highly sensitive sector for the United States, against Mexico's refusal to negotiate energy liberalization, thus minimizing pressure to make concessions while avoiding the appearance of being unilaterally intransigent.[103]

Odell also identifies a key integrative resource available to negotiators independently of "size" and the traditional indicia of power: the shrewd and creative analysis of negotiation obstacles and opportunities, toward breaking deadlocks and redefining the problem.[104] As an example, he cites the work of Ambassador Koh of Singapore in

---

[100] Odell, *supra* note 18, at 555.
[101] *Id.* at 556.
[102] JONES, *supra* note 9, at 87–88.
[103] *Id.* at 88.
[104] Odell, *supra* note 18, at 560; JOHN S. ODELL, NEGOTIATING FROM WEAKNESS IN INTERNATIONAL TRADE RELATIONS (2009), www.internationalstudies.socsci.uci.edu/files/docs/odell_05_2009.pdf.

negotiating a breakthrough in the 1978 Law of the Sea negotiations. Koh's integrative strategies included creating new and shared information, reframing the problem and identifying differences in priorities and between interests and positions, which ultimately led to linking two previously separate seabed mining proposals and a successful breakthrough.[105] This serves as in important illustration of how creativity, skill and flexibility are not the unique preserve of powerful states and their negotiating teams – on the contrary, it may be easier for small state negotiators to cultivate these virtues and capacities, and certainly necessary.[106]

The successful negotiation of the Doha Declaration, clarifying the right of WTO members under TRIPS to exercise their compulsory licensing options through trade in the face of public health emergencies, also illustrates the successful use of many strategies away from and at the table, as well as the importance of context and skillful use of background conditions.[107] Not only was the coalition within the WTO large and its cohesion essential, but negotiators also made full use of public opinion-shaping strategies, assisted by NGOs and other organizations. At the table, negotiators also used a mixture of distributive and integrative approaches to great effect.[108] Finally, the anthrax scare and resulting US moves toward its own compulsory licensing options proved fatal to the sustainability of the US position, given the vigor of the public debate fostered by earlier efforts away from the table.

In addition to the skillful deployment of distributive and integrative strategies, the structure of the negotiation process, itself a negotiated element (called in trade circles the "modalities" of negotiation) can be quite influential in determining outcomes by the way it frames and links issues. Rolland, for example, analyzes the modalities of recent WTO multilateral trade negotiations and the effects that the overall negotiation structure and various kinds of issue linkages have on

---

[105] Odell, *supra* note 18, at 560–61.
[106] Odell, *supra* note 18, at 562–63.
[107] *See generally* Frederick M. Abbott, *The WTO TRIPS Agreement and Global Economic Development*, 72 CHI. KENT L. REV. 385 (1996). It also illustrates how even a coercively negotiated agreement can still be used to defend what basic rights it did preserve.
[108] Odell, *supra* note 18, at 558.

outcomes of interest to developing countries.[109] In particular, she is critical of the "single undertaking" approach discussed earlier in connection with TRIPS, which has become the core modality for WTO negotiations since the Uruguay Round. Under the umbrella of the single undertaking, members agree in advance that nothing will be agreed until everything is agreed, resulting in "a single package of multilateral commitments agreed upon simultaneously and inseparably."[110]

While such linkage is often seen as a negotiating resource facilitating cross-sectoral bargaining, Rolland considers such a design to also disadvantage smaller members if they cannot successfully block the inclusion of items in the agenda that they are not prepared to commit to. The single undertaking means the items they desperately need liberalization on may be hostage to some level of commitment in the more sensitive areas.[111]

This dynamic has relevance outside the multilateral environment for regional and bilateral trade as well, given the relationship between negotiation design and the effective power to coerce or exploit. An example relevant to this project is the inclusion of subjects such as non-trade law reform or investment in FTA negotiations. As discussed in Chapter 2, states may feel bound to agree to coercive domestic law reforms when linked to market access commitments they must attain.[112] Similarly, investment rules are highly asymmetric and often unfavorable to host states.[113] Their inclusion in the FTA agenda can therefore be prejudicial to the host state's overall interests, since any attempt to weaken their asymmetry in the context of trade negotiations must be weighed against the risk to the trade benefits sought at the core of the FTA negotiation.

---

[109] Rolland, *supra* note 58.

[110] *Id.* at 65–66.

[111] *Id.* at 75–76 (citing David W. Leebron, *Linkages*, 96 Am. J. Int'l L. 5 [2002]).

[112] Indeed, in the multilateral context Rolland cites the inclusion of TRIPS into the Uruguay Round agreements as "coercive." Rolland, *supra* note 58, at 72. Of course, sometimes states take advantage of trade negotiation law reform "requests" to either push through domestic reforms, as in the case of Mexico with NAFTA and China with WTO accession.

[113] Garcia et al., *supra* note 70; *see also* Alessandra Arcuri, *The Great Asymmetry and the Rule of Law in Trade and Investment Agreements* (unpublished paper on file with author).

For such reasons, Barry and Reddy consider the single undertaking approach "unduly coercive," and advocate a more nuanced approach to trade negotiation modalities in which linkage decisions are "unimposed ... transparent and rule-based, and involve adequate burden-sharing."[114] In the absence of agreement on such normatively superior and cooperative approaches, it may still be possible to successfully resist the coercive or exploitative risks in such agenda-setting exercises, but this takes careful planning. Jones cites as a successful case Mexico's above-mentioned exclusion of the oil sector from NAFTA negotiations. Among other tactics, Mexico also strategically raised the issue of migration when the agenda for the negotiations was being negotiated, knowing full well that this sector was highly sensitive to the United States and therefore kept out. In the face of US refusal, Mexico had grounds on which to similarly refuse to include the oil sector.[115]

Whatever approach or blend of approaches is ultimately employed, as Rolland points out, it is clear that there is a vital link between substantive negotiation goals, the risks of negotiation and the importance of negotiation over the negotiation design itself.[116] Thus a key to managing the effects of predatory, coercive or exploitative negotiations lies in fully and skillfully utilizing the tools of negotiation theory for asymmetric parties, vigorously supplemented by the inputs of civil society, the tools of social media and a public alerted to the risks posed by such dynamics to the possibilities of trade itself.

D Recapitulation

There is nothing simple about addressing the causes of unbalanced trade agreements, since at bottom they all involve the use and abuse of deeply entrenched and vigorously defended power inequalities, a phenomenon as old as organized societies themselves. History teaches us that power and its abuse are endemic to all forms of social organization,

---

[114] Christian Barry & Sanjay G. Reddy, *International Trade and Labor Standards: A Proposal for Linkage*, 39 CORNELL INT'L L.J. 545, 623 (2006).

[115] JONES, *supra* note 9, at 88.

[116] Rolland, *supra* note 58, at 80.

a truth that Weil and others powerfully remind us of when it comes to
socioeconomic systems and their oppressive tendencies, whether they
be capitalist or Marxist, public or private, systemic or familial.

Fortunately, we have developed in law a set of tools not simply for
the facilitation of the exercise of power (inevitable), but for the restraint
of power as well (transformative). The history of economic law demonstrates that the worst examples of unrestrained power are generally
brought into line by those who also hold economic power and are thus
principally acting in their own self-interest. Such efforts are often aided
by broad popular outcry as well (I am thinking of such cases as, in the
United States, Theodore Roosevelt's trust-busting activities in the early
twentieth century, or Franklin D. Roosevelt's sweeping regulatory
response to the Great Depression). In such cases the successful self-
interested actions of powerful parties create positive spillover benefits
for the greater good. Thus, we have reasons to hope that when the
nature of the regulatory object is clear, the abuses well catalogued and
the economic self-interest of the powerful aligned with an activated
popular will, change can happen.

We are left, however, with a challenging issue: what can be done
with the legacy (and fortunate we would be if it became a legacy and
not an ongoing reality) of oppressive and unbalanced agreements
currently in force and purporting to be about trade? That will be the
subject of this final section.

IV WORKING WITH THE AGREEMENTS WE HAVE: WHAT CAN BE DONE WITH COERCIVE, EXPLOITATIVE OR PREDATORY AGREEMENTS?

> "we may properly demand that the necessity of ... change be
> intimately appreciated by those in power
> so that they may continue to approach ... [an agreement] which
> is best in accordance with right and law."
>
> Immanuel Kant, *Perpetual Peace*

I want to look in this final section at what we need to do about the
agreements we have – whether and how current trade agreements can

be reworked or reinterpreted if we want to nudge them toward genuine trade agreements, instead of what they are now. Once again, this raises some hard questions. Does everything we've reviewed and considered mean that agreements such as CAFTA are fatally flawed and should be abrogated? Or can their most onerous or egregious substantive rules be amended, or reinterpreted, such that the treaty can more closely resemble what a mutually beneficial, freely bargained agreement might have looked like, and can therefore promote a zone of more consensual bargains within its jurisdiction? In either case, is the domestic distribution of gains from trade so skewed, or the domestic regime so non-representative, that even a "fairer" bargain for the state as a whole is not likely to lead to fairer outcomes for its citizens?

Perhaps we need not toss the whole bag and start over. In *Perpetual Peace*, Kant argues that it is not necessary to destroy a legal, imperfect order in the name of justice.[117] In this, he says, prudence and justice agree. However, "we may properly demand that the necessity of such a change be intimately appreciated by those in power so that they may continue to approach the final end of a constitution which is best in accordance with right and law."[118] There are some important ways that we can respond in law and through politics to current agreements that are oppressive rather than consensual, which might be constructive steps toward our ideal of consensual trade, in Weil's sense of the term. But there won't be easy answers here.

A Abrogating or Amending the Agreement

1 Abrogating the Agreement as a Whole
One option is of course to abandon the treaty. Under the international law of treaties, withdrawal or termination options would be governed first by the provisions of the agreement itself.[119] In the absence of such provisions, any denunciation or withdrawal would be subject to the

---

[117] IMMANUEL KANT, *Perpetual Peace: A Philosophical Sketch, in* KANT: POLITICAL WRITINGS 116, 93–130 (H. S. Reiss ed., H. B. Nisbit trans., 2d ed. 1991).

[118] *Id.* at 118. Kant could be seen in this sense as foreshadowing the economic aspect of the recent US elections and perhaps other political watersheds like Brexit – the electorate's way of ensuring those in power understand the necessity of these changes.

[119] Vienna Convention, *supra* note 55, at art. 25.

customary international of law of treaties, as codified by Article 56 of the Vienna Convention of the Law of Treaties. Article 56 denies a formal right of denunciation or withdrawal where the treaty is silent, unless there is evidence that the parties intended such a right or it can be implied from the language.[120]

Fortunately, regional and bilateral FTAs generally contain broadly permissive withdrawal provisions, generally subject only to a required notice period. NAFTA, for example, whose withdrawal provisions have been in the news as of this writing,[121] only requires six months' written notice to the other treaty parties.[122] Taking NAFTA as broadly representative, there would formally speaking be no reason why a country dissatisfied with its bargain could not withdraw from such an FTA.

Of course, there is an irony here. The weaker party facing a coercive, exploitative or predatory treaty has in fact already signed and ratified the agreement regardless. Thus, the party itself is unlikely to want to exercise any right of withdrawal for the complex reasons it may have agreed to the flawed treaty in the first place.[123] This is the wrenching dilemma of coercion or exploitation at the systemic level. Even should well-intentioned third parties or academic commentators publicly consider the agreement void as a matter of civil society's criticism, as has sometimes been the case in the investment space,[124]

---

[120] This, and Article 52 discussed below, represents high water marks for the doctrine of *pacta sunt servanda* in the Vienna Convention. I say "attempts" because it is difficult to envision a state remaining bound by a treaty it intends to denounce, for lack of any argument that such a right was intended or can be implied. Thus in my view this amounts to a legal fiction, an understandable one, but a fiction nevertheless.

[121] ZEESHAN ALEEM, *We Asked 6 Experts if Congress Could Stop Trump from Eliminating NAFTA*, Vox (Oct. 26, 2017), www.vox.com/policy-and-politics/2017/10/26/16505508/nafta-congress-block-trump-withdraw-trade-power.

[122] North American Free Trade Agreement, art. 2205, Can.–Mex.–U.S., Dec. 17, 1992, 32 I.L.M. 289 (1993) (hereinafter NAFTA).

[123] However, over time, changing circumstances both within and outside states may render withdrawal a meaningful possibility, as we are seeing in the investment treaty area. *See* Clint Peinhardt & Rachel L. Wellhausen, *Withdrawing from Investment Treaties but Protecting Investment*, 7 GLOBAL POL'Y 571 (2016) (surveying growing backlash among developing countries against more egregious BITs).

[124] I am thinking here of certain highly publicized and frustrating cases in which an ICSID Annulment panel excoriates a deeply flawed investment arbitration award, yet cannot annul it on the narrow technical grounds available to it. While important as a matter of the evolution of investment norms, the losing state is nevertheless left with the decision to

this could itself risk further undercutting the parties' consent, however imperfect, and creating new dilemmas.

I am speaking here of the difficulties of abrogation as a national decision by a representative government. In fact, there may be many situations in which the people as a whole are not adequately represented by their government, and the majority of the people might in fact want the treaty abrogated. However, international law does not make any concessions to such situations, reflecting a decision to consider such matters as "internal" and not therefore an object of international legal scrutiny. Here there may well be grounds for civil society and academic commentary to expose the illegitimacy of the treaty and mobilize the tools of public shaming, even as it remains politically impossible to effect a withdrawal from it. Insofar as the other treaty party is a liberal state, there may be grounds to publicly embarrass that state enough for it to consider addressing the domestic failures of its treaty partner at least at some level.

A second exception consists of cases in which the treaty itself has been signed under duress. However, international law does not make special provision for a party to claim coercion or duress as a ground for invalidating its consent to a treaty, short of the threat or use of force in violation of the international law of aggression.[125] This also reflects a deliberate choice during the Vienna Convention negotiations in favor of *pacta sunt servanda*, and against inclusion of a principle recognizing economic coercion as rendering a treaty void or voidable.[126] Such would seem a reasonable decision in favor of stability, except when evaluated in the light of the realities of coercion and exploitation explored here. As the law stands, the requisite explicit threat or use of force is rare at the observable level in contemporary trade relations, although relevant examples can unfortunately be found in history.[127]

---

pay a now-illegitimate yet fully binding award (illegitimate for probably good reasons), or be seen as a defaulter by the international investment community. *See, e.g., LG&E Energy Corp. v. Argentine Republic*, ICSID Case No. ARB/02/1, (Oct. 3, 2006).

[125] Vienna Convention, *supra* note 55, at art. 52.

[126] *See, e.g.*, Richard D. Kearney & Robert E. Dalton, *The Treaty on Treaties*, 64 AM. J. INT'L L. 495, 533–35 (1970) (discussing rejection of economic coercion as a recognized ground for invalidity or withdrawal).

[127] *See, e.g., Opium Wars*, NEW WORLD ENCYCLOPEDIA, www.newworldencyclopedia.org/entry/Opium_Wars.

Aside from these two special cases, it is likely that if asked, the weaker state would not want the treaty abrogated, or else it would not have ratified it. Thus, the situation calls for a more complex response than simple abrogation.

2 Amending or Renegotiating the Offending Provision

Another approach that should be available under international law is the modification of the treaty or its limited renegotiation to address the offending provisions. Article 34 of the Vienna Convention states only, and in general terms, that parties may amend a treaty, which means it is therefore subject to the agreement of the parties to amend or not. It conspicuously does not make any provision for selective amendment of egregious provisions as a matter of right. Therefore, the option to amend would run into the same practical and political risks and difficulties as abrogation – why would the aggrieved state risk reopening a treaty it had already agreed to, with the same party that had imposed it in the first place? The resulting renegotiation may go worse if nothing in the underlying political and economic relationship has changed.

Similarly, Article 44 of the Vienna Convention limits a party's right to treat a provision as severable from a treaty, to situations where it can be established that the provision was not essential to the other party's consent. In the terms we are evaluating here, it means a weaker state seeking to treat a coercive provision in a US FTA as severable, for example, would in any subsequent legal proceeding have to be prepared to rebut the claim from the US that this provision was essential to its consent and is not in fact severable. Being in a position to meaningfully resist or effectively rebut such a claim in such a proceeding is unlikely given the sort of power differentials we are studying here, particularly when we consider the weakness of the dispute provisions in these very same treaties.

We are left with the conclusion that the law of treaties simply does not offer realistic alternatives through which to address situations of economic coercion or exploitation in a treaty context. While disappointing, this is not surprising, given international law's systemic bias toward *pacta sunt servanda*, the stability of borders, etc. But there may be other options.

B Creatively Reinterpreting a Bad Bargain

Kant's point about international relations in general holds equally true about regional and bilateral treaties like CAFTA in particular: the flaws revealed by a consent analysis do not render such treaties irredeemably flawed, nor must they be abrogated in the name of justice. Nevertheless, current regional trade agreements remain deeply inadequate both in their consensual (or more accurately nonconsensual) character, and in their wholesale failure to acknowledge the distributive issues implicated by the uncompensated wealth transfers effected by trade losses imposed through coercion or exploitation.[128]

If they cannot be abrogated or amended, but also must not be accepted as is, what might such an accommodation look like? There are two possibilities: the most offensive provisions of the treaty could be treated as unenforceable by a relevant international forum, or they could be interpreted against the interests of the more powerful party that imposed them in the first place.

1 Selective Non-Enforcement of Egregious Provisions

Returning to my earlier analogies to the law of contract in Chapter 2, this is an appropriate time to revisit the law of adhesion contracts. The modern approach to the unenforceability of adhesion provisions in contract law makes clear that provisions imposed by a more powerful party on a weaker party as "nonnegotiable" do not merit enforcement, for to do otherwise would be to direct the legal system toward simply augmenting the power of the imposing party.[129]

However, as discussed in Section IV, under international law this option would require treating the egregious provision as severable from the treaty as a whole. Article 44 attempts to limit the treatment of any

---

[128] Andrew Hurrell is quite critical of NAFTA in this respect: "The [NAFTA] provides a particularly telling example. If arguments about ever denser integration leading to shifting understandings of moral community were to have force, then the US–Mexico relationship should be a likely candidate. It is a relationship characterized by extremely high levels of economic and societal interdependence; by high levels of deprivation in Mexico, a good deal of which can be implicated in problems likely to have negative spillover effects on the United States; and by a rich and privileged partner well able to afford assistance. And yet the absence of any debate [over wealth transfers] is telling." Andrew Hurrell, *Global Inequality and International Institutions*, 32 METAPHILOSOPHY 34, 39 (2001).

[129] Todd D. Rakoff, *Contracts of Adhesion*, 96 HARV. L. REV. 1173, 1262–66 (1983).

specific provision as seperable, subjecting that determination to the terms of the agreement itself or the consent of the parties. Under the scenario envisioned here, neither would be likely.

However, building on his argument (discussed in Chapter 2) that TRIPS is a coercive agreement, Harris has made the interesting argument that the principle of adhesion contracts common to many domestic legal systems should be considered for that reason a general principle of law available under Article 38 of the ICJ Statute for tribunals hearing claims involving treaties such as TRIPS. If so, this might justify at least an interpretation *contra proferentem*, or against the party responsible for the drafting, in favor of developing states, as has been the case under domestic law for adhesion contracts.[130]

You may recall from the discussion of TRIPS in Chapter 2 that Harris argues that the characteristics of a treaty rendering adhesion theory relevant are as follows: (1) one state, generally a developed country, had superior bargaining power; (2) the agreement was presented largely as a form or prepackaged agreement and on a "take it or leave it" basis; (3) the receiving state, generally a developing country, lacked sufficient bargaining power to modify or reject the terms and (4) the imposed terms are onerous or unfavorable and offend norms of distributive fairness.[131] As discussed in Chapter 2, these criteria closely track the circumstances under which coercive or exploitative regional or bilateral "trade" agreements have been negotiated, and would seem to justify a finding that such agreements are treaties of adhesion.

As a first option, we could consider the application of Harris's adhesion treaty theory not so much to justify an interpretation *contra proferentem*, though that will also be discussed below in subsection 2, but instead as a doctrine justifying the weaker party in unilaterally considering itself not bound by the offensive provision of a treaty such as CAFTA. This would be consistent with how unconscionability doctrine treats egregious provisions of adhesion contracts under domestic contract law. However, this is a challenging argument given

---

[130] Harris, *supra* note 32. This principle of interpretation *contra proferentem* has been recognized by the European Principles of Contract Law, the UNIDROIT Principles and the Restatement, 2nd, of Contracts, lending weight to Harris's argument.

[131] *Id.* at 724–38.

that Article 44 expressly lays out the grounds for severability, and adhesion is not one of them, and would almost certainly expose the weaker state to economic countermeasures.

2 Interpretation Against the Powerful Party

Alternatively, if there should be a trade dispute involving one of these egregious provisions, it may be possible to raise Harris's argument for an interpretation *contra proferentem* with some effect. If the tribunal can be convinced to interpret the provision against the interests of the imposing party, this opens a small but very important window of opportunity through which to nudge a flawed agreement back toward trade.

The success of this approach depends on Harris's argument that such a principle should indeed be recognized as a general principle of law, and therefore available to international legal tribunals under the source rules established by Article 38 of the ICJ Statute.[132] They would therefore be available to trade dispute panels as a matter of their general mandate to interpret agreements on their terms and in accordance with the customary principles of interpretation of international law.[133] Harris's review of the law of major jurisdictions across three continents supports, in my view, his claim that adhesion doctrine could reasonably be considered a general principle of law and therefore a valid source of law for international tribunals addressing an adhesion treaty.[134]

If so, then this opens interesting possibilities for tribunals in such cases. One of the strengths of the *contra proferentem* approach is that as

---

[132] Under Article 38.1 of the ICJ Statute, general principles of law are a third source of law alongside treaty and custom.

[133] Harris, *supra* note 32, at 694–712. Article 3.2 of the WTO DSU, for example, states that one of the core functions of the DSM is to "clarify the existing provisions of those agreements in accordance with customary rules of interpretation of public international law." NAFTA Chapter Twenty and its rules of procedure are silent on this point, but Chapter 11 makes it clear that the rules of public international law apply to the settlement of NAFTA investment disputes. NAFTA, *supra* note 122, at Art. 1131. This depends, of course, on one's view of the role of public international law in WTO adjudication – I am of the view that the WTO Agreements, and therefore the DSM, operate within the ambit of public international law writ large. *See generally* Joost Pauwelyn, *The Role of Public International Law in the WTO: How Far Can We Go?*, 95 Am. J. Int'l L. 535 (2001).

[134] Harris, *supra* note 32, at 693–712. He reviews the law of the US, the EU, Germany, the United Kingdom, Canada, China, Japan and Korea.

Harris points out, it is itself supportive of the *pacta sunt servanda* principle, while also opening a space for equitable considerations that are already a part of international law when confronting such situations, and often through the general principles doctrine.[135] Within this space, a CAFTA or KORUS dispute panel could, for example, limit the abusive use of a safeguards clause negotiated by the United States to block imports subject to specific tariff concessions if challenged in a proceeding, perhaps conforming its interpretation to WTO safeguards criteria, for example.

Another more aggressive possibility might be for such a panel to find the challenging state in breach, but award no damages, thereby symbolically invalidating the provision altogether.[136] As discussed in Chapter 2, CAFTA provisions require Costa Rican agency and distribution contracts to be retroactively amended to submit them to arbitration, as part of Costa Rica's compliance with its CAFTA obligations. Should, for example, such a provision be judged unconstitutional under Costa Rican law, then Costa Rica could simply refuse to comply, await a US enforcement action, then raise the *contra proferentem* argument in such a setting. While this is entirely a speculative possibility at this time, it seems likely there would be strong support on many levels and from many quarters to resist such an egregious provision on freedom of contract principles, from Costa Rican domestic law to general principles of law to global civil society.

Whatever the specific challenge, the *contra proferentem* principle in adhesion treaty settings offers a promising avenue for addressing some of the most troubling dynamics in regional and bilateral agreements, in a context that respects *pacta sunt servanda* while responding to appropriate equitable considerations under international law. While such a case may never arise, or at least not for a while, the mere possibility might serve to weaken the resolve of an overreaching state, at least at the margins.

---

[135] *Id.* at 710–12, 738.

[136] *See Biwater Gauff (Tanzania) Ltd. v. United Republic of Tanzania*, ICSID Case No. ARB/ 05/22 (July 24, 2008) (zero damage award used to nullify effects of asymmetric treaty rules preventing investor misconduct from being formally considered).

V CONCLUSIONS

Safeguarding consent means recovering the object and purpose of trade agreements: to create conditions for trading societies to flourish by ensuring that consensual exchanges are protected and facilitated. What I have proposed in this chapter are reasons, as Kant might say, "not of justice but of prudence" why "those in power" (the United States in hemispheric trade negotiations, or any major developed country or system such as the EU elsewhere in asymmetric negotiations) should "intimately appreciate" the need for such changes in treaty negotiation and substance, as consent suggests.

In my view, both prudence and the nature of trade itself argue in favor of future treaty negotiations that begin with a clear understanding of the proper goal, and proceed with the type of bargaining process necessary to be consistent with that goal, toward achieving results that are themselves more consistent with that goal: a framework for truly consensual economic relations between states and among their citizens. Prudence also dictates reinterpreting, amending or otherwise reforming such treaties with all deliberate speed in favor of a more consensual kind of bargain, and we have seen some strategies that might help.

A more consensual trading system promises to open up more of trade's economic and social benefits to a wider array of the people living beneath the umbrella of trade agreements, meaning, increasingly, all of us. Trade and its pathologies outlined thus far are taking place on a global scale, with implications in all regions and economies of the world, as the global "backlash" against trade and globalization today vividly illustrates. It is to this larger global context, and the implications of a consent approach for these larger issues, that I will now turn in the next chapter.

4 CONSENSUAL TRADE AND THE TWENTY-FIRST-CENTURY GLOBAL ECONOMY

". . . market society needs to be reconstructed on a broader legitimating foundation –

in order that the world can recover by means of it."

Volker Bornschier

In this penultimate chapter I want to offer several reflections aimed at broadening and deepening the analysis presented thus far. In terms of broadening, I want to consider this possibility in two ways. First, within the universe of trade agreements, there are other major actors such as China and the EU whose agreements would also merit sustained scrutiny, and other sectors within the subjects covered in FTAs that should receive their own closely tailored consent analysis. Second, given my focus thus far on trade law, and the convergence taking place within different fields or branches of international economic law, I think it is worth considering what might be like to extend this analysis "horizontally" to include other types of international economic law agreements.

Ultimately, properly understanding the role of consent in other trade sectors and between other types of parties, and in other forms of economic exchange besides trade, requires its own careful, phenom-enologically minded investigation of these other exchanges. This kind of analysis would be a useful complement to the deeper study of coercion and exploitation in specific agreements that I mentioned in the last chapter, as the trade analogue to the common law history of deliberation concerning which contracts were too coercive or exploit-ative to enforce, and which ones could stand, albeit with modification. It is not possible to carry out either kind of analysis here. However, as I did in the last chapter with respect to the question of "criteria" for coercive or exploitative agreements, so too in this chapter I think it is at least useful at this juncture to illustrate what such extensions into other sectors might look like. For example, whether or not investment chapters are included within FTAs, and I have expressed some reservations on this point, investment agreements as a category are a major family of instruments in international economic law that raise important consent issues that deserve analysis. I do so by sketching a preliminary foray into how consent might apply in the context of investment agreements, either as stand-alone BITs or when incorporated into FTAs as an investment chapter.

Second, I want to argue for a further "vertical" kind of extension, by offering reasons why we need to look deeper *within* our polities as well for dynamics of consent and oppression as they operate on the domestic side of trade law and policy. The domestic consensual elements of trade as a policy and as a set of ratified agreements is an important additional dimension of the story of consent and trade that I can only gesture toward here. However, in the early days of the twenty-first century and in the wake of the 2016 US presidential election, there has never been a more opportune moment in which to investigate this dimension of consent.

Finally, I want to enlarge the frame yet again, to suggest that we consider consent and trade in the largest possible context, which I believe is that of the emerging global market society that we are in the process of becoming. What would it mean to respect the consensual nature of trade in a global society built around trade agreements? Why would this matter? Or, to put the matter more somberly, what does it mean that we currently live in an emerging global society structured by agreements that reflect instead the pathologies of trade?

I EXTENDING THE ANALYSIS HORIZONTALLY

A Other Sectors and States Within the Trading System

As I indicated in Chapter 1, there are many types of economic exchanges, some of which we refer to under the rubric of "trade" and regulate within the field we call trade law – exchanges involving services, for example, rather than goods, would seem *mutatis mutandis* to fit the same pattern. Others we might call something else, and I don't mean here the pathologies of trade such as coercion – I mean foreign investment transactions, for example, or finance, or lending. Such exchanges also fit the pattern of a bilateral exchange of value, and they may or may not be bargained for as well, but whether or not consent is as constitutive when money is the subject of the exchange and not the *medium* of the exchange, for example, remains to be seen.

At first blush it is not apparent why consent would not be equally central in other "trade" sectors besides the paradigmatic example of trade in goods. However, the implications of the difference in the socioeconomic footing of the exchange merits careful reflection. Starting close to home, one possibility for further work is to undertake more focused case studies of consent in other specific sectors of economic activity we now consider as part of the trade agenda, such as trade-related IP rights, services, agriculture and agriculture subsidies, government procurement, etc. D. P. Harris's innovative analysis of TRIPS, coercion and treaties of adhesion stands as important example of this kind of extension.

Broadly speaking, all of these sectors involve "trade" as we have been discussing the subject here (as opposed to "real estate" transactions, for example). Hence the object of further study would be not so much to determine whether consent is constitutive or not when it comes to "trade" in services or agricultural products (versus exploitative or coerced exchanges of the same). Instead, we would want to understand in greater detail "the conditions actually given," to use Weil's term, in these sectors, in order to better understand where and how consent is at risk in these sectors, and how likewise to best support and protect consent in these areas through, for example, more balanced and effective negotiations in these areas.

Other States
A second, related avenue for further work would be to undertake case studies of consent as it operates in agreements organized around powerful actors other than the US, such as the EU (that other global

economic hegemon),[1] or the emerging networks built around China, for example.[2] There is a spectrum of power and power inequalities among many states, and a range of norms or "cultures" with respect to how differences in power are handled. A fuller examination of consent in trade could involve a more detailed comparative analysis of how more precise differences in size and region can influence the dynamics of trade and its pathologies as they play out in economic negotiations. This all merits further study.

As I have indicated at several points throughout this book, by using examples drawn from US regional and bilateral treaty practice I don't mean to imply that the problem of consent in trade is confined to US economic relations – far from it. I use the US only as a vivid example – and the example I know best – of the kinds of power dynamics that occur when highly asymmetric powers negotiate highly unbalanced agreements in the space purporting to be "trade."

Other powerful actors play leading roles in shaping the global economic agenda, and therefore have commensurate opportunities for trade or for predation, coercion or exploitation. For example, the EU also has an extensive network of bilateral agreements with a host of developing countries around the world, many of them former African or Latin American colonies where the history of consent and its pathologies is never far from view.[3] However, the EU is also publicly committed – for its own mixed motives to be sure – to a more "progressive" trade agenda than the United States, suggesting an interesting comparative study.[4]

---

[1] *Negotiations and Agreements*, EUROPEAN COMMISSION (Feb. 20, 2018), http://ec.europa.eu/trade/policy/countries-and-regions/negotiations-and-agreements/#_in-place.

[2] *China's Free Trade Agreements*, CHINA FTA NETWORK, http://fta.mofcom.gov.cn/english/index.shtml (last visited Mar. 12, 2018).

[3] *See* Stephen R. Hurt, *Co-operation and Coercion? The Cotonou Agreement between the European Union and ACP States and the End of the Lomé Convention*, 24 THIRD WORLD Q. 161 (2003).

[4] *See, e.g.*, P. Di Rubbo & G. Canali, *A Comparative Study of EU and US Trade Policies for Developing Countries*, 13 CONGRESS EUR. ASS'N AGRIC. ECON. (2008) (finding EU policies to have created more trade across the board than US policies). This of course plays well into the EU's own self-interest in two ways: externally, it allows the EU to court closer economic ties with states resentful of their options and encounters with US "trade" policy. Internally, it can boost the democratic legitimacy of EU institutions in the eyes of member states and EU citizens, a concern never far from the uneasy institutional mind.

Shifting continents, it is generally acknowledged that we are now in an age of unparalleled Chinese global engagement.[5] This raises concerns for many about the ethics and goals of China's foreign relations, even as it seems to offer remarkable market opportunities for multinationals, investors and other global actors around the world. Such concerns are at once new with respect to China, and sadly familiar with respect to asymmetric power projection. To what extent should asymmetric negotiations between China and other weaker powers be analyzed by the same rubrics of consent, coercion, exploitation or predation, or are there different ones? And what kinds of arguments and strategies would gain the most traction to shift negotiations with China toward more consensual arrangements, assuming we find similar dynamics at work? These questions should be explored carefully and soon.

Thus, economic agreements by other powerful actors are as much in need of a consent analysis as is the US program. It may be that other powerful actors exercise their power in similar ways, or in ways that might differ in important respects. There are good reasons for making our best efforts to find out.

B From the Twentieth-Century Trade Economy to the Twenty-First-Century Finance Economy

Moving farther afield, it would be very important for our understanding of the twenty-first-century economy and its unique forms of oppressive behavior, that we undertake an analysis of the role of consent in other areas of economic activity that we don't conventionally understand as coming within the scope of what we mean as "trade." It is undeniable that in our time the activities we call finance, investment and banking together account for a huge portion of our overall economic activity, dwarfing the total value of trade, and thereby constituting a major socioeconomic phenomenon with broad systemic effects throughout our societies.[6] However, normative theorizing in

---

[5] *See, e.g.,* DAVID SHAMBAUGH, CHINA GOES GLOBAL (2013); Jeffrey Wasserstrom, *China & Globalization,* 143 Dædalus 157 (2014).

[6] For example, the notional value of all derivatives is significantly larger total world GDP. *Compare OTC Derivatives Statistics at End-June 2017,* STAT. RELEASE (Bank for Int'l Settlements, Basel, Switz.), June 2, 2017, at 2 (showing the notional amount of outstanding

these other fields lags behind even that degree of theorizing we now consider part of the trade discourse, a phenomenon that should be of grave concern to us all given the economic power and influence of these sectors.

As a starting point, we can evaluate whether foreign investment transactions, and the investment agreements that structure them, are similarly rooted in consent. Since contemporary trade agreements have also begun to include chapters on investment, this is a useful place in which to illustrate the kind of work that needs to be done.

1 Consent and Investment: A Preliminary Analysis

Recall that with trade, there are two basic dimensions to our evaluation of consent: the "market" transaction between private parties, and the interstate "transaction" of a trade treaty negotiation. Similarly, we have two levels in the investment context: an investment transaction, and a state-to-state negotiation of investment rules. Already, we can note a potentially significant difference: the "private party" equivalent in investment is actually a negotiation between an investor and a state. So, it is interesting to consider whether the "quasi-public" nature of this transaction (versus between two private parties as in my initial examples in Chapter 1) suggests any differences to the way consent is manifested or subverted in this context.

It would seem as an initial matter that the structure of foreign investment as a phenomenon is similar to trade in important ways. For one thing, parties to an investment transaction also negotiate the terms of an exchange of value. The investor offers capital on the one hand for deployment within the host state's economy, and the host state offers access to labor, natural resources, markets or knowledge capital on the other, together with legal rights.[7] The key of course is whether or not each party consents to the terms of the exchange.

over-the-counter derivatives was $542 trillion at that end of June 2017), *with* World Bank, *Gross Domestic Product 2017* at 3, https://databank.worldbank.org/data/download/GDP.pdf (last accessed July 21, 2018) (showing the world GDP was $80.7 trillion by the end of 2017).

[7] I am relying here on the typology of investment "desiderata" sought by capital, as developed by Roberto Echandi and Maree Newson. Roberto Echandi & Maree Newson, *Influence of International Investment Patterns in International Economic Law Rulemaking: A Preliminary Sketch*, 17 J. INT'L ECON. L. 847, 856–65 (2014). The "rights" the host

However, this quasi-public transaction can take several forms. It may be an actual negotiated contractual agreement, such as a concession agreement to develop natural resources. Alternatively, it may take the form of an understanding reached by an investor with a host state's foreign investment commission or the equivalent, in order to gain entry into the market under a regime conditioning access on such a negotiation. Finally, the "agreement" may only be implicit, where for example an investor takes advantage of a permissive investment regime (often established by a BIT) in which the terms of the BIT and the conditions set in the host state's investment laws form key elements in the investor's actionable expectations on investment. In each of these fundamental variations, it is worth evaluating the different ways consent or its pathologies may be operative.

The second dimension of a consent analysis involves the question of consent in the investment treaty (or investment chapter) negotiation between the host state and the investor's home state. This agreement may allow foreign investment in the first place, set limits to what any foreign investment commission may ask and set the terms for the implicit bargain the host state is offering the investor in terms of investor rights and host state duties. This level of consent may or may not parallel the similar public level of agreement in trade, between the two parties negotiating a bilateral FTA for example.

To begin with, in an investment context the element of consent is, if possible, even more nuanced. Successfully deploying investment capital abroad generally depends on a whole range of volitional acts by private and public actors: incorporation; licensing and permitting; the hiring of employees; extracting and perhaps processing resources; shipping the output; and so forth. One could easily conclude that investment transactions must be consensual or else they simply wouldn't work: lots of people have to go along.

However, the contemporary critical debate concerning the fairness of investment treaty law,[8] and the underlying history of social conflict

---

state offers are negotiated between the host state and the investor's home state, which raises an additional area for consent analysis, as will be discussed in the chapter.

[8] *See generally* Frank J. Garcia, Lindita Ciko, Apurv Gaurav & Kirrin Hough, *Reforming the International Investment Regime: Lessons from International Trade Law*, 18 J. Int'l Econ. L. 861 (2015).

that often surrounds investment, suggest reasons for concern.[9] The reality of conflict and indeed some of the very risks investment law is designed to address (expropriation law, or the full protection and security standard, for example), suggest that investment treaties and transactions cannot be assumed to be fully consensual on the part of the host state or its citizens, even if their deployment depends on a consistent pattern of volitional acts over time.[10]

This brings us to the consensual agreement between the home state and the host state. This kind of consent most closely maps onto the state-level consent we have been discussing in bilateral or regional FTAs, but there are reasons for grave concern that the consent issues are, if anything, worse than in trade. The historic inequality in bargaining power between capital-exporting states and capital-importing states, due in part to the uneven distribution of investment capital among the world's economies, has been transcended to some degree by the changes in the global investment climate since the mid-twentieth century due to globalization. Nevertheless, it has left deep marks in the structure and operation of investment treaties to this day, which the contemporary debate over investment treaty reform bears out.

The unique socioeconomic and political context in which investment agreements are negotiated strongly suggests the need for a "bespoke" consent analysis specifically tailored to the history and dynamics of the market for investment capital. However, using the concepts developed here as a starting point, we can identify at least two significant risks to consensual investment agreements. First, the inequality in distributions of investment capital means in itself that states with a significant supply of investment capital are in a position

[9] While it is risky to reason from smoke to fire, it is well-understood that social conflict is often one manifestation of the resentment and anger that come from unfair transactions. See FRANK GARCIA, Trade, Justice and Security, in TRADE AS GUARANTOR OF PEACE, LIBERTY AND SECURITY? 78 (Constance Z. Wagner, Tomer Broude & Colin Picker eds. 2006) (citing social psychology literature on justice and social conflict). Resentment and conflict abound with respect to foreign investment, but can obviously arise for many reasons including nationalism and pathologies of governance. While it would be unfair to attribute all of the social conflict around investment to injustice, the correlation at least is clear even if causation is murky.

[10] I am indebted to Federico Ortino for the conversations underlying these reflections.

to use that leverage coercively, driving highly unbalanced agreements concerning the rights and responsibilities of investors, versus those of host states. Second, the market for investment capital has significant collective action problems, in part for the same reason, which hamper the efforts of weaker states with insufficient supplies of capital to meet their development needs to negotiate more favorable rules. This can be understood as a problematic background condition, creating conditions under which a home state can exploit this weakness in order to drive a markedly unbalanced agreement, even if it has not itself created the problematic background condition.

Investment rules, whether free standing in BITs or incorporated as an investment chapter into FTAs, bear the marks of such inequalities in ways that mirror the features we have studied here in trade, as they are if possible even more deeply asymmetric than the pattern of trade rules established in the bilateral and regional trade agreements evaluated in this book. This certainly grows out of the history of BITs, which were born in an age of anxiety over the security of capital in the immediate postcolonial environment, but continue to influence the negotiating environment for investment agreements today. Perhaps the most pronounced consequence is "The Great Asymmetry," the fact that BITs give substantive rights only to capital, and merely procedural rights to states.[11] This asymmetry is important, because whatever its historical justifications, it could also be said to reflect successful deployment by home states of all the leverage they enjoy by virtue of their larger supplies of capital and the background conditions of the market for investment, allowing them to continue to drive capital-advantaging bargains.[12]

---

[11] Alessandra Arcuri, *The Great Asymmetry and the Rule of Law in Trade and Investment Agreements* (unpublished paper on file with author). *See generally* Frank J. Garcia, et al., *Reforming the International Investment Regime: Lessons from International Trade Law*, 18 J. INT'L ECON. L. 861 (2016).

[12] This may be shifting, however, as even powerful states once considered "capital exporting," such as the United States and the core European states, are increasingly also capital-importing and consequently are also increasingly subject to adverse BIT arbitrations. *See* Daniel Behn, *Legitimacy, Evolution, and Growth in Investment Treaty Arbitration: Empirically Evaluating the State-of-the-Art*, 46 GEO. J. INT'L L. 363, 393 (2015) (relative balance of cases against developing versus developed states began shifting in the early 2000s).

Much work remains to be done to develop such an account, and for this reason investment has not been a primary subject in this study. However, investment law is slowly beginning to attract the kind of normative thinking it deserves, given its profound (and profoundly important) allocative role.[13] Complementing this, I think one can at least see from the earlier reflection how a consent approach to investment might direct our attention to the degree and nature of consent underlying the investment treaties and investment transactions in question, in order to determine whether we are indeed facilitating investment, or the investment equivalent of coercion, predation or exploitation.

II DEEPENING THE ANALYSIS VERTICALLY: CONSENT AND THE "COUNTRY WITHIN THE COUNTRY"

In Chapter 3 I raised several issues concerning the deficiencies of Nicaraguan democracy in the context of CAFTA, as an example of the kind of domestic consent issue that arises in an interstate negotiation, and which in my view should have concerned the United States in its own relationship to the treaty. My focus in that discussion was to illustrate a negotiating party's reasons for monitoring the quality of consent "across the table," so to speak – in other words, within a negotiating partner's domestic society. If one is aiming to conclude a trade agreement but one's negotiating partner has foreclosed any meaningful possibility of consent on the part of its citizens, then there are reasons for concern that one is being drawn into an exploitation agreement or worse, whatever one's own motives. Such agreements may best be understood not as trade agreements, but as facilitation agreements that enable predatory practices by a country's elites against their own people. Over the long haul, ignoring such warning signs runs the risk of creating unstable economic relationships, not to mention entering into agreements that offend one's own country's norms of legitimacy.

---

[13] *See, e.g.*, Nicholas Perrone, *The Emerging Global Right to Investment: Understanding the Reasoning Behind Foreign Investor Rights*, 8 J. INT'L DISP. SETTLEMENT 673, 673 (2017); Steven Ratner, *International Investment Law Through the Lens of Global Justice*, J. INT'L ECON. L. (forthcoming 2018).

In this section, I want to return to that kind of problem, but instead of focusing across the table, I want to suggest why we may want to extend that analysis to focus on our own side of the table. In other words, I want to highlight reasons why a country like the United States should be concerned about the nature of consent within its *own* polity when negotiating a trade liberalization agreement. As I write this, US trade policy is falling into deeper and deeper disarray, as current or future trade agreements like NAFTA and the TPP become targets for a political backlash against trade and its larger context, economic globalization. In trade terms, the 2016 US presidential election was a wake-up call for many that a significant element within the US polity feel betrayed by our current trade policies, and that free trade is being imposed on them at their cost but for others' benefits.

This crisis affords an important opportunity to reexamine the internal, domestic element of consent in trade. Those of us engaging in trade from within the developed world must consider whether we have allowed ourselves to believe we can pursue trade not only without consent abroad, but without consent at home as well. The crisis reminds us that our misunderstanding of the consensual nature of trade may have repercussions *within* our domestic societies as well as between trading partners.

Addressing this misunderstanding involves looking at the intersection of economic consent in trade and the political process of reaching consensus – meaning shared consent, not unanimity – on the pursuit of a free trade policy. We can call this intersection the social contract of trade. Elsewhere I have written of the importance of acknowledging – and fulfilling – the bargains we make with others in our polity when we pursue free trade as a policy.[14] Here I want to consider how the social contract of trade is an example of "deepening" the consent analysis developed in the book, toward a deeper understanding of the many dimensions of consent in trade.

Considering this "internal" dimension of consent, as necessary as I believe it is, raises many issues, only a few of which I can touch on

---

[14] *See* Frank J. Garcia & Timothy Meyer, *Restoring Trade's Social Contract*, 116 MICH. L. REV. ONLINE 78, 82 (2017), http://michiganlawreview.org/restoring-trades-social-con tract/.

here in an illustrative manner. However, I consider it a key element for further research in considering the strength and depth of our overall commitment to a consensual – or oppressive – framework for economic exchange.

A The Social Contract of Trade

The social contract of trade involves the decisions we make as a society to pursue a free trade policy, and as part of those decisions, the commitments we make to vulnerable groups within our own society who are at risk when we undertake as a society to engage in free trade. It is grounded in what it means to consensually pursue a policy of free trade – transnational consensual exchanges – which for structural reasons having to do with national and global economies might nevertheless work to the temporary or permanent disadvantage of other members of our society. It thus includes the obligation to respect the political commitments made to secure consent to a free trade policy, in particular to compensate those within our polity who are vulnerable to trade's downside risks.

In my view, the choice to enact a free trade regime forms part of what Rawls calls the basic structure of a society: a set of institutions, policies and practices that fundamentally shape the allocation of social resources and the life prospects of a community's members.[15] It is a choice toward a set of social arrangements that we hope collectively brings us the benefits of social and economic cooperation, in this case trade. Inherent in that choice, however, is the risk that these arrangements will also bring substantial costs, in the form of lost jobs or lost wages, for particular members of our society.

The social contract of trade, as I am using the term here, consists of the obligations we undertake toward those vulnerable workers to hold them free from harm, or more precisely, to ensure they are no worse off

---

[15] See JOHN RAWLS, THE LAW OF PEOPLES: WITH "THE IDEA OF PUBLIC REASON REVISITED" 42–43 (4th ed. 1992) (linking the trade regime to the social choice for markets, and the need for fair background conditions as part of the basic structure). On the relationship between free trade and Rawls's earlier views in A THEORY OF JUSTICE, see FRANK J. GARCIA, GLOBAL JUSTICE AND INTERNATIONAL ECONOMIC LAW: THREE TAKES 70–95 (2013).

than they would have been had we not embarked on a free trade policy. This obligation has deep roots in both liberal theory[16] and the economic justifications for free trade[17], which are not my subject here. In this context, I want to look instead at how this understanding of our promises flows out of the consensual nature of trade itself.

As a preliminary matter, we can begin with the idea that if trade must be consensual in order to be trade, then this has implications for the political decision to undertake a trade negotiation agenda. What sort of implications? To begin with, it would seem consistent with the consensual nature of trade, that trade policy decisions also reflect the consent of those on whose behalf such agreements will, at least formally speaking, be negotiated. Otherwise, a trade policy decision, altering as it must the balance of rights, opportunities and burdens trading parties will face, risks working a kind of theft, or nonconsensual economic extraction, on those subject to it if there has been no consensual process underlying it, or if promises made are then betrayed. In particular, it is important that any promises made as a necessary part of securing a party's consent toward free trade be honored. This is where we can start to see the intersection of domestic trade policy and politics with the larger threads of consensual trade we have been exploring here.

In an advanced capitalist welfare society, a key site for investigating this relationship lies in the area of adjustment assistance for displaced workers. Adjustment assistance consists of a package of enhanced benefits that OECD and other governments offer to workers who have lost their jobs as a result of trade. It is designed to support displaced workers as they face unemployment or underemployment, and the retraining and relocation often necessary for them to rebuild their lives

---

[16] Aaron James, for example, calls this the Duty of Collective Due Care, one of the three equitable principles he finds inherent in the collective social practice he calls mutual reliance on markets, or mutual market reliance for short. AARON JAMES, FAIRNESS IN PRACTICE: A SOCIAL CONTRACT FOR A GLOBAL ECONOMY 17–18 (2012).

[17] See Garcia & Meyer, supra note 14, at 82 (importance of domestic adjustment policies in fairly distributing gains from liberalized trade). See generally C. MICHAEL AHO & THOMAS O. BAYARD, Costs and Benefits of Trade Adjustment Assistance, in THE STRUCTURE AND EVOLUTION OF RECENT U.S. TRADE POLICY 153, 157–60 (Robert E. Baldwin & Anne O. Krueger eds. 1984) (reviewing economic justifications for adjustment assistance).

and their communities. For many social welfare democracies, this is seen as part of the basic social contract of their form of the welfare state.[18]

In the United States, adjustment assistance, called trade adjustment assistance or TAA, is more explicitly linked to securing Congressional support for free trade negotiations (Trade Promotion Authority or TPA) going as far back as the Kennedy administration.[19] Hence we can speak of in the United States of a special or specific social contract of trade, whatever the nature of the larger more general social contract we maintain with workers. The domestic political and legal process of granting the Executive Branch TPA, and in the process agreeing to TAA, thus form an internal or "domestic" analog to the transnational mechanisms discussed in the preceding chapter for securing and protecting consent in forming true trade agreements. How we deliver (or not) on our commitment to TAA benefits following a decision to engage in trade, is a key site for assessing the consensual nature of our trade agreements and trade policy, yet it is virtually invisible in the public debate once TPA has been granted.[20]

B Betraying the Social Contract of Trade

The current political crisis in the United States has revealed that many view the process of formulating a consensus for trade as broken, and the commitment to deliver meaningful trade adjustment assistance as having been violated.[21] In the terms of this book, many are of the view that we have overlooked, neglected or actively betrayed the consent of the most vulnerable within our own polity, as we have pursued "trade" agreements that have similarly ignored,

---

[18] See J. F. HORNBECK, CONG. RES. SERV., CRS 7–7500, TAA AND ITS ROLE IN U.S. TRADE POLICY 1–3 (2013) (summarizing equity arguments); AHO & BAYARD, supra note 17, at 154–57 (reviewing in-depth equity-based arguments for TAA in the context of either a general or trade-specific social contract between government and workers).

[19] See Garcia & Meyer, supra note 14, at 85.

[20] See Stephen Kim Park, Bridging the Global Governance Gap: Reforming the Law of Trade Adjustment, 43 GEO. J. INT'L L. 797 (2012) (TAA is often misunderstood and overlooked).

[21] See Garcia & Meyer, supra note 14, at 82–84 (citing 2016 US presidential campaign poll data).

coerced or violated the consent of our trading partners. We have undermined consent both at home and abroad.

When we look at the current terms of TAA in the United States, it is sadly too apparent that we have in fact defaulted on the core promise of effective trade adjustment assistance for those whose jobs are at risk due to our decision to pursue trade. When TAA was first created in 1962, benefits were limited to training programs to promote reemployment, and some income support during the training period. Eligibility under the Act was also much more limited than under contemporary TAA programs, and many of the initial applications were denied.[22] By 1974, when Congress next revisited trade policy, support within organized labor for TAA had collapsed, the unions dismissing it as nothing more than "burial insurance."[23] In the 1980s, the Reagan administration proposed abolishing TAA completely, and the program lapsed briefly.[24]

Since then, the renewal of TAA such as it is has always been tied to new rounds of trade negotiations. Congress has renewed or extended TAA each time it has granted the president TPA or approved a new round of trade agreements, reinforcing the connection between decisions to trade and decisions to compensate at-risk workers, but underscoring its political vulnerability as well.[25] Once TPA is granted or the agreements ratified, TAA funding has tended to diminish, further reinforcing the many program defects inherent in the way TAA has been designed, and leading to widespread acknowledgment that TAA as currently constituted is a failure.[26]

All of this has had the effect of rendering TAA a political football rather than a consensual agreement. Through its failures in design and funding, our execution of this commitment has served to only undermine the social contract of trade.

---

[22] The first application accepted for benefits did not take place until Nov. 1969. *See* Ethan Kapstein, *Trade Liberalization and the Politics of Trade Adjustment Assistance*, 137 INT'L LAB. REV. 501, 507 (1998).

[23] *Id.* at 509.

[24] HORNBECK, *supra* note 18, at 9.

[25] *Id.* at 10–12.

[26] *See* Garcia & Meyer, *supra* note 14, at 87 *see also* Timothy Meyer, *Saving the Political Consensus in Favor of Free Trade*, 70 VAND. L. REV. 985 (2017).

C Restoring Trade's Social Contract

The main focus of this book has been on how the trading system might be reformed toward protecting and supporting consent abroad, and therefore toward protecting, supporting and enhancing trade itself, and not something else. In this section, I now want to briefly illustrate how we might similarly repair the consensual basis of trade at home, as a domestic policy, using the US and its TAA program as an example. I suspect however that, *mutatis mutandis*, the same basic issues and challenges are present outside the United States in many other trading states as well, as the crises in Europe suggest, and that therefore these suggestions may have a wider possible field of application.[27]

The core element in any attempt to restore the social contract of trade is to ensure that any promises made in the process of securing consent for trade, are in fact honored. This means, in the United States, that if we care about honoring consent in our domestic trade policy, we should reform how trade adjustment assistance is designed and delivered in the United States.[28] The key to a successful TAA program is worker retraining toward sustainable reemployment. Through their success European states have demonstrated that TAA works if one is serious about the commitment. By both increasing investment in worker retraining as a percentage of GDP (I shall have more to say about this later in the chapter), and offering a more effective training and apprenticeship process that better matches training to market needs, rewards early intervention (sometimes before unemployment even occurs), and offers more thorough and effective job counseling, a significant number of trade-displaced workers can find alternative meaningful employment.[29]

---

[27] See Garcia & Meyer, *supra* note 14, at 84–85.

[28] These suggestions also have implications for other countries as they consider how best to design effective compensation programs. Tim Meyer has argued that for this reason the commitment to undertake domestic adjustment policies should itself be internationalized in the form of commitments within trade agreements, thus binding all parties to a collective decision to support the social contract of trade throughout the free trade zone they collectively create. Meyer, *supra* note 26.

[29] These successful cases are being studied widely and are starting to be emulated in other OECD countries. See ORG. FOR ECON. CO-OPERATION & DEV., CONNECTING PEOPLE WITH JOBS: THE LABOUR MARKET, ACTIVATION POLICIES AND DISADVANTAGED WORKERS IN SLOVENIA 116–18 (2016) (hereinafter OECD, CONNECTING PEOPLE).

For a country as large as the United States, relocation support is another key element to effective reemployment assistance, perhaps even more important than training.[30] However, current job search and relocation allowances are woefully inadequate and should be increased beyond current nominal levels.[31] Moreover, in a high-cost-of-living economy like the US wage insurance benefit caps should be raised to recognize what a secure middle-class life costs in the United States today, and how difficult it is for workers supporting families at all age groups to find equivalent post-dislocation work.[32] Without more public investment, TAA as configured will only ensure more families enter the "working poor" rather than continue in their "pre-trade" middle class life.

The bottom line is that a well-designed and well-executed TAA program would fulfill the social contract of trade both formally and substantively.[33] However, meeting this obligation would require a deeper and more consistent commitment to funding, and here we find TAA's most spectacular failure. Overall, there has been no effort to link funding levels to data on levels of demand or need for the program.[34] As a result, TAA funding has consistently been set too low for program needs, and has fluctuated due to political trends rather than political commitments.[35] Moreover, in comparative terms the United

---

[30] Jun Nie & Ethan Struby, *Would Active Labor Market Policies Help Combat High U.S. Unemployment?*, ECONOMIC REVIEW (Fed. Reserve Bank of Kan. City, Kan. City, Mo.), Third Quarter 2011, at 44–46.

[31] Current job search and relocation allowance is capped at $1,250, which is wholly inadequate. Park, *supra* note 20, at 816 n.59; *see* Garcia & Meyer, *supra* note 14, at 88 n.68.

[32] The median US income is approaching sixty thousand dollars a year, and survey data suggests this closely tracks what US consumers feel is necessary for a "living wage" for middle class families today, and even this would not be enough in many parts of the United States. *See* Aimee Picchi, *How Much Money Do U.S. Families Need to Get By?*, CBS NEWS (Aug. 26, 2015), www.cbsnews.com/news/how-much-money-do-us-fam ilies-need-to-get-by/ (https://perma.cc/5LG2-YNQ8). The median salary for a middle-class manufacturing job for a middle-aged worker is seventy-five thousand dollars. *See* Patrick Gillespie, *$75 a Day vs. $75,000 a Year: How We Lost Jobs to Mexico*, CNN MONEY (Mar. 31, 2016), http://money.cnn.com/2016/03/31/news/economy/mexico-us-globalization-wage-gap/index.html (https://perma.cc/2YAC-B3HK).

[33] Nie & Struby, *supra* note 30, at 43, 48, 51–54.

[34] Park, *supra* note 20, at 847–48.

[35] For example, the most recent TAA reauthorization was in 2015, extending TAA through 2021 and capping the annual funding at $450 million, a *reduction* from the amounts authorized in 2009 and 2011. US Dept. of Labor, *Side-by-Side Comparison of TAA*

States is consistently near the bottom of all OECD countries in terms of adjustment spending.[36] This means that restoring trade's social contract must address funding, and not simply program design and delivery.

D Properly Funding Trade's Social Contract

Supporting the domestic consensus for trade means funding adjustment assistance in a manner consistent with its overall role in the social contract. In my view, it would be most consistent with the social contract of trade as we have formed it – as a promise from all of us to those most at risk from free trade – that the funding to support those most vulnerable to trade come from trade itself. While this could in principle be done through traditional legislative redistribution of the gains from trade, the history of trade politics at least in the US shows that we cannot rely on this for anything as constitutive as the basic bargain underlying trade's social contract.

Instead, I would argue as a key element in restoring trade's social contract and honoring consent throughout domestic and foreign trade policy, that we should consider incorporating a financial transaction tax (FTT) into all new or renegotiated trade agreements. This offers a direct way of harnessing the wealth creation of free trade agreements themselves toward supporting domestic adjustment assistance programs. An FTT with revenue earmarked for adjustment assistance would place entities that benefit tremendously from trade liberalization – major financial institutions – in the role of assisting those who suffer most from the same.[37]

Program Benefits under the 2002 Program, 2009 Program, 2011 Program, and 2015 Program 2 (Nov. 9, 2015), www.doleta.gov/tradeact/pdf/side-by-side.pdf (https://perma.cc/3YA8-MNVA); Meyer, supra note 26, at 1010–11.

[36] Nie & Struby, supra note 30 (demonstrating that the United States is third from the bottom of 21 OECD countries studied); id. (demonstrating that the United States currently ranks second from the bottom among the thirty-five OECD countries in its level of TAA as a percentage of GDP, ahead of only Mexico).

[37] For an earlier call to shift TAA funding to a transnational model, see Park, supra note 20, at 862 (arguing that the TAA should be delivered by transnational worker payments through a global adjustment fund supported by state budgetary contributions). However, Park's model failed to link TAA support directly to the trade benefits enjoyed by others.

FTT proposals are not new, and a number of these mechanisms have been adopted or proposed around the globe.[38] While a comprehensive review of the extensive literature on FTTs, and a detailed exposition of the features of an FTT such as I am proposing, are beyond the scope of this chapter,[39] the essence of the arrangement is as follows. Parties to a free trade agreement would agree that each party shall impose an incremental tax on specified financial transactions (such as securities, derivatives and currency trades) of anywhere from 0.01 percent to 0.1 percent (the rate to be the same in each member state). This is not enough to discourage productive investment transactions, yet it is enough to generate hundreds of millions for adjustment assistance for workers sharing the risks but not getting the benefits of trade's joint venture.

In terms of scope and jurisdiction, a social contract FTT should be designed to tax wholesale capital market transactions (stocks, bonds, derivatives and currency trades) between major financial institutions such as banks, investment firms, insurance companies, pension funds and hedge funds; and not "retail" transactions such as home mortgages and business loans.[40] Jurisdictionally, taxable transactions could be defined as those between counterparties when at least one counterparty is resident within the free trade area, as the EU does,[41] although in the context of free trade agreements thought should be given to whether the proposal should require both counterparties to be resident.[42]

---

[38] *See* Garcia & Meyer, *supra* note 14, at 94–95.

[39] *Id.* at 95–98.

[40] *See generally Proposal for a Council Directive Implementing Enhanced Cooperation in the Area of Financial Transaction Tax*, at 17, 36, COM (2013) 71 final (Feb. 14, 2013) (hereinafter *Proposal for a Council Directive*) (weighing the costs and benefits of taxing various transactions and institutions, and concluding that certain institutions, including refinancing institutions, should not be taxed with an FTT). It is important for political as well as normative reasons that the tax not apply to ordinary consumers at the retail level. *See* Len Burman & William G. Gale, *The Pros and Cons of a Consumption Tax*, BROOKINGS (Mar. 3, 2005), www.brookings.edu/on-the-record/the-pros-and-cons-of-a-consumption-tax/ (https://perma.cc/WA73-KXJJ).

[41] *Proposal for a Council Directive*, *supra* note 40, at 18.

[42] Particularly when the FTA zone would include a major financial center such as New York in the case of a US FTA, or the City in the case of an EU or (potentially) UK FTA, it is easy to object that applying the tax when only one counterparty is resident risks an unjustifiably large tax base.

Even with such jurisdictional and scope limitations, such a tax could generate considerable revenue toward funding TAA obligations. The EU Commission calculated that its earlier 2011 FTT proposal could generate as much as €57 billion with a tax rate of 0.1 percent on all wholesale stock and bond transfers, and 0.01 percent on all derivatives trades, with all twenty-seven member states participating.[43] An FTT with the same tax rate and jurisdictional structure, if applied in the NAFTA zone today, could yield as much as $64 billion toward adjustment costs in the NAFTA area.[44] To put this in perspective, the combined annual budget for *all* active labor market policies, TAA included, among the United States, Canada and Mexico totaled $25 billion in 2015.[45] Not only would an FTA-based FTT cover the cost of TAA as currently configured, but it would also allow for the necessary reforms and expansions without burdening the public.

However implemented and allocated, creating a trade-related FTT would be a breakthrough in trade adjustment financing and, more broadly, in mechanisms to address the social costs and inequality effects of trade. Linking such a tax to transactions within the economic zones that free trade agreements create would directly harness their wealth-creating potential and tie the funding for TAA to financial parties that benefit tremendously from the agreements themselves. Such a mechanism is rooted directly in the social contract of trade itself, and not more general calls for transnational wealth redistribution, however justified (or not) the latter may be for other reasons.

---

[43] *Commission Proposal for a Council Directive on a Common System of Financial Transaction Tax and Amending Directive*, SEC (2011) 1102–03 final (Sept. 28, 2011). This would calculate to a tax yield of 0.3 perscent of total EU nominal GDP for 2011 (€18.3 trillion), using GDP as a proxy for the tax base, although other measures such as total EU volume of wholesale capital market transactions could be more accurate. *See, e.g., European Union GDP*, TRADING ECON., https://tradingeconomics.com/european-union/gdp (https://perma.cc/3UQW-8FBV).

[44] Assuming the same 0.3 percent calculation on a 2016 combined NAFTA GDP of $21.4 trillion. *See Report for Selected Countries and Subjects*, INT'L MONETARY FUND, www.imf.org/external/pubs/ft/weo/2017/01/weodata/weorept.aspx?sy=2016&ey=2016&scsm=1&ssd=1&sort=subject&ds=.&br=1&c=273,156,111&s=NGDPD,PPPGDP,LP&grp=0&a=&pr.x=53&pr.y=13 (https://perma.cc/R94U-J2S8). Apportionment of these revenues would of course have to be worked out among the FTA participants.

[45] *Public Expenditure and Participant Stocks on LMP*, ORG. FOR ECON. CO-OPERATION & DEV., https://stats.oecd.org/Index.aspx?DataSetCode=LMPEXP# (https://perma.cc/99WY-HT27).

Implementing such a reform would fulfill the social contract of trade and render it self-sustaining, rather than subject to the vicissitudes of budgetary politics. Something as essential as consent deserves no less, and as we are learning, we neglect this at our peril.

III ENLARGING THE FRAME: TRADE LAW FOR A GLOBAL MARKET SOCIETY?

Having both widened and deepened our inquiry into both other international economic law agreements and actors, and a preliminary investigation of the social contract of trade and its relationship to consent in domestic terms, I now want to enlarge the frame yet again. Toward the end of his passionately argued book *Making Globalization Work*, Joseph Stiglitz urges us to consider a new "global social contract," by which he means "an economic regime in which the well-being of the developed and developing countries are better balanced."[46] He enlarges upon this idea with a list of policy recommendations, generated over a lifetime's work on development policy, for what such a regime might look like, and from my perspective the world would clearly be a better place if the global economy we live and work in looked more like the one he recommends.

However, in my view, Stiglitz does not go far enough, and I don't say this because of any shortcomings in his policy analyses, which I find to be quite sensible and persuasive. Instead, I mean that from a sociological, epistemic and normative perspective, globalization has brought us far beyond the interstate social framework that Stiglitz writes within as a backdrop to his policy prescriptions. We are in, to quote the much-missed Hans Rosling,[47] "an entirely new, converging, world."[48] This means that any idea of a global social contract can no longer be conceived of simply as the transnational complement to a

---

[46] JOSEPH E. STIGLITZ, MAKING GLOBALIZATION WORK 285 (2006).

[47] Karen McVeigh, *Hans Rosling, Statistician and Development Champion, Dies Aged 68*, THE GUARDIAN (Feb. 8, 2017), www.theguardian.com/global-development/2017/feb/07/hans-rosling-obituary.

[48] *Hans Rosling's 200 Countries, 200 Years, 4 Minutes* (BBC television broadcast July 25, 2017).

"domestic" social contract, such as the social contract of trade
I outlined in the preceding section.[49] Instead, as I will argue presently,
it seems undeniable to me that we are in the throes of working out what
a global social contract might mean for a truly *global* socioeconomic
space, a global social contract built around shared participation in a
global market.

Such a social contract may not – and probably should not and
indeed cannot – entirely supplant what we now consider as the domestic social contract. However, its emerging reality fundamentally alters
the space within which any society works out its own foundational
commitments. In particular, in terms of the subject of this book, the
possible emergence of a global social framework means that the question of consent is not simply a question for states in their "internal" and
"external" trade relationships. As economic exchanges become global,
the regulation of economic exchanges, and the concomitant protection – or weakening – of consent, also becomes global. We thus face the
possibility of constructing a consensual – hence dynamic and flourishing – or oppressive global socioeconomic framework.

I will begin by first summarizing the socioeconomic, regulatory and
normative convergences within the global space today, about which
I have written more fully elsewhere: the deepening of the global economy, the worsening of economic inequality, the thickening of global
social relationships, the unification of international economic law, the
emergence of global law and the integration of global justice concerns
into our ongoing conversation about development.[50] These convergences fundamentally alter the domain within which any account of
trade, including this one, must operate, since in my view they point
both toward the emergence of a global market society, within which our
aspirations for development, freedom and justice must now take place;
and toward the challenges such a society – our society – faces. I suspect
this means that trade law is becoming a fundamental tool toward

---

[49] This discussion of the boundaries between domestic and global, and its relation to the
social contract metaphor, echoes longstanding debates over the boundaries of Rawls's
liberal project. *See, e.g.,* FRANK J. GARCIA, TRADE, INEQUALITY AND JUSTICE 124–28
(2003) (reviewing what was even then an old debate).

[50] *See* Frank J. Garcia, *Convergences: A Prospectus for Justice in a Global Market Society,* 13
MANCHESTER J. INT´L ECON. L. 128 (2016).

ensuring either opportunity and fairness for everyone, or continued and deepened economic oppression, in a global market society. For this reason, a new respect for consent should make the jump to a global space alongside it.

This opens an even larger field of inquiry than this book can hope to undertake to investigate. Fully responding to the challenges of global justice in a global market society entails, in my view, a much broader approach to justice than currently in vogue, one that is at once plural-ist, relational and transactional.[51] However, insofar as consensual trade necessarily implicates all of this, we can at least begin our consider-ations. In the sections to follow, I will situate the account of consensual trade I have offered thus far into this larger frame, as one view of what it could mean to address the oppressive risks posed by a global market society. Consensual trade – or, simply, trade as we have come to understand it here – could be a key element in the evolution of our understanding of what justice requires of us in our transnational eco-nomic relationships. Reforming these relationships toward a well-functioning global market society is the regulatory and normative task of international economic law today.

A Convergences

In my view, the key legal, economic and governance convergences that globalization has engendered all point to one thing: at the confluence of these economic, social, institutional, normative, theoretical and sym-bolic trends, we may in fact be seeing an emerging global market society.[52] Understanding the role of economic law in such a society requires that we work toward a nuanced understanding of the kinds of relationships, thick and thin, that globalization forms, and the kinds of obligations these relationships engender. I will break this down into two major categories of convergence: the socioeconomic, and the normative.

---

[51] GARCIA, *supra* note 15, at 306–14.

[52] I don't mean to say that this is an inevitably teleological process, and of course the politics of the moment seem to suggest the opposite. However, I do believe that underneath the surface of politics one sees these deeper trends and processes, even as we have serious cause for concern about maintaining and deepening the progressive possibilities inherent in these trends.

1 Socioeconomic Convergence
a The Global Economy Is Deepening

I will begin, then, with perhaps the most salient of these converging trends, and one of the most controversial: the globalization of the economy. Contemporary data suggests the emergence of a global economy characterized by diminishing geographic segregation, decreasing discrimination according to source and increasingly integrated global production processes.[53] The magnitude of global economic integration can be gauged by assessing both institutions and outcomes.[54] Removal of institutional impediments is a necessary condition for cross-border integration, and in this respect, institutions (and through them, states) have largely demonstrated a commitment to global economic integration.[55]

While institutions facilitate and incentivize integration through policy-based efforts, ultimately key state and private actors must assess and respond to them, and for this reason it is significant that outcomes also demonstrate a deepening global economy.[56] Trade as a percentage of global gross domestic product rose from 27 percent in 1970 to 43 percent by 1995, and then to 56 percent by 2016.[57] Foreign direct investment has risen from approximately $10 billion in 1970 to $320 billion by 1995, and then to $1.56 trillion by 2014.[58] This surge in FDI has in turn facilitated the development of global value chains, within which nearly half of world trade in goods and services takes place.[59]

---

[53] Peter Lloyd, *Global Economic Integration*, 15 PAC. ECON. REV. 71, 72 (2010).

[54] Aseem Prakash & Jeffrey A. Hart, *Indicators of Economic Integration*, 6 GLOBAL GOVERNANCE 95, 95–96 (2000).

[55] *Id.* at 95.

[56] *Id.* at 97.

[57] *Trade (% of GDP)*, THE WORLD BANK, http://data.worldbank.org/indicator/NE.TRD.GNFS.ZS?start=1970 (last accessed July 21, 2018).

[58] *Foreign Direct Investment, Net Inflows (BoP, Current US$)*, THE WORLD BANK, http://data.worldbank.org/indicator/BX.KLT.DINV.CD.WD?end=2014&start=1970 (last visited July 15, 2016). Between 1970 and 2014, FDI as a percentage of global GDP has risen continuously, from 0.5 percent in 1970 to 2 percent in 2014. *Id.*

[59] WORLD TRADE ORG., INTERNATIONAL TRADE STATISTICS 2015 (2015), www.wto.org/english/res_e/statis_e/its2015_e/its2015_e.pdf. Global value chains allow firms to "do" the part of the process they are best at, using intermediate goods and services from elsewhere without having to develop a whole industry. ORG. FOR ECON. CO-OPERATION & DEV., INTERCONNECTED ECONOMIES: BENEFITTING FROM GLOBAL VALUE CHAINS (2013).

Therefore both in absolute and relative terms, and over time and to the present day, outcome-based indicators also illustrate the deep connections characteristic of a global economy.

This presents us squarely with a question: what *kind* of global economy are we creating?

b Global Inequality Is Worsening

For one thing, we seem to be creating a very unequal one. The problem of inequality is not new, yet globalization has intensified the nature of inequality today to astronomical proportions. The forces of inequality are global in nature and intensity. To summarize some contentious statistics, overall we see today a disturbing reversal of the twentieth-century trend toward growth with lower inequality.[60] Global inequality (between people, across countries) greatly exceeds national inequality (.70 Gini versus .40s for US, .20s to .30s for Europe).[61] While it may be that inequality *between* countries is decreasing and a lower percentage of the world's population lives in poverty (thanks largely to the gains in China and India), inequality *within* countries is increasing, at least partially offsetting reductions in global inequality. Depending how you read the data, it could be that domestic inequality entirely offsets reductions in global inequality – it could even be that overall inequality has increased despite the gains mentioned.[62]

While this is also contentious, it seems that major elements of the international economic law system as configured today favor the intensification of inequality at national and global levels. While trade has grown within this framework, and *may* decrease inequality in developing countries, such decreases come in part by *flattening* wages

---

[60] THOMAS PIKETTY, CAPITAL IN THE TWENTY-FIRST CENTURY (Arthur Goldhammer trans. 2014); Frank J. Garcia, *Capital in the Twenty-First Century*, 18 J. INT'L ECON. L. 188 (2015) (reviewing PIKETTY, *supra*).

[61] Francois Bourguignon, *Inequality and Globalization: How the Rich Get Richer as the Poor Catch Up*, FOREIGN AFFAIRS, Jan./Feb. 2016, at 11; *see also* Dept. Econ. Soc. Affairs, *Inequality Matters: Report on the World Social Situation 2013*, U.N. Doc. ST/ESA/345 (2013) (reviewing recent trends in global inequality).

[62] Christoph Lakner & Branko Milanovich, *Global Income Distribution: From the Fall of the Berlin Wall to the Great Recession* (World Bank Policy Research, Working Paper No. WPS6719, 2013) (correcting for underreporting of high income levels across national data sets leads to significantly higher levels of global inequality [.76 as measured by national Gini coefficients]); *see also* Bourguignon, *supra* note 61 (noting this possibility).

at the top; moreover, trade may be *increasing* inequality in developed countries by decreasing wages and offshoring jobs at the bottom.[63] Similarly, foreign investment increases inequality in developed countries by facilitating transfers of low-skill jobs outbound, increasing returns to capital; and inbound by increasing the skill premium (perhaps a good thing, but also promoting inequality through new elites).[64]

Even if such inequality trends were not themselves a problem (and there are many good reasons to consider them a problem, and a serious one),[65] the pattern of allocations generated by the international institutions which today frame and regulate the global economy raises significant distributive concerns, in areas as diverse as taxation, access to capital, control over natural resources, the social costs of investment, to name a few. These patterns present a host of compelling social, political, legal and normative issues for international economic law since, as the regulatory framework of the global economy, all of these issues land in its lap, so to speak. There is much work to be done to ensure that the global economy works fairly for everyone.

c Global Social Relations Are Thickening

Economic globalization is embedded in a larger framework of social, informational and symbolic globalization with immense consequences for economy, politics and society. Globalization is transforming human relationships in ways that affect our interconnectedness, the basis for solidarity and the effective reach of our awareness, understanding and actions with respect to others. I can only summarize here what I discuss at greater length elsewhere,[66] but in essence globalization is

---

[63] ERA DABLA-NORRIS ET AL., CAUSES AND CONSEQUENCES OF INCOME INEQUALITY: A GLOBAL PERSPECTIVE (2015).

[64] *Id.*

[65] *See* Dept. Econ. Soc. Affairs, *supra* note 61 (inequality poses serious threats to the well-being of people at all levels of the income distribution); THE WORLD BANK, DEVELOPMENT GOALS IN AN ERA OF DEMOGRAPHIC CHANGE (2015) (inequality one of three top challenges to development today). *See generally* PIKETTY, *supra* note 60; JOSEPH STIGLITZ, THE GREAT DIVIDE: UNEQUAL SOCIETIES AND WHAT WE CAN DO ABOUT THEM (2015); Elizabeth Anderson, *What Is the Point of Equality?*, 109 ETHICS 287 (1999).

[66] *See generally* GARCIA, *supra* note 15.

contributing to the emergence of elements of global community around a range of institutional practices and common challenges.[67]

First, globalization is building communities of risk – David Held calls them communities of fate – around the shared challenges characteristic of global life today: the natural environment, poverty and inequality, security, etc. The intensification of global social and economic interaction – in areas as diverse as global finance, refugee crises, terrorism, climate change – create common interests and can contribute to the subjective awareness of a shared fate.[68]

These build on what can be called a community of knowledge, created by global social media and the information revolution so characteristic of our everyday experience of globalization. Thanks to these infrastructures, we know so much – more than ever before – about how we collectively experience these and other risks, 24/7, around the globe, instantaneously.

Globalization is also building a set of shared understandings and practices around how we respond to such risks and to globalization's opportunities as well.[69] We see this in areas such as the use of markets and the regulation of markets through law and institutions, as well as in new and emerging regimes around challenges as diverse as climate change and global tax avoidance.[70]

Together this represents in my view a trend toward a fundamental shift in social organization on the planet.[71] One of the surprising features of this new global social space is how it resembles what we

---

[67] Communitarians cite a number of factors characteristic of communities, not simply societies: a sense of shared history and a shared future; shared understandings and practices around a range of social phenomenon; a sense of solidarity or at least common purpose; and shared sources of identity, among others. Garcia, *supra* note 15, at 146–48.

[68] Of course, they can also lead to divergence, suspicion, resentment and resurgent nationalism as well. For a heartfelt and searching examination of how these global dynamics have contributed to the causes and politics of these darker responses in recent times, *see* Kenneth R. Himes, *The State of Our Union*, 78 THEOLOGICAL STUDIES 147 (2017).

[69] *See, e.g.*, Frank J. Garcia, *Between Cosmopolis and Community: Globalization and the Emerging Basis for Global Justice*, 46 N.Y.U. J. INT'L L. & POL. 1 (2013).

[70] *See* OECD, *Base Erosion and Profit Shifting (BEPS) Action Plan* (2013), www.oecd.org/ctp/BEPSActionPlan.pdf; Fiona Harvey, *Paris Climate Change Agreement: The World's Greatest Diplomatic Success*, THE GUARDIAN (Dec. 14, 2015), www.theguardian.com/environment/2015/dec/13/paris-climate-deal-cop-diplomacy-developing-united-nations.

[71] *See, e.g.*, DIRK MESSNER, *World Society – Structures and Trends, in* GLOBAL TRENDS AND GLOBAL GOVERNANCE 22 (Paul Kennedy et al. eds. 2001). Perhaps, if not a world

used to call "domestic" space, which also consists of regions of
wealth, urbanization and industrialization, and regions of agrarianism,
poverty and underdevelopment, all linked by an overarching framework of economic, legal, political and social networks of causality,
influence and responsibility. We are in the habit of associating this
"domestic" space with an identifiable community structured by a set
of shared social norms and governance institutions, and for these
reasons contrasting it to the "international" on the basis of the
absence of such elements in the latter. However, because of globalization, we can no longer easily oppose this "domestic" space to the
"international" space "between" communities, and insist that the
latter lacks shared understandings and institutions. It is all simultaneously local and global.[72]

2 Normative Convergence
a International Economic Law is Unifying
As the global economy continues to deepen, formerly distinct areas of
international economic law are converging into a single, unified
body.[73] This development is naturally of great interest to scholars
and policy-makers of international economic law, but it has larger
implications as well. The functionalist paradigm of disparate

---

of "us," at least a world of "I and Thou"? See MARTIN BUBER, I AND THOU (Ronald
   Gregor Smith trans. 1937).
[72] See WAYNE GABARDI, NEGOTIATING POSTMODERNISM (2000) ("glocalization is
   marked by the development of diverse, overlapping fields of global-local linkages ...
   [creating] a condition of globalized panlocality ..."); see generally SASKIA SASSEN, TER-
   RITORY, AUTHORITY AND RIGHTS (2006).
[73] There is a small but growing body of literature analyzing the parallels between trade law
   and investment law and arguing their convergence. See, e.g., TOMER BROUDE, Investment
   and Trade: the 'Lottie and Lisa' of International Economic Law?, in INTERSECTIONS:
   DISSEMBLANCE OR CONVERGENCE BETWEEN INTERNATIONAL TRADE AND INTER-
   NATIONAL INVESTMENT LAW (2011); Roger Alford, The Convergence of International
   Trade and Investment Arbitration, 12 SANTA CLARA J. INT'L L. 35 (2013); Echandi &
   Newson, supra note 7; Sergio Puig, The Merging of International Trade and Investment
   Law, 33 BERKELEY J. INT'L L. 1(2015). Not all commentators, however, fully accept the
   comparison or agree with the convergence thesis, for a variety of reasons. See, e.g.,
   Nicholas Di Mascio & Joost Pauwelyn, Nondiscrimination in Trade and Investment Treaties:
   Worlds Apart or Two Sides of the Same Coin?, 102 AM. J. INT'L L. 48, 53–55 (2008)
   (contrasting the trade and investment regimes in terms of goals and political economies).
   However, in my view, the similarities outweigh the differences.

international economic law regimes established by states to address specific issues is breaking down in the face of the deepening interconnections between policy areas and the linkage issues these connections create.

This convergence can be readily mapped when one considers trade law and investment law. At the level of purpose and deep structure, trade and investment law both involve states making commitments to *each other* with respect to how foreign nationals' economic interests will be treated within the domestic legal system, for fundamentally similar reasons. Trade bargains address the question of how a foreign national's products will be treated on deployment, i.e., importation into and sale within the domestic market; and investment bargains similarly address how a foreign national's capital will be treated on deployment, i.e., establishment and treatment within the domestic market. Most importantly, the convergence of trade and investment is rooted in the evolution of complex global business forms in which both investment and trade in goods and services are deeply intermingled.[74]

This convergence also reflects the deepening of the global economy, as the global commercial integration of goods, services, labor, intellectual property and capital comes to reflect more and more the way a "domestic" economy operates. Within a well-run economy, regulations covering these disparate aspects of economic activity are harmonized through legislative and administrative action and brought into as close a working relationship as possible, for efficiency reasons. The fact that international economic law is undergoing a similar process is both evidence of the larger convergences I am charting, and an opportunity to ensure in a coordinated fashion that global economic regulation is not only efficient in the narrow economic sense, but also efficient in the broader long-term sense, sustainably supporting a flourishing global society.

---

[74] *See* Org. Econ. Co-Operation & Dev. [OECD], *Interconnected Economies: Benefitting From Global Value Chains*, at 8 (2013). As of 2011, global value chains accounted for nearly half of world trade in goods and services. WORLD TRADE ORG., *supra* note 59.

b Global Law Is Emerging

The evolutions in international economic law are part of a larger process of law's adaptation to the new global social reality.[75] Many scholars across the spectrum argue that "international" and "national" law are no longer adequate as categories to embrace the new global totality of "law," i.e., processes of authoritative norm creation, urging us to analyze law as it is emerging in this global space through notions of transnational law, global law, legal pluralism and so forth.[76] Essentially, these scholars are responding to globalization's impact on how norms are created and the kinds of norms that are emerging.

Through globalization, we see in addition to the usual abundance of "national" and "international" lawmaking, an increase in the number of bodies producing "softer" norms, often through trans-national processes, that influence or guide state or private actor behavior or facilitate coordinated regulation by states.[77] We can see such transnational norm creation in a number of areas spanning the waterfront of global social policy, from crime to tax to food safety and beyond.[78] In response, "traditional 'national' legal responses that draw on architectures of normative hierarchy, separation of powers and unity of law are likely to fall short of grasping the nature of the evolving transnational normative order."[79] Because of these long-term

---

[75] Or, as Zumbansen characterizes it, "attempts towards the development of an appropri-ately designed framework of legal analysis and regulation in light of a radically disem-bedded regulatory landscape." Peer C. Zumbansen, *Transnational Legal Pluralism*, 1 TRANSNAT'L LEGAL THEORY 141, 183 (2010).

[76] *Id.*

[77] The Basel Accords and the Basel Committee process are a good example, as is the OECD's BEPS Project, both in collaboration with the G20. *See, e.g.*, Ines Drumond, *Bank Capital Requirements, Business Fluctuation Cycles and the Basel Accords: A Synthesis*, *in* ISSUES IN FINANCE: CREDIT, CRISES & POLICIES (Stuart Sayer ed. 2010) (tracing the channels through which the Basel Accords influence central banking policy and therefore the domestic business cycle and overall macroeconomic stability); OECD, CONNECTING PEOPLE, *supra* note 29. On the soft law phenomenon, *see* Gregory C. Shaffer & Mark A. Pollack, *Hard vs. Soft Law: Alternatives, Complements, and Antagonists in International Governance*, 94 MINN. L. REV. 706 (2010).

[78] *See generally* Messner, *supra* note 71, 34–40; Peer Zumbansen, *Defining the Space of Transnational Law: Legal Theory, Global Governance and Legal Pluralism*, 21 TRANSNAT'L L. & CONTEMP. PROBS. 305, 312–13 (2012) (cataloguing global social challenges calling for transnational approaches).

[79] Zumbansen, *supra* note 75 at 153.

trends, we cannot simply distinguish types of law by their purported geographical source or effect – national or international – nor can we readily divide law's universe into two systems, the national and the international. The business of law is becoming both transnational and global.[80]

Both transnational and global approaches to law share an assumption that law in a global age will be pluralist in nature. In my view, this is a defining feature of regulation in the new global space, and I shall have more to say about this in the following sections, but at this juncture I want to emphasize that this is not a static pluralism or simple diversity of types of law, but a dynamic pluralism involving the interaction of different types and sources of law, with manifold effects on different actors and in different spaces, and subject to contending ideologies.[81] However, before turning to this directly we first need to look at how global justice discourse is itself changing in response to globalization.

c Global Justice and Development Discourses Are Transforming
The final convergence I want to trace is a kind of normative convergence, involving our postwar discourse concerning the issues of fairness raised by complex socioeconomic activity and regulation both "within" and "across" the "national." Since the Second World War and the postcolonial era, much of this discussion (where it concerns the nonnational) has taken place within the rubric of development and, toward the latter part of the twentieth century and into the twenty-first, the new rubric of "global" justice as well. These vital conversations are transforming from within and are merging toward a new integrated "post-globalization" inquiry into justice.

Conventional development discourse has been trapped in certain contradictions and assumptions that are no longer viable, if they ever were. The very idea of development began in an unstable binary

---

[80] See FRANK J. GARCIA, Globalization's Law: Transnational, Global or Both?, in THE GLOBAL COMMUNITY: YEARBOOK OF INTERNATIONAL LAW AND JURISPRUDENCE 2015 31 (2016).

[81] See PAUL SCHIFF BERMAN, GLOBAL LEGAL PLURALISM: A JURISPRUDENCE OF LAW BEYOND BORDERS (2012); Zumbansen, supra note 75. See generally GARCIA, supra note 15, at 13–21 (discussing the necessary role of pluralism in global justice theory).

structure: "we are the developed nations, you are not." To this it added a specific teleology: you want to be like us and to have what we have, in the way we have it – you exist to become us. Moreover, the dominant paradigm of development as economic growth is itself inherently unstable and contradictory, in that it implies that all countries can "develop" equally and that resources are inexhaustible, and both assumptions have proven wrong. Together this binary structure and the economic growth paradigm have largely determined the shape of development discourse for the past seventy years.

Global justice also investigates the subjects that development concerns itself with, and has also had its binary structures and assumptions. Rawls has written famously that justice is the first virtue of institutions.[82] The question of justice would thus seem natural to development as well, which has always been concerned with the institutions that set the terms within which development succeeds or fails – institutions that are themselves a subject of development.[83] However, as Gilbert Rist reminds us, justice discourse too has been marked by the binary structure, yielding a bifurcated vision for a just society: the democratic social welfare state in the countries of the North, and "development" programs in the South.[84] Rawls typifies this split: for him, investigating the justice of institutional frameworks, or what Rawls calls the "basic structure," is a key task for political theory, but conceived of as a *domestic* inquiry.[85]

Globalization has rendered such binary structures and assumptions unsustainable, for critics and advocates of justice and development alike. "North" and "South," "developed" and "developing" – all of these binaries are increasingly blurred, challenged and deconstructed

---

[82] JOHN RAWLS, A THEORY OF JUSTICE 3 (1971).

[83] Of course, development discourse has also been deeply influenced by other aspects of justice such as human rights, corrective justice arguments and other norms that add legal depth and texture to both development discourse and the justice debate. *See, e.g.*, KATHERINE YOUNG, CONSTITUTING ECONOMIC AND SOCIAL RIGHTS (2012) (analyzing the dynamic processes at international and state levels that render economic and social rights in enforceable legal form).

[84] GILBERT RIST, THE HISTORY OF DEVELOPMENT: FROM WESTERN ORIGINS TO GLOBAL FAITH (4th ed. 2014).

[85] For Rawls, beyond national boundaries, different fairness norms apply. *See* RAWLS, *supra* note 15, at 3–10; Pietro Maffetone, *The Law of Peoples: Beyond Incoherence and Apology*, 7 J. INT'L POL. THEORY 190 (2011).

through globalization's alchemical properties.[86] The most visible effects are in the economy, where globalization raises profound questions for justice and development: how is the global economy affecting growth, returns on investment, wealth creation, inequality, production and employment patterns, innovation and human capital investment within national and transnational economic spaces – in short, all of the social conditions of vital interest to development and justice alike?

Economic globalization thus also enlarges the set of institutions, actors and relationships, which justice must consider. We now must now include both domestic institutions, such as public and private law, the political process and socioeconomic structures such as the market; and their international correlates such as international law and international organizations, together with the global market and its international and domestic regulatory bodies; as well as the range of private and quasi-private actors involved in transnational norm creation.[87]

Globalization is thus critically reconstructing the discourse around global justice and development, toward a new global post-development discourse around, simply, justice. If justice is the first virtue of institutions, and institutions are increasingly transnational in scope, then so too must the justice conversation be transnational.

B At the Vanishing Point: A Global Market Society?

Together, these convergences – economic, social, regulatory and normative – point toward a newly emerging global space, with key characteristics that challenge our settled categories and create new opportunities for meaningful economic, social and legal activity. For one thing, the transnational space within which what we used to call development is supposed to take place, now resembles more closely what we think of as domestic space, than it does our traditional

---

[86] See generally Garcia, supra note 69; see also Frank J. Garcia, Transcending a Binary View of Development and Justice: Globalization, Opportunity and Fairness (2016) (unpublished manuscript) (on file with author).

[87] In global justice theory these are referred to collectively as the "global basic structure." See GARCIA, supra note 15, at 174; Andreas Føllesdal, When Common Interests Are Not Common: Why the Global Basic Structure Should Be Democratic, 16 IND. J. GLOBAL LEGAL STUD. 585 (2008).

accounts of the international context of development. Moreover, our ongoing investigation of justice, traditionally limited to national spaces, has found the very notion of national space exploded by and permeated with the global, dramatically expanding the boundaries for the justice conversation. And international economic law has grown from a set of functionally specialized regimes that structure the transnational economic relationships of national economies, into a steadily integrating framework regulating an emerging global economy through global legal processes.

Globalization is creating this space, but we have not yet fully recognized it or absorbed its implications, nor have we thoroughly examined and recast or rejected old legal and normative tools and invented new ones.[88] If we want to understand what justice will mean for the twenty-first century, we need to try to understand this new social space, which will then allow us to build toward a nuanced understanding of the kinds of relationships, thick and thin, that globalization forms and the kinds of obligations they therefore engender and support. All of this will mean rethinking law, justice and the regulation of a global economy, and understanding consent's role in all of this.

1 Emergence of Global Market Society
One way to characterize the social space that is emerging is as a **global market society**.[89] That it is *global*, can readily be seen from the nature of contemporary globalization and its transnational effects on social connections, in particular on economic transactions and business practices and the increasingly global means by which we regulate them. That it is based on *markets*, understood here as networks constituted by

---

[88] As Rist writes, development is no longer about "the success or failure of this or that 'development project' but a general way of envisaging harmonious and equitable cohabitation of all those living today – and in the future – on this planet." RIST, *supra* note 84; *see also* Volker Bornschier, *The Civilizational Project and Its Discontents: Toward a Viable Global Market Society?*, 5 J. WORLD–SYS. RES. 165, 175 (1999) (existing international agreements and regimes have not yet grown to reflect the political consequences of globalization).

[89] The debt to Polanyi in what follows is clear. KARL POLANYI, THE GREAT TRANSFORMATION (1944); *see also* Bornschier, *supra* note 88 (recognizing the emergence of a global market society and offering a critique of its current structure that points toward its progressive possibilities).

acts of buying and selling facilitated through a medium of exchange,[90] is also clear from the kinds of economic interactions and relationships that constitute it, by the institutions and regulatory structures employed to govern it (principally through international economic law), and by the ideology these structures follow.[91]

That it is a global market *society* is perhaps the most controversial characterization of the three, but in my view this is what the convergences outlined in the previous section point to.[92] One simple working definition of society could be "a large group of people sharing decisions and work around a common life."[93] At the global level, we to see evidence that work is shared through a global market, and that decisions are shared – to the extent they *are* shared, which is a problem I discuss throughout the book – through some blend of national and transnational political and regulatory processes.[94]

To the extent that globalization is understood as extending a particular version of market ideology – under-regulated capitalism or the "Washington Consensus," for example – globalization and the very idea of a global market will naturally be resisted as inimical to the interests of the noncapital classes.[95] While I agree with the substance of this critique, I think the underlying conflation of markets with

---

[90] KEITH HART & CHRIS HANN, *Introduction: Learning from Polanyi*, in MARKET AND SOCIETY: THE GREAT TRANSFORMATION TODAY 1 (Chris Hann & Keith Hart eds. 2009).

[91] I use the term ideology here in its classical, if not neutral, sense, as a set of ideas and values favoring markets over other forms of socioeconomic organization, recognizing full well the more pejorative uses of the term in connection with neoliberalism and "free market" ideology, a mistake to which I will return later in the chapter.

[92] *See also, e.g.*, KEITH HART, *Money in the Making of World Society*, in MARKET AND SOCIETY: THE GREAT TRANSFORMATION TODAY, *supra* note 90, at 91 (humanity formed a world society – understood as a single interactive social network – in the latter part of the twentieth century, massively unequal and imperfect, yet a society nonetheless).

[93] *Society*, CAMBRIDGE DICTIONARY, https://dictionary.cambridge.org/us/dictionary/english/society (last visited Mar. 15, 2018).

[94] I go deeper into this and the points in Section III.A in my essay on convergences and IEL. Garcia, *supra* note 50.

[95] *See* A. G. HOPKINS, GLOBALIZATION IN WORLD HISTORY 42–43 (2002) (dangers posed by weakened regulatory power over capitalist system). Had Polanyi lived and worked during the current era of globalization, he might well agree, given his central concern with the dangerous "fiction" of a self-regulating economy. POLANYI, *supra* note 89, at 31–32. However, I consider the equation of the two – globalization and neoliberalism – to be a mistake, as I explain here.

neoliberalism is a mistake, reflecting an understandable normative judgment about the global spread of under-regulated capitalism as a *particular* form of market society, more than a considered judgment of the idea of a global economy or a market society per se.[96] Equating markets and market regulation with a specific – and contested – market ideology masks the power of the market *as an idea* that cuts across social models, ideologies and levels of development.[97] For our purposes here, it is the ubiquity of the market itself as idea and practice that is significant from the perspective of shared understandings and practices, not its often-controversial nature.

Neoliberalism notwithstanding, market societies have certain structural weaknesses and are prone to certain kinds of oppressive tendencies, such as the tilt toward inequality that Piketty warns us of, and which we see playing out globally today.[98] In response, market societies seeking some degree of social stability and sustainability develop social practices or domestic institutions capable of supplementing and mitigating the rigors of capitalism even minimally, for example by compensating the "losers" through some form of wealth transfer.[99] Aaron James calls this the practice of mutual market reliance.[100] By this, James means something beyond the shared practice of relying on a domestic market model: the mutual reliance on the emerging global market itself, as a transnational market that lives in, through and beyond the sum of each state's individual markets. This shared practice is itself generative of a broader set of global social relationships and practices that deeply inform the nature and challenges of regulating a global market and keeping it roughly fair.

---

[96] In this sense, I read Polanyi not as an indictment of market society understood as a society relying on markets for economic organization, but as an indictment of a society organized by markets – neoliberalism, in other words. The task, which this project seeks to contribute to, is to reassert the primacy of society over economy, even (especially) in a market society. *See* POLANYI, *supra* note 89, at 259.

[97] DON SLATER & FRAN TONKISS, MARKET SOCIETY 1 (2001).

[98] *See* PIKETTY, *supra* note 60; see also *supra* notes 60–65 and accompanying text (growing inequality); *see also* SLATER & TONKISS, *supra* note 97, at 34–35 (noting disorder, irrationality and oppressive behavior as endemic to market societies, not "transitional" problems).

[99] SLATER & TONKISS, *supra* note 97, at 120.

[100] JAMES, *supra* note 16.

The emergence of a global market society has profound consequences for how we approach transnational problems of politics, economics and law.[101] "Global market society" can be a contentious term when confused with current neoliberal market ideology, but is a progressive term, in my view, when properly understood in terms of individual and communal freedom and opportunity. As Sen has written, the freedom to participate in both the market for labor and the market for products is a key freedom, intrinsically and instrumentally, and therefore a cornerstone of development.[102]

Realizing this freedom depends entirely on how the global market is regulated and according to what norms. This opens up new challenges and avenues for economic law, which I have argued plays an essential role in establishing and safeguarding markets through defining and protecting consensual economic agreements,[103] to play this role on a global level toward a truly *global* network of consensual exchanges.

C Consent and Justice in a Global Market Society

As I have argued elsewhere,[104] a global approach to justice will have three elements: it will be **pluralist**, embracing the moral diversity of a truly global conversation; it will be **relational**, capitalizing on the social architecture of the new global social space; and it will be **transactional**, by which I mean it will protect and support consensual economic exchanges as a pragmatic, market-friendly approach to ensuring opportunity and fairness from the bottom up, so to speak.[105] I will focus the remainder of this section on situating our discussion of

---

[101] For one thing, it shifts the frame through which we try to understand relations between advanced market societies and societies still transitioning from traditional to market principles, such as most Middle Eastern societies.

[102] AMARTYA SEN, DEVELOPMENT AS FREEDOM 6–8 (1999).

[103] SLATER & TONKISS, *supra* note 97, at 105.

[104] GARCIA, *supra* note 15.

[105] By "market-friendly" I mean norms of justice compatible with the logic of markets – hence less easily shrugged off by powerful market actors insofar as they depend on markets themselves – rather than norms that facilitate the social irresponsibility of such actors. *See infra* notes 107–108 and accompanying text.

consent into a larger framework as a transactional approach to justice in a global market economy, an economy that is only minimally governed at present by global institutions such as international economic law, and yet which so deeply influences our life prospects.

1 The Transactional Mode of Justice

In the Transactional Mode, just behavior is considered a function of the nature and norms of a specific transaction (like a contract for the sale of goods or the negotiation of a treaty), embedded within a specific set of social practices (like a body of contract law, a set of treaty rules, treaty membership or mutual reliance on a market).[106] This mode presupposes no other relationship but that sort, and derives its norms internally from the transaction itself and the practices that embed it. At its best, such an approach gives us an alternative, more market-friendly route to reaching some of the kinds of structural outcomes we might associate with a just global order, but through an understanding of what fairness means *within* economic exchange itself, and therefore an understanding of the behaviors that undermine this kind of fairness and therefore undermine the nature of commerce itself (as well as, cumulatively, the possibility of a just economic order).

I want to state clearly at the outset that by describing transactional justice as "market-friendly," I do not mean norms conducive to shifting risk away from control or profit, which individual market actors might consider to be characteristics of a "friendly" regime, in the narrow self-interested meaning of the term. On the contrary, I consider that counteracting this tendency for those with control to shift risk while securing profit to be – following the work of my teacher Joseph Vining – at the heart of the social purpose of economic regulation.[107] I mean, instead, an approach to justice that is deeply compatible with the nature of markets, i.e., built around consensual

---

[106] GARCIA, *supra* note 15, at 279–80.
[107] JOSEPH VINING, FROM NEWTON'S SLEEP 287–90 (1995); *see also* Larry D. Thompson, *The Responsible Corporation: Its Historical Roots and Continuing Promise*, 29 NOTRE DAME J.L. ETHICS & PUB. POL'Y 199 (2015) (citing the contributions of Joseph Vining toward our understanding of corporations in social life).

exchanges themselves, and therefore not a theory of justice that can be easily rejected as exogenous to market rationality.[108]

In order to understand what a transactional approach to justice might mean in a global market society, we need to return to the place of consent in the market-based relationships – transactions – that increasingly constitute our converging global social reality.

2 Consent and Convergence

If I am correct that an investigation into the nature of trade as a human experience reveals that many aspects of current trade law and policy mix what is ostensibly free trade with something else – exploitation, coercion or predation – then this not only has important normative and pragmatic implications for global trade policy, but also offers us a radically different take on the fairness of economic relationships in a global market society, one that builds on the possibilities created by the converging trends I have sought to highlight.

How does consensual trade reflect the deepening of the global economy? To begin with, consensual trade presupposes global economic ties, but it goes a step farther and reflects the need for a unified approach to economic regulation in such an economy (thus reflecting the unification of international economic law) as well as a unified approach to the norms and expectations inherent in a global economy built on trade, or to put it in Aaron James's terms, built on the shared practice of mutual market reliance.

In this sense, consensual trade also reflects the thickening of global social relationships. Thickening social relations mean it is no longer adequate to consider only the consent of those within our societies to the regulatory structures we are building – we can no longer afford to consider the consent of those outside our societies, but nevertheless impacted by these regulatory structures, to be irrelevant. We simply know too much about how our political, economic and legal decisions and regimes affect the lives and prospects of everyone else around the globe.

---

[108] See Bornschier, supra note 88, at 170–71 (addressing injustice in a global market society needs a "deep-seated rationale" that "follows the logic of the construction of justice within market society."). Consent is at the heart of this. See SLATER & TONKISS, supra note 97, at 18 (market society is revolutionary in that it creates social obligations mediated by contract, i.e., by individuals entering into consensual agreements).

How is consensual trade a brake on inequality? Grounding economic transactions in consent can affect both the fairness of the bargains people will agree to or not; and the compensation aspect, or social contract of trade, that if adhered to, will mitigate un-equalizing tendencies. In other words, if everyone's consent matters, then bargains that will intensify inequality seem less likely to be agreed to, and mechanisms such as Trade Adjustment Assistance, which can mitigate trade's effects on inequality, will be incorporated into the overall social bargain embodied by free trade.

How is consensual trade related to global or transnational law? It identifies a site of transnational norm creation within a global market society, and offers a metric through which to evaluate the resulting norms for fairness: do they reflect and embody consensual processes of norm creation?

How does consensual trade build on our new understanding of development and justice in a global space? Here is where the Transactional Mode of justice comes into its own.

The key to a consent approach being a part of the justice project is the argument that a flourishing trade system that respects the consent of its private individual and state participants will incidentally also be a more just system of global economic relations, since individuals and states will have fewer reasons to accept bad bargains, and will instead negotiate and conclude more equitable bargains at the transactional and treaty levels. A truly consensual system of trade will therefore promote similar outcomes to what we have sought to promote through the global justice debate, but through a route that ideally cuts across normative traditions, does not assume a difference between "development" and domestic justice and seems intuitively plausible to any market participant, thus fitting into the larger social and economic norms of an emerging global market society.

IV CONCLUSION: THE IMPORTANCE OF PROTECTING CONSENT IN A GLOBAL MARKET SOCIETY

A consensual basis for a "fair" economic system thus has an intuitive market-based appeal that can make it useful for structuring a global market system. Insofar as markets thrive on consensual exchanges, so a global market society will thrive on a shared global understanding of the role of consent in exchange. Recast this way, trade agreements can do more than promote fair bargains: they can begin to answer the larger question we face of how to construct a more just global economic order within conditions of pluralism. A network of truly consensual trade agreements can serve an important ordering role in global socioeconomic relations, by establishing a pragmatic, commerce-based rule of law among peoples who do not necessarily share any other sociopolitical loyalties.

A consent-based theory of trade, understood here to sound in the Transactional Mode of justice, can thus help meet the need in a global market society for a pragmatic and market-friendly approach to economic fairness, which can have a positive influence independently of the reforms to larger, more institutional relationships foregrounded by Justice as Relationship. A consent analysis offers us a way to understand and develop the implications of such an aspiration, harkening back to the work of Kant, Locke, Smith and others regarding the tremendous potential inherent in self-interest as a force for good in a well-regulated system.

CONCLUSION

I SUMMING UP – WHERE HAVE WE BEEN?

This book has been an investigation into the nature of trade as a human experience – one investigation among many possible lines of inquiry. I have focused on the relationship between consent and trade – the social fact of consensual exchange, more than the theory of political consent – and offered a view of consent, understood this way, as constitutive of trade itself. In other words, as I have said many times, consent makes trade, and not something else.

I have also sought to illustrate how trade law and policy today are unfortunately riddled with examples of that "something else": predation, coercion and exploitation operating under the guise of trade. These pathologies of trade, as I see them, are in one way or another a violation of consent, but nevertheless proceed under the color of lawfulness (courtesy of the doctrine of formal consent in international law) as operative patterns of economic exchange between states, despite their underlying dynamics.

To illustrate this, I offered examples in Chapter 2 drawn from multilateral, regional and bilateral trade agreements, involving states across the spectrum from superpower to small island economy. What unites all of these examples is the use by strong states of disparities in economic power to force bargains which seem not to be in both parties' economic self-interest, and yet which are agreed to formally, either because actual consent was never sought or necessary (remember Weil's insight that consent cannot be sought where there is no power of refusal), or because consent was coerced, or because the more powerful party exploited unfair background conditions (sometimes of the powerful party's own making) to secure a kind of reluctant consent.

Having illustrated these dynamics in Chapter 2 by reference to the WTO, CAFTA, KORUS and CTPA treaties, and argued in Chapter 1 for why consent matters on purely pragmatic grounds even to powerful parties who might otherwise not be unsettled by coercion or exploitation, I considered in Chapter 3 the two main questions that follow naturally from such an analysis: how did we get here, and what can we do about it?

I began by arguing that, in my view, the single most important step we can take if we want to aim our negotiations toward actual *trade* agreements, and make best use of what opportunities we have to shift current treaties in this direction, is to simply clarify in our own minds that trade is consensual, and that any other kind of nonconsensual or coerced or exploitative economic exchange, whatever we call it, is simply not trade. In other words, the most important pragmatic move we can make, in the classical sense of the term, is to shift our understanding of what it is that we are about when we undertake to trade, or to negotiate a trade agreement.

I followed this with a radical new way to think of the object and purpose of trade agreements, and with that in mind illustrated what consensual trade might look like through a number of provisions that should be in consensual trade agreements, and others which should not be. Since moving this way means reforming trade negotiations, I also offered a number of suggestions, drawn principally from the negotiation literature, for altering the dynamics of trade negotiations when power asymmetries are involved, and a number of suggestions for approaching the problem of existing agreements, including suggestions drawn from the adhesion contract literature. Doubtless there are many others, and it may well be that further study of the role of consent in trade, and of specific economic agreements, will uncover new options tailored to specific kinds of treaties and specific parties and regions.

The fact that, in Hans Rosling's term, we are in a "totally new, converging world," means we must expand the analysis of trade and consent I have offered along a number of fronts, which I laid out in Chapter 4. We must first extend it outwards into other domains of economic law and into economic agreements negotiated by other key economic actors today, since together these domains and these agreements form the most comprehensive transnational economic regulatory regime for the emerging global space that we have today. We must also deepen the analysis into the consensual relationships and agreements that in principle *should* underlie – and in actual politics often *have* – our liberal societies' internal decisions to engage in trade, or, as I have called it, trade's social contract.

This is all the more important when we consider that through transnational economic and social activities, and through international economic law and other forms of regulation, we may be in the process of creating an emerging global market society. I concluded Chapter 4 with my reasons for thinking so, and a role for consensual trade in this emerging global space. Safeguarding consent could play a crucial role in such a pluralist and market-driven society, as a way to ensure a kind of fairness within an environment that must recognize a number of competing normative and economic rationalities.

If we don't consider this or other kinds of alternatives to what we are doing now, we risk seeing through globalization the weaknesses and violence inherent in capitalism played out on a truly global scale, rather than its tremendous emancipatory and progressive possibilities if well regulated. In this, as in many things, Weil was uncannily prescient, so it seems fitting to return to her again in this Conclusion.

II CONSENT AND OPPRESSION IN A GLOBAL MARKET SOCIETY

As we know too well, capitalism has the power not only to unleash tremendous individual and collective economic dynamism, but also tremendous social and environmental destruction, given that it operates on a logic that, if not regulated, will inexorably bring about its own crises and in the process a vast amount of suffering.[1] Recognizing and respecting the subtle yet critical role that consent plays in mitigating the oppressive tendencies of capitalism can therefore be key for promoting a more sustainable long-term socioeconomic system for everyone concerned, workers and capitalists alike. Insofar as capitalism depends on

---

[1] *See generally* FRITZ SCHARPF, GOVERNING IN EUROPE (1999) (charting the self-destructive contradictions inherent in capitalist societies).

thriving markets, it will in the long run depend on consensual relationships. Oppressive relationships might in the short run facilitate extractive or predatory capitalism, but will inevitably collapse, as we saw with the Spanish *encomienda* system in the New World, the *Ancient Regime* of eighteenth-century France, American slavery, nineteenth-century European colonialism and the 2007 Global Financial Crisis, to name only a few recent examples.

When one considers Weil's work on consent and oppression in economic relationships in light of her seminal essay on the *Iliad*, one is struck by the essential relationship between capitalism and the empire of force she so powerfully documents in the *Iliad*. James Boyd White writes about the empire of force as an ideology, a way of imagining the world and oneself and the others within it, that is always present in war and required by it, but present also in our lives whenever people deny the humanity of others whom they destroy, manipulate or exploit.[2]

This unfortunately dovetails well with the nature of capitalism and the global capitalist system as currently constituted, in its tendency toward unrestrained competition and exploitation that can threaten workers, consumers, citizens, other capitalists – in short, all human beings involved in the enterprise. The risk is that a system for improving coordination among market actors, and therefore improving the richness and efficiency of the market and increasing the well-being of society, becomes a system for the commodification of human beings and the debasement of human desires into market demographics.

The risk is not confined to capitalism, though. As Weil realized through her own journey into and out of Marxism, all economic models and systems have a tendency toward the empire of force – they can turn people into objects and operate according to an ideology of oppression and exploitation that if not understood and resisted will crush all people in its path.

It is hard to ignore the historical parallels as well. Weil wrote during the rise of fascism and during a time of global economic depression due to the triumph and collapse of early-twentieth-century under-regulated

---

[2] JAMES BOYD WHITE, LIVING SPEECH: RESISTING THE EMPIRE OF FORCE 13–50 (2006).

or "robber baron" capitalism, and I am currently finishing this book during an era of tremendous nativist and populist backlash against twenty-first-century under-regulated neoliberal economic globalization among both developed and developing country electorates. The parallels between the under-regulated capitalisms of the twentieth century and the twenty-first century seem clear.[3] There is similarly widespread concern that as in the twentieth century, so too in the twenty-first, the reaction against the kinds of "trade" agreements this capitalism produces will lead to fascism, or at least the emotional and nativist reactions which can hasten us toward it. For these and other urgent reasons, we must ask similar questions today to the questions that preoccupied Weil over half a century ago: what is this sociopolitical development we call the global market doing to human beings? What is the nature of the order it creates?

This suggests a vitally important reason for bringing the notion of consent into the very heart of the global capitalist system and its architecture: the rules framing the market itself and therefore the heart of any emerging global market society. Globalization itself is a conditioning factor in the exercise of economic power and control, given its impact on the possibility of simultaneous real-time coordination of economic production around the globe.[4] If we don't look carefully at the consensual or oppressive nature of its rules, then it doesn't matter whether we are increasing income or GDP per capita, etc. – all good things, no doubt. We have done so through a system of oppression that denies the very foundation of that which we seek through trade to nurture – human well-being.[5]

Weil was also eerily prescient about the nature of globalization as a form of capitalist organization. In *The Analysis of Oppression*, she wrote that as social forms of economic organization emerge, people are paradoxically freer from their servitude to nature, but increasingly

---

[3] THOMAS PIKETTY, CAPITAL IN THE TWENTY-FIRST CENTURY (Arthur Goldhammer trans. 2014) (2013).

[4] The extent to which power can be effectively exercised by any one person depends in part on "the objective conditions of the control exercised," including "more or less rapid methods of transport and communication." SIMONE WEIL, *Analysis of Oppression, in* SIMONE WEIL READER 126, 141 (George A. Panichas ed. 1977).

[5] *See* JOSEPH STIGLITZ, MAKING GLOBALIZATION WORK 285–93 (2007).

subject to the dominion of others and the very system they have evolved to free themselves from nature. "Systematic coordination in time and space becomes possible and necessary, and its importance increases continually."[6] If one considers that globalization is often defined as the transcendence or elimination of time and space, or as the possibility of global production *instantaneously* coordinated in time and space around the planet,[7] then one can see why a global system of production can become the ultimate form of human domination, even as it seeks to become the ultimate form of human economic productivity and therefore liberation from the constraints of nature.

This makes it critically important for us to understand how economic globalization its current form resembles the nature of oppressive social systems as Weil identifies them. Weil attempts to account for the expansion of oppressive social systems in terms of the inner logic of power itself.

> Every power, from the mere fact that it is exercised, extends to the farthest possible limit the social relations on which it is based; thus … commercial power multiplies exchanges. … [T]he extension of exchanges has brought about a greater division of labor, which in its turn has made a wider circulation of commodities indispensable; furthermore, the increased productivity which has resulted from this has furnished new resources that have been able to transform themselves into commercial and industrial capital.[8]

This echoes the globalization debate, where one often hears the argument that the growth of the global economy and the aggregate wealth it has created is its own argument for the desirability or beneficence of the global economy as currently constituted.

Weil's analysis suggests instead that this is but a reflection of the internal logic of social systems, which extend themselves with an appearance of growth until they reach a point of collapse.

> [P]ower can extend the foundations on which it rests up to a certain point only, after which it comes up, as it where, against an impassable wall. But even so it is not in a position to stop; the spur of

---

[6] *Analysis of Oppression, supra* note 4, at 132.

[7] *See, e.g.,* MANUEL CASTELLS, THE RISE OF THE NETWORK SOCIETY (2000).

[8] *Analysis of Oppression, supra* note 4, at 143.

competition forces it to go even farther and farther, that is to say to go beyond the limits within which it can be effectively exercised. It extends beyond what it is able to control; it commands over and above what it can impose; it spends in excess of its own resources. Such is the internal contradiction which every oppressive system carries within itself like a seed of death ...[9]

If this is so, we have reason to be concerned over the conflicts, protests and tensions surrounding economic globalization, the global financial crisis and its severe disruptions and political impasses such as the collapse of the Doha Round of WTO negotiations and the apparent disintegration of domestic public support for trade agreements across many polities. These may in fact signal the beginning of that over-extension – Paul Kennedy calls it "imperial overstretch"[10] – that the current framework for globalizing the economy, understood as an oppressive system, would be prone to, according to Weil's analysis. Weil's analysis also suggests that we have broad systemic reasons for concern over the implications of a nonconsensual system of international trade regulation for the sustainability of our global economy, and compelling reasons to undertake a consent-based analysis of international trade, and a consent-based reform of its underlying principles, structures and dynamics.

Consent in particular is key to the resistance to oppression needed in a global system of economic production, because it directly addresses the root condition of oppressiveness characteristic of contemporary economic relations: "However tied and bound a primitive man was to routine and blind gropings, he could at least try to think things out, to combine and innovate at his own risk, a liberty that is absolutely denied to a worker engaged in a production line."[11] Transposing Weil's simplistic yet resonant metaphor from the production line to the world of global economic exchange, when current patterns of transaction and regulation are premised on nonconsensual agreements and create an environment favoring nonconsensual

---

[9] *Id.* at 144–45.
[10] PAUL KENNEDY, THE RISE AND FALL OF THE GREAT POWERS (1989).
[11] *Analysis of Oppression, supra* note 4, at 149.

transactions, the loss of individual liberty and innovation that consent would safeguard are as restrictive as any production line.

For Weil, the resulting "social question" is clear:

the mechanism of this transfer [of power from nature to society] must be examined; we must try to find out why man [sic] has had to pay this price for his power over nature; form an idea of what would constitute the least unhappy position for him to be in, that is to say one in which he would be the least enslaved to the twin domination of nature and society; and lastly, discern what roads can lead towards such a position, and what instruments present-day civilization could place in men's hands if they aspired to transform their lives in this way.

The essential answer, from the perspective of economic relations, is to safeguard through law the power of consent over the transactions and exchanges that most intimately affect one's own life prospects.

In Weil's thought, consent is also the key to the larger question of social justice. Reaching back to Plato, she writes that justice in fact consists of mutual consent, and the pursuit of justice is the pursuit of conditions allowing for the possibility of consent, or refusal, to obligations.[12] Thus in this sense consent is not simply the key to trade being trade, and not a form of oppression: consent is key to the entire project of global justice, namely the fairness of global economic relationships.

However, and this hearkens back to the Transactional Mode discussed earlier in Chapter 4, rather than operating from an external substantive standard of justice, a consent approach grounds fairness in the basic fabric of economic transactions themselves: do they reflect the mutual consent of the parties? Extending this to the macro level, do the transactions occur within a framework of rules which themselves are the fruit of consensual negotiations among states? Have we consensually created a global regulatory framework that itself respects the consent of its participants?

Thus, through a consent analysis of trade we can evaluate not only whether our trade relations are indeed about trade, but also the extent

---

12 SIMONE WEIL, *Are We Struggling for Justice?*, *in* SIMONE WEIL (Eric O. Springsted ed. 1998) (referencing Plato's *Symposium*.)

to which our trade relationships are in fact contributing to a just economic system, or perpetuating an unjust economic system. These are the kinds of questions this project has sought to raise and to begin to answer, by developing an approach through which to analyze the consensual nature of trade and trade regulation, and through which to suggest strategies for "creating conditions where it is absent."

Finally, and in the largest sense, how does consensual trade reflect the possibilities opened up by a global market society, and answer the needs of a global market society? We have a multitude of concerns about the nature of contemporary economic relationships and transactions – their freedom and their fairness – since in the aggregate they form the global economy itself, and the global market society which that economy builds, and which it is embedded in. What about the opportunities?

Perhaps we can approach these opportunities as a question of market efficiency in the fullest sense: can consensual transactions over time promote a more efficient allocation of resources than the opposite, when social externalities are fully accounted for? We can also frame this as a question of freedom, following Smith and Sen: do our market relationships embody and promote the greatest degree of individual economic liberty? Are we embracing the new regulatory possibilities that convergence within international economic law open up, and ensuring that the emerging global law of an emerging global market society is both internally coherent and anchored by norms of justice at both global and local levels?

Insofar as markets thrive on consensual exchanges, so a global market society will thrive on a *shared global understanding* of the role of consent in exchange. It is my hope that a consent theory of trade, suitably extended, can help meet the need in a global market society for a pragmatic and market-friendly approach to economic fairness that has reasons to appeal to any market actor's long-term self-interest, and which can have a positive influence independently of any other reforms to larger more institutional relationships motivated by other approaches to fairness. Perhaps in this way our efforts to understand and respect consent can help us achieve a global market society's progressive possibilities.

INDEX